REVIEWS OF A LEGACY OF MYTH

In Jay Carson's candid and compelling memoir, *A Legacy of Myth*, the poet, professor, and one-time bad boy shares his journey as he celebrates 50 years of sobriety. This richly detailed memoir, interspersed with poems, short fiction & non-fiction, ranges from self-deprecating humor to dead seriousness. Raised in a Pittsburgh family of privilege awash with alcohol, Carson notably remembers his mother's counsel: "Have a drink, Jay, and take a nap." Instead, after some years of denial and struggle, the author saves his life through his steadfast commitment to sobriety and to helping others. Jay Carson has an unmistakable gift for friendship and kindness. His poetry is especially engaging and there's hard-won grace and wisdom throughout this book. You might want to buy one copy for yourself and one for a friend.

— Joan E. Bauer, author of *Fig Season* and *The Camera Artist*

Good humor, heart, humility, wisdom. Rarely does a memoir so perfectly balance all four. We're in good hands with Jay Carson, as he generously guides us through lost Pittsburgh and his own wondrous growing pains. If you're nostalgic for your own hometown and our humanity, this is the book for you.

--- Heather McNaugher, author of *Second-order Desire* and *States of Emergency*

Jay Carson's memoir, A Legacy of Myth, chronicles his passage through a complicated family legacy, active alcoholism, recovery, and career and personal failures and triumphs. Jay explores the myths and narratives that shaped and influenced the course of his life and his growth beyond myths that outlived their utility. "I have done the work," he writes, "struggled through and come to terms with my life's controlling myths, and reached a peace." Laced throughout with Jay's compelling poetry and short fiction, A Legacy of Myth is unwaveringly honest, courageous, and forthright in search of the truth of his experience, regardless of where that search leads. I have known Jay for many years, and this compelling memoir has given me an invaluable opportunity to know him better.

---William Pollak aka Billy Price, singer and recording artist

ACKNOWLEDGMENTS:

I am deeply grateful to the following who made this book possible:

Phil Terman, William Pollak, and Heather McNaugher for their fine editing skills

Jim Morris for his incomparable technical editing

John and Evan Carson for their cover photography

Robert Qualters for the use of his remarkable painting *Persephone*

Judy Robinson for her inspiration throughout this project

A LEGACY OF MYTH

A Memoir

by

Jay Carson

Dedicated to my family and friends who made my life possible, rich, and happy

Preface

This is a memoir of myth, real and fictional stories that embody the cultural ideals with which I grew into whom I am today. Throughout this work, I use the term, myth, not as falsehood, but in the larger sense as a body of stories told within a group of people to explain their culture, especially the most mysterious, basic and inexplicable elements of it. Some of the myths found in this work are truer than the facts, fiction, poetry, or narrative in which they are presented. While this memoir is an account of what I have done and what has happened to me, it is also an examination of how various myths have impacted and, in some cases, created my life. For they are powerful. Among those I examine are myths of social/economic/race superiority, others involving faith and religion, workaholism as well as other more personal myths. I have wrestled with all of them, winning over some, embracing others, and sometimes coming to a respectful draw in understanding them and myself.

Chapter I

MY FAMILY AND THE MYTH OF NOBLE LEGACY

I begin with my family. Like many Americans I have stories about distinguished relatives from Europe, but as they say: *Dukes don't emigrate.* Aristocracy is either too happy or powerful to leave, or they get executed at home. Nonetheless, I will tell you of some of my family myths. True or not, they are what shaped me.

My Father

My father's mother was a Siebert. That family came to Pittsburgh in the 1830s from the Alsace Lorraine region between and fought over for centuries by the Germans and French (Alphonse Daudet wonderfully captures this tension in his great short story, "Le Derniere Class" depicting a last French class after Prussians forbid teaching French in Alsatian schools).

The Siebert's and their descendants thrived in Pittsburgh, founding an early boot/shoe factory and owning a number of farms along the Allegheny river. Siebert Road in the North Hills of Pittsburgh is named after them. They married other German and French immigrants. My father enjoyed recounting how some of these children, coming back from school, would tease one French sympathizing grandmother telling her they had learned of German victories during the Franco-Prussian War of 1870. These same children would the next day tell tales of French victories to their grandfather, a Prussian sympathizer. Who was winning in these children's stories had to do with who their favorite grandparent was at the time. In an attempt at peace, my great-great German grandfather planned to name one of the small streets in his large plot of land on the Allegheny River in Lawrenceville in honor of his wife's birthplace, Strasburg Way. He never got around to that, but he did name another small street Berlin Way. It's still there.

The family built a large house on the Allegheny River in what is now Lawrenceville. The house was grand enough for a ballroom on the third floor, where my grandparents were married. Years later that house became an office building for Armco Steel. Dad didn't mention much more about their wedding except to say his mother Matilda Magdeline Siebert lost her entry in the Pittsburgh Social Register to marry John B. Carson.

My father's father, John B. Carson, was born and raised in a farming family in Saxonburg, Butler County, Pennsylvania. We claim to be distantly related to Rachel Carson. John B. attended Butler Academy and while his older brother fought in the Civil War, he helped on the family farm. In the peace that followed, my grandfather became a clerk in Humboldt's store in Butler, a small town some 40 mile north of Pittsburgh. Scots-Irish himself, he learned German to deal with the many German speaking farmers who were customers. Wanting something more in life, he came down to Pittsburgh. Smart and entrepreneurial, John Carson saw a way to capitalize on the thriving steel economy of late 19th century Pittsburgh. He borrowed enough to start a merchant tailor store downtown where he served a large number of newly rich industrialists who wanted to look as successful as they were.

John B.'s fluency in German allowed him to draw upon the skills of immigrant German tailors who helped make the store very successful. He took the middle initial "B" to distinguish himself from another Pittsburgh John Carson. My grandfather happily counted among the elite Pittsburgh industrialists who frequented his store, Henry Clay Frick. Suits in the Frick family home museum still bear the Carson Merchant Tailor label. One family myth is that Frick supposedly told John B. to "beg borrow or steal" (my father's terms) every dime he could to buy stock in the burgeoning United States Steel corporation. That tip paid for my father's, my own, and my son's educations and start in life. Nonetheless, John B. was disappointed that he could not quite buy a partnership in the new US Steel.

My father, John Stanton Carson, was born in the Monongahela House, a premier hotel that numbered among its guests Abraham Lincoln and John B. My grandmother was Matilda Magdalene Siebert, whom I only got to know through her portrait by Aaron Gorson which hung in our living room. My own mother said several times to me and my brother she was happy that she had no female issue that she might feel she would have to name either Matilda or Magdalene, and sure to be nick-named "Tilly." My father was named after his father, John Carson, with his best friend, William Stanton, nephew of Edwin Stanton, Lincoln's Secretary of War, donating the middle name. William Stanton was a successful real estate developer in his own right. Stanton Avenue in Pittsburgh's East End is named after him.

My grandfather was happy to live in the Monongahela House hotel and be close to his business. The family story was that at the age of two, my father nearly fell down the hotel elevator shaft. My grandmother insisted the family move to safer quarters. John B. refused. She then took her son back to her parents' big house in Morningside, now the parish house for St. Raphael's Church. My grandfather stayed in the Monongahela House hotel. It's hard to believe that elevator safety was the young couple's only problem. My father claimed John B., like the reputable husband he presented to the world, visited his Matilda every afternoon for tea. I find it hard to believe that a separated man would have tea with his wife daily. Myth is a powerful force in my family.

German and English by blood and French by culture helped define my father who could be disciplined: Phi Beta Kappa at Haverford College, Harvard Law graduate, respected attorney, sophisticated in manners, tri-lingual, well-traveled, and widely read. He maintained that a Siebert ancestor was Axe Man to Napoleon III – not an executioner but a sort of Secretary of the Interior/Forestry. This civil servant supposedly escaped Paris with Eugenie, Napoleon III's wife, after the Franco Prussian War. My father, called Stanton, even for a time, formally by his children, sometimes achieved a more democratic nobility: he was scrupulously honest, generous, and caring in that reserved 1940s way, but was thwarted in these virtues because he was emotionally abandoned early in his life, then later developed a too great fondness for alcohol. In this poem, I recall those problems and note that he was a gentleman and often good to me.

Locks

I sleep near my father's hair,
curling next to my bed on a shelf.
His soft four fingers of silky blond
lie in a grey box now broken,
still showing a small but distinctive crest
for the Pittsburgh aristocrat
he never became.

His parents took more from him
than that grasp of hair: hot-housing him
in the child purgatory of the Monongahela House Hotel;
his mother died early; his father's mourning

obliterated all but his merchant tailor business.

My father's childhood was briefly saved
by his grandmother's farm, idealized in his telling
of sweet lettuce patches, cucumber sandwiches,
a gardener who blew the foam off his beer reward
into the face of a cat named William Howard Taft.
And by his mother's brief vitality, cancer growing slower
than the spring radishes.

And they left him less: an eternal thirst
for love and whisky, a rage
at injustices done to others and himself,
and a few irreplaceable memories.

My father's hair is tied by a small piece of string
so I can touch where once the ancient and loving oils

of my grandmother's hands worked;
the string is as dried now as worn compassion,
yet it doesn't crack and blow away.

Matilda Magdaline, my father's mother died when he was 10. In the selfish way of children, I never thought about it much until, as an adult, I did say to him that losing his mother at such a young age must have been tough. His second wife said what my own mother probably tried to shield us from: "He was *devastated*," she emphasized. After his mother's passing, my father lived with his father, John B. who had given up the Monongahela House Hotel and bought a house in the school district where my father was already enrolled. They lived at 230 N. Negley Avenue, a very nice neighborhood at the time. Barney Dreyfus, founding owner of the

Pirates Baseball team lived down the block and occasionally took the neighborhood children to games.

This new location allowed my father to go to a nearby school, Fulton, with his favorite cousin, Chick Siebert, whom he idolized. My young father, on hearing that Chick broke his arm, spent a whole afternoon looking for it, mistakenly horrified that the arm had come completely off. Chick also provided older-brother protection at school. Something of a nerd, my father was grateful for Chick's help. I knew Chick much later and was completely charmed by his infectious warm personality. I can still see his tall frame entering the Duquesne Club where it seemed everyone wanted say hello to him. At one of our summer lunches, he took off his boater straw hat as he approached the coat room and sailed it to one of the attendants, much to everyone present's pleasure as the attendant jumped to catch Chick's hat calling out, "Hello Mr. Siebert." Several of us clapped, especially me. I wanted very much to be like Chick Siebert.

One of the dangers from which Chick protected Dad were the tougher, less intellectual Irish boys in the neighborhood. My father remembered being taunted as having "swallowed the dictionary." My mother was Irish, and in family disputes she and I, often on the same side, despite our fondness for Chick to say nothing of my father, wistfully rooted for those tough Irish kids.

My father went to Peabody High School which had an accomplished alumni/student body, including the great literary critic Malcolm Cowley and the distinguished rhetoric and literary scholar, writer, and critic, Kenneth Burke, who developed the powerful rhetorical concept, argument by identification: you will agree with someone's argument in as much as you identify with the person making it. (The best explanation of the successful political career of George W. Bush. "I'd like to have a beer with him," many voters said or felt.) My father said when students flunked out of Peabody, they went to Shady Side Academy, and when they flunked out of Shady Side they went to ELA, East Liberty Academy, or as my father called it, Education's Last Attempt. By the time I went to Shady Side Academy, it was because Pittsburgh public schools were no longer so strong academically.

Dad spent his freshman year at Penn. He was disappointed at not being rushed by Psi U, which Dad said was the most prestigious fraternity. I doubt this was his only disappointment at that large university; he decided to leave. Rather than heading to smaller Lafayette where his cousin Chick was a graduating senior who encouraged Dad to come, he transferred to equally small Haverford College where his old friends from Peabody, Willard and Charlie Mead, were enrolled in his year. The Meads were Dad's life-long friends and often visited our house. Williard became a teacher at Shady Side Academy where he effectively taught me a senior English class. Haverford was and is still a small Quaker college that takes its education role seriously. My father thrived there, both because of its gentle spiritual environment and its serious academics. He was moved by the regularly scheduled religious Meetings where individuals, touched by an inner light, would spontaneously speak. Dad recalled with a small smile that the faculty were more often moved to speak than the students. That spiritual experience had some effect on my father, who remained a church-goer all his life, even if often through radio broadcasts from Shady Side Presbyterian Church.

My father's father died in his freshman year of college, making him an orphan. When he returned to Pittsburgh, Dad found his home was being turned into a boarding house; "to maximize the value of the estate," his father's executor told him. My father rarely complained or even talked of his youth, but these losses, even of his home, must have hurt him deeply.

On summer vacations, some of his college and later law school friends joined my father in travelling around America and Europe. This shared travel helped compensate for his lack of parents and a home. My father's other male first cousin, Christian, once told me that Dad visited him at his Camp Hill home occasionally on short college vacations. He said "Stanton sometimes just sat in the living

room looking so sad." This next poem tries to capture some of his character and his compensation with love of trains and travel.

Railroad Bill

I have always lived within the sound
of the Pennsylvania Railroad
which moans, then sings, and rides me at night
to the sound of my father's voice,
trembling at the trains he knew and those
he rode in childhood and growing and passing.
The ones to meet his father in Cape May, or
to carry a gift to my mother in New Mexico, or
to come and lift my brother and newborn me in California.
He'd given up the car for good in the Sonoran Desert
simply at the urging of a billboard showing cool happy people
in a sleek frosty-looking Santa Fe car and captioned:
"Next Time, Take the Train."
Sometimes, Santa Fe, Super Chief, and Dad crossed America just
  for the hell of it.

He'd worked hard-sweat labor
in a railroad roundhouse repair shop
summers in college although he didn't need a dime.
Orphaned, he lived financially easy
emotionally hard, eased by the trains.
He knew the diesel roads, the steam numbers, even old 97
and 143, the FFV serving the first families of Virginia.
His voice would catch

at the sighing steam of the Pittsburgher
leaving for New York
or telling my fourteen-year-old self
how to change trains in Chicago
and catch the Panama Limited to New Orleans
and to order the gravied grits in the dining car.

My father and I coupled to New York's Pennsylvania Station
Pennsylvania side, first as a family then just us.
But I had to pass to my brother Terry
and miss traveling to Paris
to ride the *Train à Grande Vitesse* to Nice.
My brother said that travel month wore him down ten years
which transubstantiated into Dad's delighted grin.

My father did many fine things for me:
taught me driving-wheel morals, beautiful language,
and how to build a flagman's sense for trouble
and a lineman's backbone for hard times.
But I must admit that on hearing the keening
of a Pensy mainline highball,
as we packed Dad into the final black carriage,
I found myself humming "Hobo Bill's Last Ride."

After Harvard law school, my father continued travelling, once taking one of the first flights from London to Paris, which had to unexpectedly land in a French field because one of the passengers was airsick. Dad said she wasn't the only one getting sick on that bumpy harrowing ride. He was also happy to recover in that French field. My father settled back in Pittsburgh. He toyed with the idea of going to Boston or New York, but his cousin Chick argued that their family helped build Pittsburgh, and he belonged here.

Although Dad returns later in this memoir, I will finish this "Father section" with the following poem which suggests our unique relationship.

Dad's Calling

In my early twenties, my father
strode into my bedroom
shouting *Get up, get up.*

Half-dressed, sprawled on my bed,
I was still high from a drinks party
and sure there was some emergency.

The chance to be a good son.
I formaled up quickly, coat and tie,
ready for anything. I waited by our hallway door.

My father dressed now in pajamas, came out
of his bedroom upstairs and looked down at me.

Where are we going? I asked in my addle.

You are going to bed, he said seriously.
*I woke you up to get you to get
yourself together for bed.*

Late in his life, my father
took to calling me in the deep night.
Often high and with a problem.
I was no longer drinking.

Once, he called to ask
if I could come and get him - surprisingly,
at his office downtown,
from which he'd retired
seven years before.

I was bone-tired from working sober hard,
but felt another chance
to be the good son.

As I was girding up to go get him
a fading martini recollection sent me
a helpful suggestion:
I told my father: *Go to the window
and tell me what you see.*
He described, not the downtown scene,
but the building across the street from his Shadyside house.
So I talked him into turning around, seeing his bed,
and lying down in it.

Neither of us ever spoke
of these two instances,
never to say
I was the good son.

MY MOTHER

My mother was Catherine Donnelly Carson, raised with seven sisters and two brothers on Mount Washington. Her father was a successful grocer, and his daughters were successful children achieving a number of college degrees and good jobs, unusual for women at that time: Mayme, Manager of the federal tax desk in

Pittsburgh; Nancy, Director of Home Nursing in Allegheny County; Betty, owner/operator of Hamilton Press; Peg, Sister of Mercy, MA in English and M.A. in Education, teacher, and archivist for Carlow University; Alice, AT&T manager, Bina and Pat married early after college. My mother was second oldest but clearly the leader. She paid many of her sisters' education expenses from her own salary, and helped in their career and personal paths. Kay, as they called her, even ran a sort of intellectual/social and etiquette workshop for her sisters. They deferred to her all of her life.

The brothers were not as easy. Jim, the oldest had, some success behind the scenes in politics and was a great companion of my mother who adored him. Jim introduced her to much of the social, and especially political, life in Pittsburgh during Prohibition. She recalled being taken to the "Holy Mary Mother of God Club," an Irish Speakeasy. Before I knew him, Jim died in a freak accident in California: crushed between two cable cars in San Francisco. Hugh Donnelly, the second boy, showed great promise as a student and tennis player. Alcoholism cut both possibilities short. He was a handsome Black Irishman whom I romanticized and felt close to. This next poem which jumps ahead in my narrative and tells much of my own and my brother's character, pays a little homage to Uncle Hugh:

Good Friday

That smoky spring morning
reminded me of fall, heartbreaking
in its promise and surety of end.
It was Good Friday.
Before Jesus' inheritance,
when it was all on the come:

his bet and belief way back then
and mine that it would be ok even though

I was nineteen and mostly wondering
the oxygen of women
and why my miracles
always tasted of bourbon.

One latest busy question:
why we stop at red lights.

I dealt the traffic tickets in a semicircle
on my brother's kitchen table
like blasphemous apostles
while he finished
the cigar he had lit at the police station
for our confidence.

Nine stop signs, four stoplights, and
a weak little "too fast for conditions."

Two screaming days later,
I dutifully drove them
and a sack of dollars
out of my parents' house
downtown to the fixer,
my uncle, who got sober with Blackie Reilly, really:
If you had only come to me sooner-
I date the secretary.
Could have stopped it right there, free.
Now I'll have to deal with the Greek,
And believe me, it will cost.

Hugh Donnelly stayed sober, repaired his family relations, even coming to my high school graduation, and lived into his late sixties.

CHAPTER II

STANTON AND CATHERINE AND THE MYTH OF CALIFORNIA

Dad joined the law firm of Wright and Rundle. My mother, then the firm's office manager, said he was an easy hire since J.M. Wright didn't initially pay him anything on the pretext, "He doesn't need the money." My mother lobbied for a salary for the new man, showing for the first of many times how much Stanton needed her. Nonetheless, my mother loved to tell my brother and me how father and Wright made a powerful pair, my father carefully and relentlessly researching cases behind the scenes and Wright dramatically appearing in court and winning for old and attracting new clients. My mother romanticized this as a reification of Sydney Carton, the self-sacrificing character in Dicken's *Tale of Two Cities*. Actually, this harnessing of my father's talent probably kept him from fully developing as an attorney, especially one who attracted new clients. Another way myth has been very powerful in my family.

My parents, having met at Wright and Rundle, were immediately interested in each other and began dating. They had an active social life which included a lot of drinking

Their attraction was electric. And sparks flew of both love and anger. I could see that, even as they aged. Both were good looking: a college friend on meeting my father said he looked like Humphry Bogart; my mother had that Irish pale fair skin with sparkling green eyes and what my aunt Mayme described as a very nice figure. They were both witty, and capable of much charm. Unfortunately, alcohol got between them. It made my life both hard and sometimes very amusing. My mother especially had an amazing sense of humor. I try to capture some of that and the difficulties it could cause in the following:

Mother's Days

The last time I saw him, he was lying drunk
on the floor of the Holy Mary Mother of God Club,
my mother said of a just-elected politician.

I never thought of her as so incisively aware
or wickedly funny
until I started to drink with her.

Much younger, I had learned
to avoid interrupting
her long afternoon hangover sleeps.

If you could walk with me
hobbling around that house
so not to wake angry that ecstasy,

you would know why I prayed so long
through my endless marriages
for warmth, even purgatory.

Or maybe I'm just blind to myself
and who my mother really was.

"I think you have yellow jaundice,"
the Chinese intern once told my mother,
and she replied: "How would *you* know?"

They married and like many Americans, my parents were subject to the American myth to go West, specifically California. In the late 1930's, they rented a house on Pomona Drive in Long Beach. My mother was happy there but my father became less and less enchanted with starting his law career over, (including a new California bar exam). Dad began a midcentury version of a bi-coastal commute, visiting on holidays and the summer while my mother became a more permanent resident of California. Both my brother and I were born there, and I have often wondered how our lives might have turned out had my family stayed. The Beach Boys grew up only a few blocks away. (I can't sing, but I am pretty good at making friends). But we came back East before any of our lives changed much at all. What I do see is my father repeating his own parents' family volatility, separation, yet ongoing commitment.

ME

I was born on October 23, 1941 (same birth day as the late-night host, Johnny Carson, sixteen years earlier). I am John Stanton Carson Jr. I have been called Jay since my mother named me for more singularity. One pleasant family myth is that I was born on the same floor of Good Samaritan Hospital as Mary Martin's daughter, Heller. My mother claimed I was chosen (over Heller) as the demonstration baby, the height of my theatrical achievement. Nurses I have known since have told me they always choose boys for demonstrations.

My brother, Terry, exhibited an early and dangerous rebellious streak by walking two blocks from our Pomona Drive home to the beach when he was supposed to stay in the back yard. In his defense, other unsupervised youngsters were calling him over. After playing and getting sand in his eye, he started home across Ocean Blvd., blinded. An old truck just missed him but the bumper caught his shirt and dragged him some twenty feet down the street. Luckily, the man stopped and got help. Terry was hospitalized for a short time, but ok. Years later, when I told my mother I remembered all that happened, she told me I couldn't remember it because I'd been with one of her friends six blocks away for the afternoon. Repeated stories had made me believe that I was there. I was creating my own myth. But an underlying truth does emerge: my parents' negligent supervision of both my brother and me, probably caused by drinking.

Our life in California came to an end on Pearl Harbor Day, December 7, 1941. Fearing a Japanese invasion, my mother wanted to get us away from the West Coast. Most of the available transportation was taken up by the Army and other fearful Americans, complicating any travel plans. Eventually, we did get back to Pittsburgh and my father. After fears subsided, my mother, brother, and I returned to California for another two years until both my parents decided to settle in Pittsburgh. Their settling was neither ordinary nor complete. My father maintained an apartment closer to his office where he slept and lived during the work week. The living arrangement was just normal to me, but not others. After too often seeing shocked or too-knowing looks, I learned early on not to mention my father's apartment to my grade school friends and especially their parents. I have come to believe that my father just didn't want the bother of young children around more than on weekends.

CHAPTER III

PITTSBURGH AND THE MYTH OF THE HAPPY FAMILY

We lived in the East End on Kentucky Avenue in Shadyside. Although it was a beautiful modern (for 1947) center hall house on a lovely street, vestiges of the pre-WWII era were all around us. We had visits from the vegetable huckster, milkman, and knife sharpener. At first, most of these came to us via horse drawn vehicles. This added charm to our youth, allowing us to sometimes feed sugar to the horses and get ice from the milk man (his only refrigeration for the milk). The horses also provided us horse manure, street obstacles for walking and riding our bikes around. A big old red stable, in its day, providing carriages services for a number of local houses, stood directly across from our new home. The owner, now horseless, still lived in the upstairs apartment. I could see him in his wife-beater undershirt putting out and pulling in bottles of milk and beer from the window sill, perhaps his only refrigeration. Within a few years of our moving in, the stable and land were sold, and a considerably sized apartment complex started to be built. This construction site provided my neighborhood friends and I with great illegal places to play and an endless supply of bricks, which we stopped stealing because of our storage capability and our exhausted imaginations. We finally could not figure out what to do with them.

One great advantage to our new home for me were two kids my own age: Liz and Gil. Their families fit into the individualistic nature of the of the neighborhood. Liz's father was the court beat reporter for the *Pittsburgh Press*. He was tall, handsome, and supposedly distantly related to the great Confederate cavalry general, Jeb Stuart. He also drank a lot and was often poured out of a cab on Friday evenings. Liz's mother was a faded Southern belle and a fabulous (in every sense of the word) story teller, mostly exaggerations or outright lies. I remember hearing stories about myself, about to be taken to London, for example where my family could shop for things, some for me, unavailable in the U.S. (We never took such a trip.) I knew these tales were not true, but I loved them because they were so much more fun than what happened in reality. In short, Liz's family lived in a dream world, a myth that after a while became untenable.

Raised to Be a Debutant

My oldest friend, Liz, ended up a cleaning woman in hospitals.
Aristocratic dreams swirled
in her parents' ancient linage heads.
Father from Virginia's planter class
that you could guess seeing his tall supple frame
nobly erect as if saddle-ready
for Light Horse Harry Lee's brigade.
And a Greek and Latin learning air,
almost redundant marks of breeding.
All crushed like cotton twigs underfoot.

Her mother from West Virginia coal and commerce people
whose boom imploded in a mining bust.

Having exhausted the last of their meager inheritances
on a big falling down house, private school, and music
lessons for my friend, they were out:
of money, prospects, dependable relatives, ideas.
So, the father drank and the mother lied.

Even as a child I knew she was lying
But she was so accomplished, I preferred her stories,

some about our childish pranks,
to more harsh, boring reality.

Jeb Stuart should have been Elizabeth's father's ancestor.
Her mother surely was a friend of Jimmy Stewart same
hometown, after all.
We kids reveled in her back porch fantasies
sometimes interrupted by Liz's father being poured out
of a Yellow cab and helped up the steep back steps.

Liz couldn't take ski trips over Spring vacations
like her private school friends,
and couldn't fit in with classmates' private golf club parties.
So, she dropped out, started going to rock bars,
and married a truck driver.

I could go over the other husbands who
wouldn't measure up to a family that had founded
churches in Richmond and had to mortgage their ramshackle/
for gin and doctors. Nor is this about Liz's marital problems.

It's about a secret snack we had:
those little candy Dots in which we would put toothpicks
and sell to our childhood friends for a penny each,
laughing at the taste of our ingenuity.
We promised to meet when we were 30
and make a business, a life, of selling our irresistible treats.

Liz was just put in a home for the forgetful
and I know she has a lot to let go.

> I rarely see a package of those candies
> without remembering how delicious they were
> even when occasionally the toothpicks poked through
> and cut my tongue.

My other great childhood friend Gil was one of four boys living in an old mansion on Fifth Avenue where his father had a very successful laboratory that produced the gas mask used by the US Navy in World War II. He also invented perhaps the first remote-operated toy car. Very family oriented, they had a large back yard where we played softball, climbed on monkey bars, ran around a pond, and decorated for Halloween a small play house. Gil was my friend throughout my life, but we drifted apart as he moved West and became even more of a social and environmental activist.

Gil's Song

> He was what I wanted to be
> long before I knew it:
> successful student, lawyer,
> musician, motorcycle dude. More than all those
> Gil, slight of stature, was a heavy-weight freedom rider,
> almost run off a bridge by swerving vengeful KKK
> while he tried to get the vote to those who had none.
> Later, revitalizing scores of river areas
> with his friend, Interior Secretary "Stu" Udall.
>
> It goes without saying I was none of the above.

The damnedest thing,
the infuriating thing: He cared about me.

We'd grown up together,
friends since five. I made him
swear then that we'd meet at twenty-one
and sell pieces of jelly licorice
on toothpicks to make our millions.
Even then, I sensed Gil liked me
and only humored my plan.

We invented a game of bar tag
on his backyard monkey bars,
one of my wins because
of my slick nylon jacket.

Later, if I drove past in my new ritzy car
with a new glitzy girlfriend,
he still invited me to his string band's benefit
for revitalizing our local river.

Out West, Gil opened a high-rise law firm
successful enough to support
his considerable storefront help
to indigent natives and an aching earth,
saving grassland and repairing wetlands.
I slid as easily as with my nylon jacket
to jobs where too little thinking
and too much cocktail were expected.

But I was still somehow relieved and infused when we met

and he tried to reach me, with maybe how to see and study birds,
or show me how too many untended cattle destroy a small stream,
or what a good senator or governor can mean.

When we were twelve, I almost
broke his arm in horseplay, or maybe in envy to prevent him
from doing what I already knew he would.
Weeks before his death,
Gil, inexplicably and, of course, purposefully
draped that arm around me.

After a few years of seeing us only on weekends and complaints from my mother, and a rent rise in the Royal York Apartments, my father moved in with us, full time. I remember some big changes. No longer could we listen to The Life of Riley and Fiber McGee and Molly, among other radio shows, at night with our mother, lying crossways on my brother's bed. After my father's moved in, Terry and I were mostly left in what I call now "benign neglect." I was seven and by this time, used to withdrawal of parental supervision and care. My brother, however, marked this as the beginning of his rebellion towards the family. From then on, he often seemed uncomfortable with all of us.

Our parents continued to travel to Europe. That meant full-time maids for my brother and me. When we were babies and toddlers, it had meant a nursery home called something like Maxata, which my second wife called "Baby Boarding School." I don't remember that place. Terry remembered not liking it at all. When we were older, our in-home maids hired for the duration of my parents' trips were nice and tried to keep us happy with schedules we liked and good food.

I remember having a run-in with one of the African American maid's children, a girl about my own age. At eight years old, I tried to win the argument by saying "you are just mad that you are not white." I got my first diversity training from that girl's mother. I had fallen into perhaps America's most dangerous and evil myth, the superiority of whites. I was told in no uncertain terms that Negroes were proud to be Black and I had no right criticizing on the basis on their color. That maid would sometimes have a few friends and relatives in to drink beer at night. I was a little scared. But we were fine with and to each other after that.

Since my parents came back from one of those trips well after Labor Day, they instructed another maid (white and Irish) to pose as my grandmother and sign me up for Sacred Heart Grade School. All went well, and I was able to start my education in first grade at the age of five since I would be six before Christmas. Now, I feel I should have been held back. But that wasn't the thinking at the time, especially in our house. I saw classmates being registered with their parents and felt what I now know as abandoned. My father on more than one occasion pointed out that Terry and I got more attention than Winston Churchill who was brought in to see his parents only at tea time for less than a half hour. It took me some years of therapy to see how wrong both Winston's and my parents were.

CHAPTER IV

GRADE SCHOOL AND THE MYTH OF CATHOLIC EXCLUSIVE ACCESS TO GOD

At Sacred Heart Grade School, my classmates and I were seated by our perceived intelligence as well as our classroom accomplishments. I was in the slow row. My mother disagreed. She had various ways of correcting these "mistakes" in my grade school education. One was to send some whiskey and/or a ham to the sisters' convent. In this case, Mother put on her armor, a Kelly-green suit, and visited in person. Her interlocutor was my first-grade teacher, a nun whom my mother referred to ever after as "Farmer." Still in the classroom, I remember their meeting as short, perhaps warmed up with an earlier delivery of whiskey and a ham. The next day I was in the smart row. I was and am still not sure why I was in either. I was learning something about the American success myth: gifts and powerful personalities can often smooth the way

I had a few outstanding teachers at Sacred Heart, one of whom supported me when it probably opposed her Catholic commitment. Although my mother was Catholic, because my father was Protestant, the nuns would not let me receive my first Holy Communion with my classmates. When the other children went over to the church to practice, Sister Antonia, a beautiful petite young nun stayed back and soothed my hurt feelings. I can still see her sitting next to me in one of those small wooden desks, saying softly it would all be alright. When my mother learned of my exclusion, she called a powerful connection she had at the rival St. Paul's parish, and the problem disappeared. I practiced and then received Holy Communion with my class. Another myth was laid to rest, the power and indomitable nature of my local parish priests and nuns.

But another dangerous one was seeded: it's not what you know or believe; it's who you know.

I had one outstanding teacher, Mrs. Sullivan. She was tough and looked it, steel grey hair atop a tall powerful body; but I learned a lot. We even had a class party celebrating her at the end of the year. She taught me one of the great secrets of teaching: to establish a community in class and then create an "us" (the class)-v.- "them" (everybody else) pride. The pride was in how much we cared for each other and for learning, no matter what others thought. I remember she created a competitive atmosphere where you never felt you lost much; there was always the next lesson to win at. Years later, I imitated that approach in my own teaching with some success.

But mostly I found Sacred Heart Grade School teaching to be tedious, angry (if you didn't understand something, it was not the teaching, but your fault), and overly focused on the Catholic saints. I learned math pretty well because there was no saint to get lost in. But my English studies were so abysmal that when I applied to Shady Side Academy, my English grades on the entrance test were very low. A good summer school teacher whom I would again meet at Carnegie-Mellon University years later helped nearly double my score.

At Sacred Heart, I did alright with grades and the strict discipline. But I saw some scary stuff. I remember a young woman who made the mistake of wearing a see-through blouse (she did have a bra on) get humiliated in front of a class of 50 students by a nun. I also saw my friend, Lindsay, having a ten-pound paper cutter thrown at him, for lord knows what infraction. My brother had his difficulties with the discipline. He was once confronted by the Principal for sneaking into school late. She slapped him. Terry returned the slap, but given how her habit overshadowed her face it was probably more of a punch. Anyway, he was expelled. My parents must have been on his side because they didn't make much of a fuss, and Terry transferred to the good neighborhood public school, appropriately for him named, Liberty School, which he liked and where he did well.

Some people had trouble with my brother, and our relationship was not perfect, but all through our lives I could feel his love. I change Terry's name in the poem for a reason that will be obvious.

Michael

My brother was a tough customer,
once confronting a sympathetic friend
who said, after our mother's long illness
and death, *Maybe it was for the best.*
Michael growled, *Maybe it wasn't.*

He once drank a few hours away
with Lee Marvin and complained
that Lee was unpleasant and obstreperous.
I recounted this to that same friend
who answered, *What did Lee say?*

But he was Michael the archangel to me
when I was out of money or friends
or full of enemies, one of whom
was a big 8th grade paperboy when
I was in fourth and who caught me in a garage
and roughed me up pretty good.
On his route with a load of papers on his head,
he wasn't tough enough to scare Michael

who socked him so hard papers flew
like peace doves all over Fifth Avenue.

I could never return such a favor.
When death came after him,
I could only buy his favorite flowers for the funeral.

Years before, Michael bought a mountain cottage
and immediately gave me a key. One Saturday we planted
daffodils all day

which I can still glimpse, blazing,
as I drive by on Route 22, these many years later.

We also lived close to the East Liberty business district when it was the fifth busiest "downtown" between New York and Cleveland. At that time, it was home to five movie theaters, two bowling alleys, a hobby store and lots of other businesses fascinating to young people.

The following poem looks at my life near East Liberty and foreshadows my first marriage and my interest in art.

Something in the Eye

Always my shining safe, after-movie place,
Woolworth's was even more brilliant
in the darkness of January's
late afternoon snow.

Cold numbed, film-full gaze,
I stumbled into the women's department:

rings and their glistening quartz stones
as larcenously luminescent, and high as my eyes.

It stunned from the middle of a careless pile
like my pretty Aunt Ann amidst her sisters.
One shop girl talked to another,
her hair as alluring gold as the rings' settings.

I want that ring . . .
for my mother. "It's too small
for your mother; it's a girl's ring."
My sister, then. I want that ring.

Before I married, my wife
talked me out of watching a Lakers-Celtics game
to pick our china. Her planned hour turned
into three as I brought plate after lustrous plate

for her rejection - until the one
I broke and walked away. It was the day before
the last film we saw as single people:
the one about the empty Hermitage Museum.

In seventh grade we had to fill out sort forms announcing where we were planning on going to high school. Even though I had done so poorly on the English entrance exam, Shady Side Academy had accepted me, which I wrote on the form. My 7th grade nun teacher yelled a question: "Do you know that you know that you misspelled Academy and that Shady Side is a Presbyterian school?" I was a short-timer, so I thought, but was too cowed to say, maybe I could spell Academy if I had gone there earlier.

Like many of my schoolmates, perhaps the chief thing I learned at Sacred Heart Grade School was guilt. We believed we were bad children and probably should go to hell. (How little I thought about the "holy family of Jesus, Mary, and Joseph" the nuns thought we should be thinking about so often. Why did I do so badly on tests of material not well taught? Why was that young girl humiliated for wearing a see-through blouse? What had my friend Lindsay done to get a 10 pound paper cutter thrown at him? My biggest complaint with the Catholic Church to this day is the constant repetition that the Catholic Church is the only true church and the only way to true spirituality. (We were actually encouraged to try to "save" our non-Catholic neighbors with "explanations") This claim of exclusive access to God has driven many people who could have found spirituality elsewhere to complete avoidance. Several of my friends who don't go to any church explain their avoidance by simply saying they were raised Catholic. I have had much success finding spiritual help in Protestant churches particularly Presbyterian churches. More about this later.

CHAPTER IV

SHADY SIDE AND MY OWN MYTH OF FAMILY

Shady Side Academy (SSA) was a revelation in many ways. I knew no one. Many of my new classmates had gone to the Shady Side Junior School and others knew each other from various groups including the Jewish community. Many were connected socially by old Pittsburgh families and country clubs. As mentioned earlier, my family roots in Pittsburgh go way back and my father's mother was in Pittsburgh's Social Register. Because of general contrariness and alcoholism, my parents had largely isolated themselves. We belonged to the Pittsburgh Athletic Association, where we knew almost no one well and the Duquesne Club for my father's downtown lunches where he was able to be charming and control his drinking enough to eat with colleagues. But no tonier country clubs. I think now, although I was getting better at covering it, I suffered a real introversion from all the turmoil at home. And I often felt alone and neglected. The following poem tries to capture that sense, starting at a young age.

Frozen

Snow covered branches
ice tree skeletons
as if rising from winter's graveyard
haunting all warmth,
recalling stark solstice from my boyhood
when I would have Christmas
in my room alone; small standing tree
I purchased from my allowance
decorated with the leavings
-cracked ornaments, wrinkled tinsel-
from the downstairs family tree:
A big prickly pine for big prickly people
who, weary of fighting,
would leave beneath their tree for me
large negotiated peace offerings:
play guns – for protection? bicycles – for escape?

For my private Christmas,
I would buy some small presents

at Woolworths, a maple sugar soldier
a tiny silver key chain
from me to me.

And for the full effect,
I'd open my windows,
so the snow came right in.
I'd rest my feet on the hot radiator by the window
warm white flaked socks.
A quiet dead peace.

The hell with the expense, the waste.
The hell with Them.

We did have some good times as a family. I remember the best being our vacations at Spring Lake, New Jersey where we went yearly in August to the Monmouth Hotel for ten years. My parents had made some good friends there and were able to hold their drinking and anger in check. I was very happy for them and for me and Terry that we had a normal, even good, time. It was a great hotel with a terrific beach. I still remember learning to body surf and spending whole afternoons practicing that new skill. I made friends with other young people and with some of the people who lived in Spring Lake; chief among them was Andy Taggert, the child of a Scotts family who had a small restaurant near our hotel. He introduced me to other locals, and I had a terrific time in that beautiful seaside town, going to small community dances and parties.

Unfortunately, our vacation travels to and from Spring Lake were bracketed by train trips to New York. We would start in Pittsburgh with a long dinner waiting for the Pittsburgher passenger train to be ready to board. Those dinners would be long boozy affairs for my parents, especially my father who would inevitably lose the train tickets, and then be pretty much unable to do anything. My mother would have to find the tickets and get all of us on board and to our compartments. Complicating things, my father was usually argumentative. I was always sure we would not get on the train. Today, I love to travel. But I am still nervous at the beginning of a trip.

How could I do better, especially in this new intimidating prep school environment? Not be isolated, make friends. I had been complimented especially on my sense of humor. Certainly, I had developed the skills of a diplomat by negotiating around three bigger and sometimes dangerous people. Despite my brother's love, he had a bad temper, one reason I could not use him as a model. Another was an arrogance in talking about how much money we had. The nuns had taught me at least that such talk was in bad taste if not sinful. Looking around at my classmates at Shady Side sealed the deal for me. Even I could see and hear (Nick is right in *The Great Gatsby*: some voices are full of money) what my brother didn't understand: many of my schoolmates were far richer than we were and didn't say much if anything about it.

I used what skills I had and did pretty well in making friends. Starting with Eddie Byrnes, tall, blond, athletic, later the captain of our track team, whom I met bicycling to Shady Side summer school on. He taught me the back way in through the football field. That fall and for the following four years, Ed and I sat next to each other in Shady Side's "Presbyterian" chapel. Two Irish Catholic boys. To this day, I kid Ed that, when I am around him, I have an unnatural desire to sing Protestant hymns. Another early friend was Bill Robinson. We were both in the same English class and became almost professional grifters in our ability to get library passes so we could spend our free classes away from the dreaded study hall, a huge room full of seventy or so desks and young men hating being there. Sometimes they were upper classmen quietly hazing/teasing newer students. I learned several new words and sexual possibilities in those long study halls. They were usually presided over by faculty members who often overlooked or missed the whispering undercurrent.

Shortly thereafter, I widened my connections to a group who became life-long friends and some of whom appear in the stories below. In a way, I did too well. None of this was clear to me at the time, but I was beginning a process of building a new family, one that was more dependable and kinder and liked me. And one that making myself fit into became wonderful at the time, but probably too important long after it needed to be.

I needed that new family's support a number of times in our new and sometimes difficult surroundings. In one instance I stepped on the Senior Campus a small grass quadrangle in front of the main classroom building, Rowe Hall. My punishment as a freshman was that the seniors "depantsed" me. They took off my pants, ran them up the flagpole, covered me in mustard and ketchup and chased me around that campus. One odd memory is that, mostly for bravado, I kept using profanity about the condiments they were putting on me. To this day, I remember the captain of the wrestling team saying to me almost like a psychologist, *You swear a lot*. Looking back, I am still somewhat amazed that no faculty stepped in to help me. I had to borrow a shower, pants, and a shirt from a boarding classmate to return to class. I was chastised by the teacher of my math class for being late. We were all part of a larger myth growing out of the English boarding schools. A certain amount of bullying is good for initiation. It helps new people grow and connect. I did feel more a part of my school and less afraid. But I think there are other ways of achieving that end.

A nucleus of about eight of us formed early in our freshman year. Charmed by some of the Roman history we were learning, we quickly named ourselves *the Mob*. Central to planning was Jim who became my best friend then and thereafter. He was a stocky, serious looking, (claimed at one point to be part American Indian) and a great student, but with a wicked sense of humor. We pulled the usual high school pranks and more. At one point, we were nearly thrown into jail and out of SSA for breaking down a door to a party to which we were not invited. My father proved a brick that night, stopping the police from taking us in, and calling the door owner to calm him down. And he neither disciplined or reproved me, even suggesting I skip the group visit and apology to the door owner. I mark that up to my father's myth about him and me being too special. Part of the myth was that we were very much alike. We did look alike and appreciated each other's conversation and sense of humor, his being much drier than mine. He also liked that I had friends whom for the most part he trusted, after all they were from Shady Side Academy. He lacked friends. This myth taught me the wrong thing: that I didn't have to be accountable. The positive was my father's protection. That and my connection to my friends started to make me less afraid, but also less responsible. The following story tries to capture that incident and some of my sense of our group, although for the sake of the plot it distorts my father's role and character.

MOST WANTED, 1972

The portrait is still there, hanging between the French doors. My grandmother, maybe in her fifties, done by Gorson. Aging, still looking pretty, loved, and at home. I was snooping around an old desk as I waited. I found a cartoon that my grandmother sketched which fell out of the family Bible. On ordinary faded drawing on paper a mustachioed, top-hatted man orders out a lined-faced woman with his finger. *Too old, doesn't want me, and I can't go back to my parents*, she says in the caption, finished off with my grandmother's ornate signature. I re-hid the cartoon somewhere in Psalms.

As I finished reshelving the Bible, the first of our gang, Rodney, breezed right in one of those French doors, always the earliest and brightest of us. Then Oliver came downstairs. He was from West Virginia and boarded at our Valley Preparatory. Ollie, the Animal, was staying the weekend with me. The living room filled up with the rest of us as we made our plans about a party. Initial news did not look promising.

"We weren't invited," Devon said. How Devon always had the information on all parties mystified me.

"Well, aren't these guys our classmates?" I asked.

"One thing a decent private school ought to provide is access to classmates' parties," Ollie added, taking my side.

"It's George's girlfriend's party and they don't want us." The words stung my sophomore self.

"Such a school ought to provide access to girlfriends too," Rodney chimed in. "Especially girlfriends."

"How do you know they don't want us?" I pressed.

"I called George," Devon said. "It's just a small, closed party while the parents are out. I've been there: pretty girl, full liquor cabinet. Only an ancient grandmother whom they keep upstairs, mostly asleep."

Very few people want you when you are a fifteen-year-old boy. Too old to be taken care of at home. Too young to hold an outside job or drive. Not able to pair off in couples, we hung out in a large, chaotic group, trying to appear tough and looking for just enough trouble to handle without bloody lips and knuckles and outside of police stations —which is to say, not much. We were annoying rather than dangerous.

With some sense of self-knowledge, we called ourselves *The Mob* after the Roman rabble in our history books. We did, of course, want to pair off with girls, but that, too, had to wait until we could drive. What we could do was go to parties. Often over-chaperoned, these Pepsi, chip, and record affairs were usually pretty deadly, just a small, dusty oasis in our social desert. Unless, of course, the parents were not there, when liquor bottles might be opened and girls touched.

The Mob was just the kind of group not to be invited and often wasn't. Because of ignorance of the party or geographical problems (again, no cars), we often overlooked these slights. But if the party was relatively close and we knew the actors, our rules changed.

"People don't invite you to a party," Rodney pronounced, "for one of two reasons: either they don't know you or they don't like you. If you go anyway, they probably won't know you any better, and they certainly aren't going to like you any better."

"Rodney's right," Karl, the Bear, said. "Let's just go."

"I'm for it," I said.

The rest—Ollie (the Animal), Devon (Chief of Intelligence), Dean, and Ed—agreed.

Although cool and masculinity were hard to maintain on a bus, it was raining. We got there in about ten stops, earning lots of dirty looks for three obscene songs sung at the tops of our voices.

Devon, with all the information, found the house with little trouble.

"Maybe we should ask politely first," he said.

"Yeah," Rodney answered, "and maybe you can get a date with the grandmother."

The perpetrator of our disrespect was a girl from Highland Park who had invited her friends. The guys were our classmates, proving that the old school ties only went so far. The parents were gone. The oldie upstairs probably would not interfere with liquor flowing or girl touching.

The Mob knocked on the door. There was no answer, but we were relentless with the heavy brass knocker.

The door then opened a crack before it started to close. But we had the Bear in our front line. Then, with Devon, Rodney, and Dean's help, the crack widened, then started to close again, protection from invasion being a basic human urge. It was a lever/fulcrum issue. *The Mob* surged but the defense held.

With all the pressure from the other side, we broke what had looked like a pretty solid door.

Whereas it is often difficult to slip into a party when not invited, it's impossible once you've broken the host's door. Like the Roman commoners after Caesar's death, *The Mob* fled.

It's not easy to scatter when using public transportation but we managed. I was already back in my house with Oliver when the doorbell rang. I was surprised to see a policeman. I figured we'd done less damage than we had or that broken doors were part of the cost of raising daughters.

"Yes, Officer? What's the problem?"

"I would like you to identify some people." I honestly believed him that we were off scot-free. Ah, youth!

"Do you know these two?" the officer said, referring to Devon and a much weaker-looking Karl sitting in the back of the police car. I was tempted to say "No!" just for the fun of it. But then I started to smell the trouble and fessed up.

This was getting to be no fun for any of us. Even the cop looked a little uncomfortable. In retrospect, I guess bringing in some pain-in-the-ass juvenile delinquents isn't exactly a fast lane to promotion.

"Get in," the cop said.

"Where are we going?" I asked.

"Down to old number five," he said.

"Is this some kind of railroad game?" Ollie piped up in his native West Virginia accent, possibly the most suicidal response I have ever heard. Now the cop looked pissed, and I was really getting worried.

"Get in!" he repeated.

I was faced the dilemma of telling my father, or rather pleading with him for help, or going to the police station. Dad could have a terrible temper but jail is jail.

"I've got to go back in and get my jacket," I said. And the cop let me.

"Dad, Dad," I implored into his study, "a cop outside is trying to take us to jail."

He didn't even ask me what I had done. He was a lawyer and maybe thought that knowledge might hurt his ability to defend me.

The cop came to the door again, and my father started to talk to him.

I faded to the kitchen with Ollie. The Animal and I quietly got maybe our last beers for a while. When we came back the cop was standing there like some kind of customer. My father was on the phone, trying to talk down the parent of the party-giver, the now broken-door owner. Turns out this guy was also a lawyer, so things were going a little rougher than with the cop. But reason, or luck, or my father's skill prevailed, and the cop left, promising to take the two in his back seat home. I never saw my father in court; he must have been pretty good.

But then he started on me.

"What the hell were you thinking? Invading homes. And telling cops not to play railroad games; that almost cost you a night in jail. Of all the doors to break down in Pittsburgh, Bill May's is the worst. He is a real son of a bitch, but luckily, I know him and promised to pay for the door. You, young man, will be earning that money working for me. But there might be an additional problem: his wife's mother supposedly had some kind of an attack caused by your invasion."

All I could say was that I was sorry, which I really was. "Do they think she'll be okay?" I added sympathetically.

"Hell, May's been complaining about her for years at the Duquesne Club Bar. He probably doesn't really care or want her around. I know, I've seen enough of that in my time."

As we headed up the stairs, Ollie clapped me on the back. "Why so glum?" he chortled. "Thanks to your dad, it's all working out fine. I'll help with any work you have to do."

"He doesn't really want me helping. Hell, Ollie, even the cops don't want us," I mumbled.

Mr. Bill May lived up to his mean reputation by raising hell with our school headmaster and nearly getting us kicked out. But mercy prevailed; eventually our probations ran out.

After we stopped our pranks, we soon were driving and going out with girls who seemed to want to be with us. We looked back on our earlier capers with humorous condescension.

But vestiges of *The Mob* live on. I am told that Karl called Mr. Bill May every year on the day we broke his door, yelling into the phone: "Happy anniversary, *The Mob*."

What isn't so funny to me anymore is never learning what happened to Mr. Bill May's mother-in-law. I asked his daughter, the party-giver, a year later. She just looked down and walked away. Later that fall I was trying to help my father put on a storm to a French door. He also looked down and walked away when I nodded to my grandmother's portrait and asked if she had been kidding in her cartoon: *Too old, doesn't want me, and I can't go back to my parents.*

At fifteen I knew I would get older and have at least someplace to go. For a while, anyway.

The End

Something else started making me feel more at ease in the world: My friends and I began to drink. It was a time before much public knowledge about the dangers of alcoholism, although I had much anecdotal evidence from my family. Our parents didn't object and even thought it was better to have us drinking in their houses than out in cars or parks. They thought we would learn responsible drinking in their homes. They were wrong. My own and many of my friends' parents were often not good models themselves.

Whatever their theory, we drank a lot in our parents' houses and not often responsibly.

In my sophomore year of high school, my mother contracted a vicious bone disease that put her in Mercy Hospital for a year (a hospital stay that wouldn't happen today). To my surprise, my father visited her nightly for several hours. For me, that meant I had the unsupervised run of our house until around 10:00 PM. The maid fixed me dinner, and there was an endless supply of beer that I now believe my father kept to assuage my temporary loss of parents. He had unpleasant memories of the early deaths of his mother and father. I generously invited my friends over. When my mother returned home, she asked if I was trying to turn her house and home into a bar and grill. I asked if she was trying to turn my bar and grill into a house and home. We were both only slightly kidding.

I made life-long friends at Shady Side; the education was, for the most part, excellent; I participated in sports, although not willingly. But the campus was beautiful; and I entered into a world of many very smart classmates and some pretty rich ones as well. Our teachers were "Masters" and our class levels were "Forms," giving the whole experience an English boarding school vibe.

Athletics were required every day, every season, for me, a constant difficulty. I did participate in the lower forms and am glad I did. Largely because it allowed me to learn about sports, something lacking in my family, removed some of the mystique, and allowed me to feel reasonably comfortable in locker rooms ever after. However, slight and uncoordinated, I did poorly. I did try to avoid athletics. One of my tactics one season was to become a football team manager. Being in charge of the footballs, and water (in a bucket - way before bottled water), and taking roll was more trouble than I had expected. The worst, of course, was derision from my classmates on the team. My other tactic was excused absences to work on publications, the school newspaper and yearbook. That experience cemented my interest in writing. I try to bring them and other experiences together in the following:

On My Way

On my way to being a poet
I rocked in my grade school bed,
my arms around my shoulders
to the rhythms of radio-found blues
and parent-abandoned Beethoven records:
my child-made Mother's embrace.

On my way to being a poet
I stopped playing football to become a water boy,
avoiding those well-aimed high school cleats.
No one wanted to be the water boy,
cowardly but surviving bucket lugger.

On my way to being a poet
I stopped in a bar
and breast-fed myself bourbon
to rock again in the music
and hide the water boy.

On my way to being a poet
I became a rhetorician
to argue myself
out of all the confessing
and to convince myself
into becoming

my frozen father and forgetful mother.

On my way to being a poet
I have burnished and sung stories
to get you to realize
that I am a poet
to get me to realize
being a water boy was worthwhile.

Early on, I was lucky enough to have an English teacher, Dick Gregory, who was a true master of grammar. His book on the subject couldn't get into print because publishers complained it was too difficult. Under his tutelage I went from knowing nothing about the subject to becoming very good at it. I once corrected some ambiguity in the instructions on one of Mr. Gregory's grammar tests. That is, I corrected the teacher who, impressed, then raised my grade. He took a personal interest in me and helped me adjust to a strange and difficult new environment. Later, his grammar instruction was an enormous help in my own teaching.

One upper-level English teacher, Mr. Innes, had a strong New England accent to match the Harvard satchel he carried everywhere. If we worked hard in class and finished early, he would read to us from different books, underscoring the reward element of reading. My favorite was *Wind in the Willows*. During one chapter reading, our Harvard accented teacher turned to a friend of mine, who was having difficulty keeping quiet his run-in with the local police. Mr. Innes, looking directly at my friend, Gus, pointedly read "And no more unfortunate incidents with the Police, Toady." That same teacher had enormous credit with many good colleges and universities and used that power to get us in. Sometimes, to keep his credit with these colleges and universities strong he would not recommend someone who desperately wanted to go to a particular school and whom Mr. Innes believed would not do well there. He liked and helped me despite my less-than-stellar academic record. Others were not so lucky. A classmate told me that once when I was over-cheering a pre-football rally, our headmaster (whom I had satirized in a cartoon in our school paper) said to the well-respected Harvard master, "That Carson is such a show off." To which my guardian said in his New England accent which I can still hear, "Oh, Jay is all right."

The math teaching was also excellent, but the science not so much. Many of my classmates were so smart, great teaching did not matter. I was in the second tier and depended on at least good teaching. There were several of us in the same boat. To accommodate us (and not have so many failing science students) the school created a less challenging "Physical Science" course that got us all through. We were the bad boys, talking, acting out in class, and it was fun.

My most interesting and influential teacher was Mr. Hightower. A true Southern gentleman, he had grown up near the Faulkner plantation in Mississippi and recalled Willian Faulkner crashing a small plane on the Hightower plantation. His mother served the great novelist lemonade while a car from Faulkner's home came to fetch him. The first Hightower not to be mayor of his local town, he was from-central-casting: tall and lean, thoughtful. Most importantly he had a great feel for literature and ability to teach it. Once, when asked if *Hamlet* was worth another of our classes he responded, "My God, man. it's worth your whole life." I also remember him mesmerizing the whole school in chapel by reading a scene (from Faulkner, of course) of newly-freed slaves marching north. He taught seven of us our first literature seminar in an unusual post-graduation class. The seminar took place in the Shady Side library on Sunday summer evenings. I loved being in all that great dark wood and among protecting books, looking out on a beautiful campus. And talking about great literature. All of us were impressed, but I was hooked and knew then what I wanted to do for my life's work. My friend, Jim, who though he liked the class was less impressed, saying Hightower belonged in an antique shop. I see now I was buying into another kind of myth, the great character-teacher.

The overriding feature through all of my time in high school was I was a poor student. Lack of supervision at home and parents' drunken arguments took their toll on my studies. I was no longer in the "smart row" as I had been in grade school. And my mother could do nothing about it. I had also taken up drinking with some energy. My brother, three forms/grades ahead of me, was already failing out of Shady Side. Terry got a girl pregnant and decided to join the Marines Corp. I did not want to do any of those things so I buckled down enough to get through.

I had been a good and cooperative student in grade school. But now, I was having fun being the bad boy, the drinker. Drinking also made me feel more at home with my friends. My best friend Jim tells me that I led him down the garden path to drinking. There may be some truth to that, but somehow, we drinkers always find each other.

Also, my friends and I started dating. At first, dating was a long slow stuttering process, some of which never went away. I was lucky in my junior year to find Jan, a terrific girlfriend. She was a good looking blond, kind, and with a good sense of humor. I was a sexist: a boy in the 50s, with no sisters, at an all-male prep school. I remember seeing Jan's paper on John Milton's *L'Allegro* and *Il Penseroso* and being shocked at how good it was, far better than I could do. I was getting another lesson in equality and another myth was falling.

The best part was that she was interested in me, partly because of my bad boy image. Our first kiss occurred after she kept talking at the end of an evening. I finally said "Oh, shut up" and kissed her. I was in love in that heart-breaking teenage way, learning to open up and connect – a long process for which I didn't even have the vocabulary. Here's an earlier example from my 12-year-old self. I am proud to say my great poet/editor partner, Judy Robinson, teaches this poem in her CMU Osher adult class:

Baking the Ginger Boy's Tongue

"What do you want?"
The white uniformed voice feeds
my anxious sweet hunger, but iced
with the fear of women's words.

"Them, the ones next to," I said.
"Crumb buns? You want crumb buns?
Or the flopovers, which?" Her voice knife sharp
as the red nail of her finger stabbing at the cakes.

Her ruffled pink collar an old
poisoned plain for her mountain head,
a bumpy nose more sure than Sister Pancratious
smelling out my neck and side sweat.

But my brother warned me
of the rancid taste in feminine scented,
sweet words. And how to lower
to Bogart's lip and tongue swagger.

"I can't give you any until you say."
Her eyes bulge at me,
like muffins rising in the tin.
Finally, timed and done, I rise.

"Crumb buns, crumb buns,"
I cry quickly, through slitted mouth,
cut open for the first of many times,
by the cinnamon of desire.

Jan and I dated into our Freshman college year. I even hitchhiked (once with some crazy guy on a schedule and on speed) from eastern Pennsylvania to Boston to spend a weekend with her. Unfortunately, the distance and one of my SSA classmates and good friend, a terrific guy who was in college nearer Boston and who became a well-known doctor, finally got in the way. All three of us have remained friends.

As well as English literature, I became interested in school publications. Writing humor columns under my nom de plume, "Alphonse," I got some real pleasure both from the writing and classmates' recognition. I was chosen as co-feature editor of the *Shady Side News*. I was also an editor on the yearbook, the *Academian*. I was finally finding my way to belong, as a writer and in a community of writers.

I boarded on the Shady Side campus during my senior year. A nucleus of our group going all the way back to the *Mob* were all in Ellsworth House. My best friend Jim was down the hall with another more studious classmate, and I roomed with Richard G., (Dinks, a nursery name that held on well into his adult years) Hamilton. It was a good experience for me, preparing me more for college life. Dinks was a true rebel. He looked a little like and had some of the mannerisms of Marlon Brando. My friends, who were neighbors of his family, said his parents could not control him. Of course, we all thought he was great. One of my favorite memories of Dinks was his capturing two moths and putting them under his armpits. He then went out to see the night faculty proctor, saying it was time for a shower and raised his arms. We all watched these two poor gassed moths spiral out of Dinks's armpits to the floor.

A few years later, Drinks and I, on a weekend whim, drove to Cape Cod to visit some friends. We were drunk and I had lost my glasses. Dinks drove the whole 12 hours up and back. When we got there, he called his parents who had specifically told him not to go anywhere as they were throwing him a birthday party that Sunday, and giving him a car. No birthday party and no car. But that was Dinks.

"We are what we pretend to be" the old saying goes. I was developing my party image a little too well. A counselor later called me, at the age of 21, a "mildly acute alcoholic." My senior class informal picture was of a down-and-out-on-the-pavement drinker buying a literature magazine. My girlfriend Jan was embarrassed by it then; I still am. With my weak grades, I was going to have trouble getting into college. Very luckily for me, my father's first and closest cousin, Chick, was on the board of trustees at Lafayette College. The school was not as selective then as it later became, and I might have managed getting in by myself. My family connection made it a lock. It was a great break, but I was starting to learn the wrong thing about a myth I had developed, that bad things don't happen to cool connected guys like me. I was also passively acquiescing to the evil myths that surrounded me and made my life easier. One of them was the muted antisemitism at Shady Side which had a quota system that mirrored the same quota system in force at Princeton and other ivy schools. My friend, Mike Liberman revealed all this and more in a blockbuster article in the school paper, the *Shady Side News*. The following poem addresses some of those unfair myths I benefitted from.

Lucky You

>my Jewish friend replied
>to my comment that I
>am divorced from most of the antisemitism
>she witnesses and fears daily.

> For I have been a WASP, raised
> in the patriarchy with a faux love
> and respect-but true advantage
> thrown at me everywhere, benefitting
>
> from cheap black mother-maids
> as a child, easier passage to prep
> and college schools, and not
> much trouble finding work
> that certainly wasn't back breaking;
> open invitations to all neighborhoods,
> country club invitation friendly,
> and some powerful friends,
> brokered by an influential father.
>
> I wasn't the guy who made
> all that discrimination.
> I was the guy it was made for.

All in all, Shady Side was a great experience and I was accepted into a very good college. Even so, I had to pass my final exams. Remember that Physical Science course I mentioned earlier? Well, they softened it to get us through, but they still expected us to work. So, the bad boys had to buckle down. I sometimes give the impression that I was as carefree as Dinks, but I got hives in my last night of nervous study. Passing that test made a nice ending to high school.

After graduation, my group started getting invited to debutant parties. A very well-connected and close friend, Claud, had coached me on which dancing school was a feeder to the deb party lists, and he may have had connections who recommended me. (I used to sneak out of that dancing school and go up to the Hill to listen to jazz at mostly-black Crawford's Grill and the Hurricane with two other bad boys.) Claud and I were close friends as partiers and drinkers but also as music lovers, for example, alone among those we knew, early fans of Bob Dylan. Besides Claud, I also knew some of the girls who were "coming out" and their parents who seemed to like me. So, I was happy to accept the twenty plus cocktail parties or big parties/balls that summer.

The following short story gives a sense of what the big parties were like for me.

TO DIE FOR
by
Jay Carson

When, in the middle of the dance, his drink flew up in the air and the contents rained down on the lovely auburn hair and pink dress behind him, I was barely surprised. Hugh had been doing those kinds of things for years. More worrisome was that the lovely auburn hair and pink dress belonged to my girlfriend, Alison, whose party this was. She looked up, only partly confrontational until she saw who did it. She then just went back to her furious dancing which had only partly to do with me.

More concerning to me was Alison's brother, who looked very angry. I saw he was sitting in a corner chair, his hand wrapped in cocktail napkins. There was a broken glass on the floor; he must have cut his hand on that glass, undoubtedly recently filled with brandy, his favorite. There was a small darkening red stain on the wall next to him where he'd smashed it. As his supposed friend and for Alison, I knew I would have to go over to him. But I wanted to finish the dance, which on top of all my liquor seemed especially exhilarating. Hell, the whole party was chaos, but tastefully deceptive chaos: Everybody got plenty to drink and eat, the little peccadillos were accepted, but you better not take off your tux jacket. Bleeding was surely not to be done.

Even in the sixties, I thought debutant parties were hedonistic excesses. Before the dance was a dinner where a nationally famous folk group played for those 50 people close enough to Alison and her family. And Lester Lanin, flown in from New York, played his famously long and smooth melodies at the dance, giving out their eponymous hats as the night wore on.

The country club itself was deceptive, looking from the outside like a small New England house, but leading inside to a balcony that opened down upon a huge dining room and ballroom. Gracious steps on either side made entrances dramatic.

My date, Alison, had found a towel and was drying her hair. She looked at me accusingly. My time was up; I went over to her brother.

"Morgan, what the hell did you do to your hand?" I asked.

"Goddamn this place and my sister. All night I hear nothing but 'Can we have a picture with Alison?' 'Does she need to refix her hair?' 'Can Dad have a dance with Alison?' The hell with them all."

My capacity for amazement was stretched a little more. "You're jealous of your own sister's coming-out party?"

"Coming out like hell," Morgan said. "After tonight, she'll go right back in. To her little New England school, to her dumb friends, to her boring room."

My friend, Hugh, pushed another guy into Morgan "accidentally," and Morgan yelped. Did I catch a grin from Hugh?

"Come on," I said, "let me get you up to the bathroom. The one upstairs, away from your parents."

"And put your hand in your pocket," I said. What was another ruined tux jacket?

We went up those gracious steps and down the hall. An attendant appeared and helped clean and tape up the cuts, which weren't all that serious. No need for a hospital or even to go home. Morgan's righteous indignation apparently stopped at the possible loss of a party and attention.

Coming back, I looked out from the top of those steps and didn't see the party below as my usual funny image of penguins and flowers. It seemed an ugly distortion. I remembered the phrase I had recently learned in French class, "still life is la nature mort," dead nature. Too much booze.

Coming down the steps, I saw her, Roberta Anderson, daughter to allegedly one of the world's ten richest men and good looking to boot, with lovely dark brown hair and those high cheek bones that always got me. We had shared a table at another party and spent the night talking about our favorite books and movies in pretty nice agreement. Maybe the booze again, but I thought she liked me. Unfortunately, she was with some out-of-town buff, suntanned guy who looked as if he had just come off the slopes at Gstaad.

I dropped Morgan off at his parents' table where they'd give him just what he wanted: total absorption. They shot me the family-only look. More Morgan. Poor Alison.

So, I headed out into the ballroom to see if I could have a dance with Roberta. Remembering Mr. Buff, my courage flagged: One last drink, I thought, as I went to the bar again to dip my cup in an endless stream of liquor.

By the time I did get to the ballroom, she was dancing with an older man. This guy was laying down the steps impressively. I was awestruck with his dancing and could see Roberta was also impressed. She was more than keeping up and really enjoying herself.

If I were to start going after Roberta, I could see there was a line. All this exertion wasn't so easy on him, though. His face was getting redder and redder. But they were gathering a small crowd of admirers which seemed to redouble their efforts.

Turned out that it was her neighbor and family friend, who stopped in the middle of a dip, pulled Roberta up, grabbed on to her, gasped for breath, and collapsed. The maître d' with two waiters lifted him up from the floor and carried him to the porch. That was the last we all saw of him. The word was that he died later that night, but as my friend Hugh said, whether she was to die for or not, he went in Roberta's arms.

The collapse was discreetly handled, Lester Lanin kept playing, and the bar stayed open, but the party was over for a lot of us.

I walked Alison to my car to take her home and didn't ask how Morgan was going to make it. After I started the engine, I had to get out to throw up. Only too late did I realize I was in my car's headlights as well as Hugh's car lights who rolled down his window and cheered me on.

God, I thought, I had come a long way from my Catholic grade school days.

It was a bad one followed by dry heaves. It took me a long time that night and after to get all that poison out.

THE END

My friends from those years are still a mystery. I'm not sure why I got them, but feel very lucky to have them. Competitive, sometimes jealous, but supportive enough to make, for me, a new family. We made enough excitement to be amusing but not enough to really get in trouble. "What's up for high adventure?" my best friend Jim used to ask. Aside from being adventurous, he was, as I said, wicked smart, also very witty, a wonderful conversationalist, and someone already developing a world view. One of the most important things he taught me was to start paying attention to my own needs.

At the end of that summer, our chosen adventure was a trip to Cape Cod to visit a classmate whose family had a house in Hyannis Port. We were pretty good house guests: Jim was able to carry on intelligent and amusing dinner conversations, and I dated our classmate's sister. We went to parties, drank too much, put Nixon stickers on the Kennedy yacht. All the things spoiled young men were supposed to do, or did any way. It was the youth myth: you can do anything you can get away with that is somewhat fun and doesn't cause too much disturbance or grief. Our friends did other parties and drinking and some even ended up in jail for disorderly conduct. Of course, they got out right away, so it was a conversational coup for them. Looking back, I am both appalled and jealous of that youth. It was dangerous: we drove drunk most of the time, were disruptive much of the time. But we suffered few consequences. Most destructively, we told ourselves, or I told myself, we could get away with this kind of conduct indefinitely.

CHAPTER V

LAFAYETTE AND THE MYTHS OF IMMUNITY AND WORKAHOLISM

I started at Lafayette College in the fall of 1959. Lax, as usual, I had not sent my room reservation early enough. As a consequence, I had to take a room in a private home nine blocks off campus. That daily walk often, with an ROTC uniform proved to be too much.

One afternoon, I decided to take a look at what I was missing and did a walk through the newest dorm. As a piece of luck, I met the young man, Peter, tall, thin and easy to talk to, who also found me interesting to talk to. An immediate sense of kinship was reciprocal. He was ensconced in a big single room on the 4th floor. Being both gregarious and sick of the nine-block walk, I suggested to Peter on our first meeting that for the full college experience he needed a roommate, me. To my surprise, Peter went for it and got maintenance to move in another bed. We established a great friendship throughout our Lafayette experience and after. Among his generous acts, he included me in his father's invitation to see a Pittsburgh-New York game of the 1960's World Series at Yankee Stadium. (Wonderfully, the Pirates won 3-2. Incidentally, much of the student body at Lafayette at the time, were New Yorkers. We were all willing to bet on our hometown team. I cleaned up when Mazeroski hit that great home run and the Pirates won the series.)

Fraternities were important at Lafayette. This was partly because the school had yet to build a dining hall large enough to handle its freshman class. We were immediately in "rush week," looking over fraternities we would like to join and them looking us over. It was pretty serious business: in the first six weeks choosing a living group for the next four years. We would eat lunches and dinners at prospective fraternities. A friend's father sent an introduction for me to ritzy Zeta Psi but we failed to spark an interest in each other despite the charm of their taking care of many fraternity bills by placing them on a bulletin board where visiting alumni would take them down and pay them. One story told of Puerto Rican house boys working in the Zate house into the 1950s, the decade I entered Lafayette (1959).

Lafayette had no women and up to that point had few Jews. That changed our freshman year when a large influx of Jewish men was admitted. I later heard from an elderly faculty member that admitting Jews was a classic way for a college to raise the general level of intelligence and hard work among its students. This became a mismatch with the fraternities, most of which admitted few or no Jews, some by national charter. I was a bit of a pain during rush week because I asked how many Jewish brothers the fraternity had. I was becoming an Irish liberal even then. This didn't go over too well and I was frozen out of a few houses, which was ok with me. I actually thought and entered conversations about joining the one

Jewish fraternity on campus to make a statement and experiment in diversification. I then had second thoughts about making my college career social life a big experiment. Besides, as I think any Jew or Black will tell you, who wants to be the only one. But I was seeing college social life through the myth of the pure white fraternity.

I did become interested in Delta Kappa Epsilon. The Deke house appeared in at least one John O'Hara story with good reason - it was imposing, charming, and a little mysterious. A number of successful Americans were Dekes, some from Lafayette, including William Simon, former Secretary of the Treasury. But by my time there, the Dekes at Lafayette were also known as big partyers. I remember with some nostalgia being dressed in a three-piece suit and popping champagne corks on the heads of Theta Delts at football games. We had to go through the usual fraternity nonsense, but it seemed worthwhile if it meant hanging around such cool guys, many of them prep school graduates. After a while, the nonsense started to not seem so nonsensical, marching around that great Tudor house singing *A band of brothers with arms locked firm and tight*. I was buying into their brotherhood myth.

Our pledge master, Jack, started a cocktail hour before dinner. Again, I felt like I had arrived: we entered his suite through a mysterious totally black room, and drank good scotch before dinner in a storied house. I was having a good time over cocktails and dinner with the brothers and my pledge class buddies. But by the time I got back to my dorm room, I was ready not to study, but to go to bed or have a few beers. My Shady Side education was just good enough to make me arrogant: Most of the things that came up in classes I had studied at least a little. And I had learned to write acceptably. I was beginning to understand the import of the name: preparatory school. Rather than using that head start to really grow intellectually as some of my friends did, I just got lazier. I was settling for what were called "Gentlemen C's."

The following slightly tongue-in-cheek poem captures a little of my educational difficulties:

Attention

*...and that, ladies and gentlemen, is the reason
that all European intellectuals ever since
have been either existentialists or communists.*
I've been looking for the first part of that sentence
ever since I woke up in that class.
Everybody *I* knew in the class
either cut or, like me, didn't pay attention.

It's happened more than once:
*.... is the most important writer of the 20th century.
.... is the only way we can save this economy*
or was it *this planet?*

I did finally read the first part of *The Sun Also Rises*
enough (3) times to figure out Jake Barnes had *an accident
in the war* that made him impotent;
he wasn't just being coy with Lady Brett.

I'd like to hear your thoughts on paying attention
but I would probably miss the first half.
So, like Jesus said, save
the something or other for last.

The cocktail hour difficulty was solved for me when the Deke house burned down. Although we did have some meetings and were encouraged to stay in contact, I started to drift away and spend more time with my dorm buddies, especially my roommate Peter and one of the RA's, Dick Webster. Dick was from Towanda, PA and had started his education in a one-room school house. He became a hometown big star earing a scholarship to Lafayette and distinguishing himself there with honors and awards, as well as a major role in student council. He was such a hero back home that much of the feature page of the town newspaper was often devoted to him. Coming from where he did (one of the bars in Towanda was called the Bucket of Blood), he had not had the educational advantages I did but made great use of what he had, so that by the time I met him he was much smarter than me. I think of Dick as the quintessential successful and caring American.

My Deke experience came to a final end during hell week. We pledges were taken off campus (a clear violation of college rules) to a farm house where we experienced the usual degradations, including picking up torn pieces of paper off freezing cement floors for an hour at a time, being chased through corn fields and generally hearing that we weren't good enough. Mostly, I got through with doled out gulps of scotch from Pledge Master Jack.

And then I started to think. What the hell was I doing - simply repeating my high school alcoholic activity and mind set. All the brothers seemed to be Economics majors (the easiest major at that college at that time) with little interest in the arts. And they drank just like my friends at Shady Side. I thought I should do something different in college.

So, I just walked out of the farm house to a neighboring farm house and called a cab. I went back to my dorm. The next day, two of the brothers came to my dorm room and tried to talk me into coming back, assuring me of only one more light hell night. But I had had enough of them.

I wondered for a while what would have happened if the house had not burned down, if I had gone back. But I was pretty sure of my decision. I'm still sure of my decision, but even now I wonder about my complex relation to group affiliation. I recently examined that puzzle in this poem.

Belonging

I people pretty well
alone or in their groups

even though, after shopping among them,
I have found little of purchase.

They are so full of themselves,
one by one or in their clans
protected by their secret words
or things or knowledge:
the Greek phrase in college
like *crotheum* something or other
BMW and *Benz*; crypto currency,
golf, only the best country clubs.

Or they are perhaps a group of Givers:
singing in cathedrals or chapels,
delivering tampons and tinned tuna
to the poor, taking stock of sins inside:
a Giver's momentary lack of goodness, assumed,
your apostasy or blasphemy, appalling.

Or they are politicats, always
listing their side's inalienables, your inconsistencies,
endlessly purring some human savior.

> Still, I tried, oh, God, I tried
> to belong, and succeeded
> sometimes: that secret word, *crotheum*,
> is from my college fraternity.
> And I have rushed good clubs
> and been an Episcopalian, paid tithes,
> served food to the poor,
> asked for forgiveness, voted correct.
>
> But always, I tell myself to leave - -
> excision before shunning?
>
> *Why are there no blue meats?*
> my friend once asked rhetorically,
> then answered: *Some problems cannot be solved.*

I had already been changing my focus to my friends in the dorm, especially Peter and Dick. One of Dick's chief projects was the yearbook. He asked me if I wanted to be an editor, writing the captions for all the informal photos. I agreed and started a long connection with the Lafayette yearbook, The *Mélange*. The work was fun and I even liked the name which carried forward the long and charming French tradition at Lafayette.

Dick also asked me if I would be interested in his fraternity, Theta Xi. I had dinner at their house a few times and was impressed with the diversity of the brothers' backgrounds, majors, and interests - unusual for a small Presbyterian college in the 1960s. I was able to spend time with one of the first people of Asian descent I would know, a Colombian, Catholics, Jews, WASPS, Engineering, biology, government and law, and English majors. One of my favorite New Jersey brothers was one of the best card players/dealers I have ever met, despite missing a thumb. There were of course the usual weekend parties and drinking, but nothing like the sustained access I experienced at my previous fraternity.

Theta Xi asked me if I wanted to pledge. As impressed as I was with them, I had already done all the pledging I was going to do, and was not interested in the fraternity beyond its social aspects. After some deliberation, they invited me to be a social member: knife, fork, and beer keg. I accepted and the arrangement worked out beautifully.

By this time in my sophomore year, I was the Scheduling Manager for the yearbook, which involved arranging the taking of all but the formal senior pictures. It was very time consuming, but fascinating. I learned something about photography (moody available light pictures were in, and I liked setting them up.), and I learned more about different kinds of writing, especially for an audience beyond teachers. Everybody wanted a good picture of themselves in yearbook so I had a sort of carte blanch to almost anywhere on campus including all the fraternities and school dances. I met Louis Armstrong whom I photographed at Lafayette's big Spring dance. I still remember his raspy voice over our handshake: "How you doing, young fella. How you doing?"

I also learned to work hard. I was dateless at that meeting with Satchmo, because of yearbook and class commitments. One of the reasons I was so over stretched was that the editor-in-chief was unable to delegate or even get others to work for him. For example, his managing editor was his pledge master at his fraternity so my editor in chief never wanted "to bother him." My Editor in Chief also was a terrific photographer and spent too much time in the darkroom. I remember him spending a whole afternoon trying to photographically remove the acne from a friend's face for the perfect picture. (This was long before the ease of digital photography.) I ended up being the de facto Managing Editor along with my Scheduling Manager job along with anything else that was needed.

My studies suffered but my drinking didn't. I still managed to get to and get drunk at all fraternity parties. I was starting to drink reward beers at night, supposedly after I had finished studying.

I was also discovering the pleasures of Lafayette's geographic location: about equidistant between New York and Philadelphia. I would on some weekends go to either for dinners and shows, mostly music. The folk music revival was in progress, and I loved it. I was able to see, hear, and sometimes briefly meet, Jack Eliot, Bob Dylan, the New Lost City Ramblers, and Joan Baez. One weekend, Pete Seeger with the great blues singer, Lightning Hopkins, was in Philadelphia Town Hall on Friday and in New York Saturday night. I saw both shows which were great with the caveat that Hopkins was just being rediscovered and was a little stage struck, cutting into Seeger's time on stage. But I had other chances to see Pete.

By this time, I had made another friend, also a yearbook volunteer. When I became Editor-in-Chief in my junior year, Rich Bonelli was my managing editor. We spent a good deal of time together both because of the yearbook and similar English Major schedules. Rich also liked to drink. On our first night out after some yearbook layout work, we drank 10 cent drafts (those were the days) for hours at Dutch's College Hill Tavern. Finally, Rich said, "I always wait for the other person to quit." I knew I had a real drinking companion. Rich was also culturally knowledgeable and I was learning a lot. We became life-long friends and I was sorry to lose him to cancer a few years ago. I try to capture some of our experience in the following poem.

Camouflage

Walking along Forbes Avenue,
I was suddenly barked at by a giant bush which then
jumped out at me.
Turned out to be some college student in carefully
constructed camouflage, meticulously applied
leaf by leaf, assisted by a side-kick camera woman
who caught my surprised face.

But that's not all that jumped out at me.
Flashback: New York, 1962;
I was ready for Lenny Bruce,
a show at the Village Vanguard
with my friend, Rich, who was teaching me
about the right wines and foods, Shostakovich, *Catch 22*,
all a Midwestern sophomore needed to know.

We were testing my petit bourgeois background
with the great foul and honest comic. He won,
and I walked out after 15 minutes of riffs
on one word, *Motherfucker*.

Outside, I had second thoughts:
Rich was still inside the club, loving Lenny.
They wouldn't let me back in. Rich had driven.
I was stuck in NYC.

I wandered around 5 or 6 streets,
having a beer here or there
until I got broke and lost.

> High on beer and low on prospects
> I started around a corner,
> past a trash barrel, out of which Rich
> jumped up, newspapers still stuck to him.
> He was thrown out of the club for rushing the stage.
> Laughing uproariously, we drove out of New York.
>
> I remember Tennessee Williams said
> *Sometimes, God is there so suddenly.*
> He came and took Rich real fast, camouflaged him
> as a dead person last year.

Starting my junior year at Lafayette, I moved into an apartment off campus with a new fraternity friend, this one from Colombia, Carlos. He was a great roommate, both as a friend and an interesting man. He was an International Studies major who could talk intelligently about world affairs especially those having to do with South America. Carlos also offered to teach me some Spanish, but we got no further than my learning to order really powerful cognac-infused sangria. Certainly, his language skills did come in handy when we learned my music appreciation teacher had a Spanish speaking girlfriend. Carlos would translate her letters to him and help him compose letters to her. We kidded that their relationship went better when my grades in the music course were better. There might have been some truth to that. Later that year, I crashed Carlos's Corvair in a drunken attempt to master the car Ralph Nader called "unsafe at any speed." Carlos was incredibly forgiving and gracious about it. Sometime later, I learned his best friend in Colombia had died in an auto wreck the previous summer.

My mother became seriously ill that winter necessitating my return to Pittsburgh. When I first received the call, I was frightened and somewhat paralyzed in inaction. Within an hour, Carlos got me a ticket on a plane out of Allentown-Bethlehem-Easton airport, and drove me there at an insane speed in time to catch it. I was so stunned and scared, mostly of my mother's health but also of flying. My kindly older seatmate asked if it was my first time in a plane. I said it was. He said not to worry and then placed one of his hands over the other as if one was the plane and the other the ground. He then clapped them together and said: *It's nothing: bumpety, bumpety, bump, no ground.* Even today, when I am nervous about a plane take-off, that description still calms me.

After that harrowing day and time, my mother recovered. In about ten days she was out of danger. I then flew back to Easton. Afraid of bothering me at such a difficult time and without my contribution, Carlos couldn't pay the gas bill. I will never forget him on my return to our apartment: under two blankets, saying with his charming Colombia accent: *Don't worry, Buddy Jay, Spring is coming.*

It was very full year. The yearbook was demanding, as were my English major courses, ten days of which I had lost. I was struggling with a particularly wicked Victorian Writers course, taught by William Waite Watt, who would sign papers that he graded W^3. He was a well-known composition scholar whose book, referred to as the *little green bible*, was well accepted in the rhetoric world. (I would run into and re-examine that book later - in my graduate rhetoric studies.) He was also a poet specializing in light verse, regularly published in the *New Yorker*. Dr. Watt had little patience with undergraduates who were not very serious students. Given how little time I had left over after the yearbook work and drinking and now a trip to Pittsburgh for my ill mother, I found his course to be nearly impenetrable. Rich and I took the course together, and he pulled me through.

The *Mélange* yearbook remained a great experience. We were able to get the important work done with some creativity and fun. On one picture of downtown Easton, PA we superimposed a dirigible with a string attached to a little boy in the picture. (We later took out the string; we kept the dirigible.) I did resist Rich's attempt to put a Heinz ripe tomato-as-graduate, complete with mortar board hat) image (a promo from Heinz Ketchup that year) in the graduate section with all the other seniors - alphabetically in the H's. I kept thinking of someone with a name adjacent to Heinz reviewing his yearbook with his family and seeing a big red tomato face sporting a graduation hat as if a classmate. They would be thinking *what kind of school did I/he go to*.

The year came to a dramatic conclusion. Our *Mélange* yearbook dinner was luckily off campus. On campus was a wild party growing out of control involving several fraternities. Carlos was accused of throwing gotchas (pants down views from under the naked butt and through the legs) on the roof of the Theta Delt House.

All this was unknown to Rich, Webby, me, and the rest of the yearbook crew who merely ended up at our apartment continuing to drink with only a mild visit by the Easton Police. I found out about it over bloody Marys at the Young Republicans Club the next morning. We had all been skating on thin ice for a while. Carlos went out too far. I probably would have been in the same trouble if I had been on campus with him. In some way, that yearbook work had saved me all year from drinking too much – and it did it again. I thought about that and started to build another myth, this one of workaholism: hard work could prevent too much drinking and connected trouble.

To help my roommate, I contacted my cousin, Chick, who was still on the Board of Trustees. Because some town girls were on campus and felt threatened and their parents were rightfully furious, nothing could be done. Luckily, Carlos landed on his feet. He was allowed to finish the academic year and was accepted shortly thereafter at Colombia University in New York to both finish his BA and complete an MA. Adhering to my charmed youth myth, although really bad things were threatening, still none were happening to us, at least none that we couldn't escape from.

At the end of that year, I talked my parents into letting me travel to Europe with Carlos. We went for six weeks and had a wonderful learning experience. On our "student grand tour" we saw substantial parts of Germany, Italy, France, Spain, and Switzerland. We met, among others, Algerians and American expats in Paris, and German nationalists in Munich who mistook me for a German because of my blond hair and sharp features. These Germans became angry that I didn't talk to them - I did and do not know German and couldn't understand them, making them think I was just being a snooty German student - all this was explained to us by a bi-lingual acquaintance later. Finally, we met a wonderfully happy and funny British newlywed couple in Nice.

Also, because of Carlos's connections we had an elaborate lunch at the Colombian Embassy in Madrid. Afterwards, the Ambassador took us to a window to look out on some men supposedly working on a water pipe on the street right outside the embassy. The Ambassador then told us that during a recent student uprising (this was still Fascist Franco's Spain), one smart Spanish student escaped arrest by running to the Colombian embassy for sanctuary, all embassies being off limits to the police. The men outside the Embassy fixing the water pipe, obviously secret police, had been fixing that pipe since the student had arrived 18 months before. We always wondered what eventually happened to that student. I hope he lasted it out until the more forgiving post-Franco government.

It was really a great trip in a unique moment in history: aside from our Colombian embassy experience, bullet damage still marked buildings in Munich, the Algeria crises was still apparent in Paris (near the Palace, I was picked up off my feet by two very tall French paratroopers for getting too close to De Gaulle's seat of government), and we were able to get a beautiful two-room suite, with shower, in Madrid for $2 a night. I still remember my first trip to the Louvre and the Prado, and seeing opera in the Baths of Caracalla. We were also able to visit long-time friends of my parents in Lausanne. And I was blown away by my first bull fights. What courage and brutality. And what an understanding of parts of the human heart.

On the ship back, I met a number of international students coming to the United States to study, many of them black Africans. In an attempt to acclimate them to life in the US, workshops and seminars were given on life in America and ways to successfully negotiate it. One, for example, was on how to use university dental schools for free help with teeth problems. Another was on race relations in the US. Of course, and maybe necessarily (so as to not scare the Africans) the seminar was something of a white wash: the myth presented was U.S. race relations used to be bad and now they were so much better. I will never forget the redheaded white French woman in a leather skirt asking: "I would like to know how many American here have had a black to their dinner table." Dead silence. Until a Southerner from Vanderbilt said in a not-quiet-enough voice, "Does my maid count?" All of a sudden it hit me that these black Africans had very little idea what they were in for in 1960s America.

That underscored the issue that my country and I have depended so much on the labor of Blacks and have given them so little in return: the myth of white entitlement. My personal experience was formed by the maids we had growing up. How they provided so much of our family life. I tried to celebrate that in the following:

Home Maid
for Dell

Long ago, my parents left us to others,
so that like Topsy we would just grow up.
A Black maid paid attention
to my brother and me until,
at the end of her long hours of work,
she made that wonderful meatloaf, peach pie,
asking about our friends, school,
answering all the hard work with a smile
and a dignity I did not know,
telling us we were all a great family.

A friend once asked why
I spoke so respectfully of Dell.
I answered simply, *she not only had more class than
anyone in the family, but than anyone we knew.*

To say I loved her like a mother
would be like saying I had another.

But more often than appreciating, I was complicit in the white patriarchy, ignoring and even abusing Blacks. Part of that attitude was my learned sense of what I and my circle of friends could get away with.

WHITE HOT JUSTICE

Everybody said my father
was a fine attorney

and he bought me through that childhood.
He worked hard to be mostly
fair with us all, but left a sense
of the imperfection of justice, once saying:
*I suggest that what you think is equity
is really the Lone Ranger.*

When my friends and I went to the whorehouses
on the Hill, we all wanted Billie.
Sometimes the pimp or madam
would have to call her in
and she would show up
in an elegant dress
or what I thought was.
She was so beautiful in her dresses,
and then caramel skin, the first time
I noticed black women's
nipples were so dark.

When she said, *What do you want, honey?*
her shock of strawberry hair
floating over those marmalade words,
I couldn't tell her.
Sure, I was a tough
locker room boy, beered up,
who could say *half and half,*
straight fuck, even dare *around the world.*
But when she asked what
I wanted, I was afraid,
of more than of the razor fight
downstairs, of the police
who had already threatened jail,

of the tales of brain-rotting syphilis.

In a dream I wear a wig
the color of my ghostly skin
and pound a mahogany gavel.
I say unaccountably,
take her to my nursery.
Her eyes are now afraid.

In the jury box,
My father stands up.
Stop this endless tyranny.

I entered my senior year somewhat relaxed. Rich and I had been offered editorship of the *Mélange* for an unprecedented second year, but again without pay. I said I would not do it for less than $5000. That was probably high (when $5000 was $5000) but I didn't want to do it anyway. I wanted to be a more serious student in my courses.

Throughout my time at Lafayette, I'd been more interested in my course work than I have indicated here. I read course descriptions carefully and asked upper classmen whom I respected about the best courses. It was hard to go wrong in the Lafayette History and English departments at that time. I still remember a terrific two-course American history series, taught by Professor Welch, incidentally, a son-in-law to the fine American novelist, John P. Marquand. Welch's courses were "Reconstruction to WWI" and WWI to the Present," the present being 1963 although we didn't get that far. I can remember great lectures such as "Chet at the Helm," about the presidency of Chester Arthur; and "Billy, Amy, and God" about Billy Sunday, Amy Semple McPherson and the American religious revival.

I also remember a philosophy course that spent some time emphasizing the problem of evil; In that section of the course, Dr. Resnick would come into class, take off his sport jacket, loosen his tie and bark out: *Is God all knowing, all powerful and all loving? Then how can evil exist?* He would then proceed to show logically the two can't exist, that in fact free will and such a God are incompatible. That course challenged my spiritual belief system, eventually (years later) making it stronger by underscoring the importance of faith. Other standout courses for me were a history of ideas course and an economic history course, which I took during the same senior year semester. In the morning, Dr. Gendebien taught us how the modern world came about through great ideas; in the afternoon I learned from Dr. Welch it was all about the pursuit of money. Those two positions began my journey of learning that intelligence has much to do, as F. Scott Fitzgerald noted, with keeping two opposing ideas in the mind at the same time and still functioning,

I kept my streak going senior year by taking a Milton and modern novel course, both taught by Cleveland Yauch. He was terrific, a natural along the lines of my high school teacher, Hightower. I remember Yauch saying that he started to prepare his courses by working on Milton and then taking breaks with modern novels. But he found himself having difficulty in concentrating long periods on preparing the modern novel course, both because of the writing style and subject matter. So, he ended up breaking the modern novel preparation up with more close reading of Milton. The idea of reading Milton as a break for anything was a revelation to me. But as the semester and my reading went on, I began to understand it. Yauch taught both courses brilliantly as well as connecting well with students. At one point, he interrupted his lecture saying, *some of you are thinking that you could teach this section of Milton better that I am doing now* (which was exactly what I was doing). *You are doomed*, he added, and then after a pause: *to be teachers.*

I also have fond memories of an international law course I took just to experience a teacher who had helped to create the League of Nations. Not the United Nations, the League of Nations, begun after World War I. He knew Eleanor Roosevelt who visited with him. (She had died in 1962, only a year before I took the course). In short, our teacher was very old. In one lecture, he was discussing the concept of the citizen soldier - something new (since Napoleon) in the international order. At one point in the lecture, he seemed to just fade off, not asleep, but no sign of life. Kenny, whom I've mentioned as a Theta Xi fraternity brother, witty guy and wonderful card player, was also in this course and often sat next to me. During our teacher's brown out, Kenny turned to me and said *We have to leave*. Why? I asked. *He's dead.* Kenny said. I answered that our teacher was only thinking. Kenny said again*, He's dead,* and then added*, and we're going to be blamed for it. We have to leave.* We went back and forth a few times until our professor became amazingly alert. I was waiting for him to say something profound, proving my point that he was pondering some great question. Finally, he did become alert, referencing his earlier discussion of the citizen soldier by stating unimpressively, *Gentlemen, he who fights and runs away, lives to fight another day.* That same faculty member gave me an hour of great advice about which eastern law schools that might be good candidates for me and might find me a good candidate. Old, yes, but he was sharp as a tack in that office hour.

I also (re?) learned some manners, especially in my art history classes all taught by Dr. Gaertner. He started several early classes with a lecture on manners. We were told we would be seeing a lot of slides with the overhead lights turned off. *You may sleep, but you may not snore,* we were told. As for outside class when we were meeting young ladies, *always carry two handkerchiefs, one for you (and when you use, don't look at it, you know what's in there); the other for Mary Sue* (our mythical girlfriend whom Dr. Gaertner seemed sure we would never have because we were such uncouth louts).

Although I did spend more time on classwork, I still was spending too much time drinking. Rich and I were also suffering from the romanticized myth of the alcoholic writer and teacher, vocations we seemed to be preparing for. I remember thinking that the best teachers I had were either alcoholic or homosexual. The very best were both. I can't use the word, "partying," about our lives because it did not often seem like a party anymore. Rich and I often drank together, both in Easton and nearby New York or Philadelphia. We did have some fun but the ominous cloud of alcoholism increasingly hung over our antics. We spoke of it only rarely. I touch on it obliquely in the following poem.

The Hawk of South Jersey

We met in Dutch's Tavern
as editors planning the literary magazine,
the beers showing up, disappearing
as if vaporized.

One of us said *I always wait
for the other person to quit.*

He taught me about Shostakovich and Wagner
about Lenny Bruce and Joseph Heller
and, slapping his haunches, what aged beef
to order in Mercanti's Blue Room in Philadelphia.

I looked out for him through
that affair with the crazy pregnant woman,
stealing for her rent and the drugs.
We sat drunk, swearing 5 A.M. in June in Philadelphia
unable for the third day to drive ourselves to the Jersey line.

Sundays at the Young Republican Club,
Bloody Mary's to beer, 10 a.m. to midnight,
playing car tag with real cars,
stealing cars, slowly, one beer at a time,
gambling them away.

Taking dope, smuggling dope,
check fraud. "Cash" I called him.
What do you mean "no money"?
gotta lotta checks, lotta ink;
lotta money.

I have lost him now.
Thirty years of recovery and twenty
of therapy taught me to divorce:
to be only me.
I am alive with family and friends,
sober; nice they tell me,
responsible as hell.

But I miss that antic tower
when we were stuck, deformed,
occasionally able to fly out
past the cathedral gargoyles
and see so much of little known Paris.

Lafayette was wonderful for me. I had great courses, many of which helped prepare me for teaching, but some of which just improved my mind and made me a more responsible citizen. I met interesting people, many different from my Shady Side group: I met Otto, a German immigrant from Long Island whose family bought, then improved delicatessens and sometimes flipped them. Otto left after the first year but always made me welcome in his deli and home on Long Island, a great resource since I had often spent all my money in Manhattan bars. I met a guy whose father was a landlord in Freehold, New Jersey, and may have rented to Bruce Springsteen's family. And many others, Carlos's chief among them. And, of course, my original roommate, Peter, and dorm proctor, Webby, who remained life long friends.

This is not to say I had turned my back on the kinds of friends I learned to like and love in Pittsburgh. At Lafayette, I was lucky enough to meet many who were similar: John Cooper, my first friend at Freshman orientation, is one of the nicest guys I ever met. I still enjoy seeing him and his fraternity brothers at reunions.

I keep up with many of my friends after Lafayette. But sometimes we drift away:

Mustangs

The tiny horses are all gone now
that once hung around the necks
of the sophisticated beer
that Carlos and I sipped in Switzerland.
Not even a shred of string left

that went through their little necks
to hold them on the beer
and emphasize the rich label.

Carlos and I were like young brothers that summer,
him showing off for me, picking up
all those European women and walking
across the slim hand rail on the bridge
over that cataracts feeding Lake Geneva,
me terrified of losing my longed-for sibling.

We collected a bunch and passed those horses back
and forth when we later visited each other,
me dropping them off in Medellin,
and Carlos leaving little plastic horses in Pittsburgh,
with lint from our pockets and then our children's
and at each stop somehow more got lost.

Then wildly reduced, they became
as lost as Western mustangs, as our friendship.
We had changed.

I the young brother who nearly cried in confusion
at the whore's hangout bridge in Munich
had learned to choose and marry a beautiful wife
and to tether an opponent to a decent standstill in tennis.

Older brother Carlos had nothing to do but host us in Cartagena
to a beautiful party weekend with so much family
we could only tell bowdlerized versions of our adventures.
at a magnificent, safe, beach weekend.

> A fine last roundup as the herd
> was being culled to nothing.

I kept up with many of my college friends years after at regular and more informal reunions in Easton, Philadelphia, New York, and the Jersey shore.

My *Mélange* yearbook experience had allowed me to stretch myself in literary, artistic, and social ways I hadn't known I could. I knew many class and schoolmates from all parts of the campus which allowed me to learn about and participate a little in school politics. I was invited to help in writing and laying out the Lafayette newspaper, including total control of one humor issue. A very nice honor was being elected to the Lafayette senior honorary society with the cumbersome name, the Knights of the Round Table, usually referred to as KRT. My father once asked me if I was a Knight. Both of us broke out laughing.

As my undergraduate life came to a close, I was under subtle pressure from my father to go to law school, as he had. It seemed easier than trying to find a real job. So, I took the LSAT. I have always done well on standardized tests and did on this one. I applied to a number of law schools, including Harvard. (What's the point in being an American if you can't apply to Harvard?) I got accepted to most (not Harvard) and made the boring, less brave, and easy choice to stay in Pittsburgh. My LSAT score qualified me for a scholarship. My father told me to leave the scholarship for someone who really needed it, that he could and would pay for my law school tuition. I like to remember how kind and generous he could be.

I was characteristically slow getting out of my Lafayette apartment. Rich and I would start our packing each day, then meet with a six pack of beer, and that would be the end of packing. I was a little worried that I would never get out of Easton.

When I came back to Pittsburgh, I still faced the problem of me. The partying and crazy drinking continued. It was a pretty wild summer. I share a representative example in this fictionalized account of Dan.

THE SKUNK AFFAIR OF 1962

It was hard for Dan to believe that he had lost the directions to the Sewickley mansion. At twenty, he felt he ought to be better at directions, especially to great potential party places like Sewickley, and a mansion anywhere. Even harder to believe was the array of listings in the white pages under the name Alexander Hamilton Chislett. Supposedly a direct descendant; maybe Hamilton had left enough of the first Bank of New York to pay for all the buildings these telephone numbers suggested: stables? The party would be too late for riding, but from the stories, you could not be sure about those people. The garage, no. The main house? Maybe. There it is: Dan remembered Roger had told him it would be in the gymnasium. Dan thought he was kidding. Dan had met some rich guys at Negley Academy, but their own gymnasium? *Hell*, he thought, *I'm really JV around these guys.*

Dan's father, a tax attorney, had known a little about the Chislett's—*iron and steel—in both finance and demeanor*, he had said.

As for the stories, Dan had been told by a number of his friends to watch out, that Alex was a son of a bitch and sometimes violent (could he really have gone after a guy on the open hearth of his father's steel mill?). But every time they'd met, Alexander Hamilton Chislett had been very deferential, "the soul of propriety," Dan's father would say. *You are probably meeting him before the family's legendary alcoholic gene kicks in: 11:00 p.m., I'm told,* the thoughtful attorney said dryly. But Dan knew his father was pleased that Dan was making these rich, if somewhat irresponsible, friends. Maybe that's what law taught you.

After the phone book research, things went easier. Picking up Billy, Dan's best friend, and the drive were a breeze given the decreasing traffic, to say nothing of the decreasing six-pack under the front seat of his father's '61 Cadillac convertible. Cruising down Ohio River Boulevard, top down, the red and white interior leather flashing in the last of the sunset, Dan felt like he and these new friends didn't own but somehow controlled the city, or the worthwhile parts anyway. Maybe someday he would own a piece of it. Maybe that's why his father was so forgiving. "Benign neglect," Dan later laughingly called it to a therapist, after Senator Daniel Moynihan's advice to Nixon's programs for the poor.

Two bad turns, and questions to locals, including one to a Sewickley black and white Chevy police car, Dan and Billy carefully kicking beer cans back under the car seat—and they were at the gates. Dan thought the success was his smooth politeness, but then thought again it was the Chislett name. Through it all, Billy, the faithful sidekick, was keeping up with the directions and discretely passing the crisp beers and muted moral support.

"Are you sure we were really invited?" Dan asked.

"You worry too much. What difference does it make?"

"A lot, I would think."

"People don't invite you to parties for only two reasons: they don't know you or they don't like you. If you go, they probably won't know you any better at the end of the party. And they certainly won't like you any better. So go."

Once on the estate, some questions to a heavyset hired-hand type led them to the gymnasium, a freestanding building that looked solid enough to Dan to be maybe 1920s. When, he'd decided, all good things were made.

Then it was the usual for an all-guy party—keg, some pretty good foul jokes, yelling, improbable plans for getting laid. Without too much past success, as far as Dan could tell from what they were saying as well as his own experience. Except for the Chislett family having their own gymnasium pool sealed over by heavy wood cover (*There's a newer, bigger inside/outside being dug out downstairs,* one of Chislett's kiss-ass buddies said), the evening was nothing to remember until they started home.

Alex Chislett lived up to Dan's memory of him: polite, even gracious—almost as if he were watching himself. Which might have been the case, given Roger's story of Alex being picked up two days ago by the Sewickley police. He had apparently been singing some obscene songs in front of some townie girl's house near the business district; it was midnight and, luckily, Alex was merely shirtless.

Right before they left, Dan was intrigued by a discussion that almost started some time ago when Roger asked whether everybody was a social climber.

"Right," Alex said. "Name me one person who is not a social climber."

"Yeah, I bet you can't name one." The kiss-ass guy jumped in.

"Queen Elizabeth," Billy said.

Everybody laughed. And Dan felt warm being part of the smart guys from the city. Billy did that for them. But Dan somehow regretted that they stopped talking more about the topic that interested him.

Aside from their love of beer and whiskey and their ability to procure it, Billy's quick wit and Dan's access to his father's black Cadillac convertible had been their chief assets in insinuating their way into the group. Both Dan and Billy had been at Catholic primary school. Both were acutely aware that no Catholic had yet been accepted at the two best country clubs in the area. Almost by accident, they had found each other with some of the best socially connected people at Negley, their new prep school. Dan later wondered how accidental it had been. Even at twenty, he noticed that drinkers tended to find and seemed to quickly like each other.

After the party, finding the Cadillac in their drunkenness was harder in the complete darkness of the summer. Dan decided he had to take a piss, letting go on a flower bed somewhat removed from all the buildings—but not far from a skunk which he probably hit. In return, the skunk let fly back all over Dan.

"Thank God the top's down," Billy said. "You really stink."

"But my driving is still pretty good. I'll just throw my shirt in the backseat."

After about ten minutes, Billy said, "It's not your shirt, the skunk aimed lower." At the next light, Dan slipped off his pants and tossed them in the backseat. Dan loved how the night air felt against his skin as they drove on.

"Let's get a pizza," Dan said as they were entering back into the East End.

"Just have to push it," Billy answered.

"Me?"

"All of us."

Dan pulled up in front of the Pizza Pub on Walnut Street, waiting a few seconds for Billy to get out.

"At least keep your shorts on," Billy said as he walked into the bar.

Ten minutes later - having driven around the residential streets, and taken his shorts off because of the implied dare - Dan pulled up again in front of the pub.

Billy was standing there; he came around to the driver's side and pulled out a Camel pack. "Pizza, not done. Want a gret?"

Dan took the cigarette and the stares of some onlookers. Both pleased him. Billy flicked his Zippo on his pants and lit his own cigarette.

"How about that light?" Dan said.

"You got to come and get it."

Nude, Dan got out of the Cadillac and walked the three steps to where Billy stood in the middle of the street. Chuckling and shaking his head, Billy lit his cigarette. "Jesus," he said.

And with all the swagger he could muster, cigarette dangling, Dan got back in the car.

In what seemed like seconds to Dan, police cars appeared round the corner - lights and no sirens, he remembered—in front and behind. And a police officer at his car door.

"Get out of the car."

"I don't think…"

"I'll do the thinking. Get out of the car," the cop repeated.

Dan did as he was told. He threw away the cigarette.

"God, now he's littering," an old passerby said, in an offended voice.

Billy materialized out of the crowd, carrying the pizza box like a shelf.

"Did you tell him about the skunk?"

"Shut up, kid," the cop said, slamming the pizza box against Billy's chest. Dan thought he could see some red on Billy's shirt. Had he started eating that pizza?

"I was hit by a skunk and couldn't take the smell. It was all over all my clothes."

Why did you get out of the car in front of the Pizza Pub?"

"I was just getting a light for my cigarette."

A few awful few moments seemed like an hour of silence. Dan could not think of one word that would help him.

"Where do you live?"

"Around the corner and down six blocks."

"Get in the car," the cop said, "and go directly home. I catch you around here like that again..." The cop's voice trailed off ominously.

Billy jumped in only seconds after Dan, and in five more minutes of silence, as if a word would break their luck, they were pulling the big car into Dan's driveway and down into a back court.

"Why did he let us go?" Dan asked, confounded.

"Bringing guys like you, especially naked, into the station is not exactly what you get promoted to sergeant for," Billy answered.

"Do you think he believed me about the skunk attack?" Dan asked.

"Oh, he believes in skunks all right."

* * *

Although Dan was sure that Billy saw him, they never mentioned the figure standing at the top of Dan's driveway leading to the back court as Dan turned the lumbering black car around; the lone man in silhouette looked to Dan oddly like a scarecrow in an empty field. Dan was sure it was Alex Chislett, who must have followed them all the way in from Sewickley. Alex never mentioned

Dan's nude appearance on Walnut Street or his nakedness now; nor did he mention the cops, even his own party. Instead, he started talking about how he had an address for a girl, an Asian foreign student, short on funds and willing to spend the night with the right guys for the right money.

Neither Dan nor Billy ever brought up any of this again. Perhaps they thought Alex's appearance out of nowhere was too absurd, or maybe even a hallucination, or just not funny. Maybe neither wanted trouble with a Chislett, or maybe each went to see the poor immigrant girl later that summer. Sometimes on the street they'd pass Alex Hamilton Chislett's Mercedes, out of which neither the rich young man nor his army of workers could get the last of the faint smells of old beer, wine, sweat, even vomit, a naked decomposing blight that seemed everywhere then.

THE END

CHAPTER V

LAW SCHOOL AND THE MYTHS OF SPORADIC HARD WORK AND BAD THINGS DON'T HAPPEN TO COOL AND CONNECTED GUYS LIKE ME

Although I wasn't excited to go to law school, I had no other plans and could think of few other options. I was also becoming concerned about being drafted into the Vietnam conflict. Occasionally, I would think romantically that I ultimately would become a writer and ought to have great experiences including war. Then, common sense would remind me that I was abysmal at ROTC which was required for my first two years at Lafayette. And I hated it: meaningless marching, and discipline. Learning how to take apart and reassemble an M1. I now see that as an arrogance: why shouldn't I have some knowledge of how to defend my country? My increased drinking suggested to me that I would not be much of a soldier. That drinking also suggested that I would not have an easy time getting and holding a regular job. But I still seemed to be able to do school, and law school seemed a logical choice.

In the fall of 1963, I entered the University of Pittsburgh Law School. I had been accepted at a few other places, including Tulane and still sometimes wonder what might have happened if I had gone there. But I had been told that schooling in a Pennsylvania law school would be an advantage in taking the Pennsylvania Bar Exam. That assumed I would practice in Pittsburgh. I was still too much of a home boy.

I followed the school suggestion that I room my first year in the on-campus dorms, the three then-new ones on Fifth Avenue. They were so new they were unnamed, simply called Towers A, B, and C.

Because of their cylindrical shape; students called them Ajax, Babbo, and Comet.

I was in Comet, luckily only two doors away from my old high school classmate, Jay Ruffner, the only other Jay I knew. We soon formed a group including Pete Veeder, another high school friend, and Wally Knox from Erie, both only a few floors away. We all took the same classes together and took our evening breaks at a wonderful bar across the street. The Pitt Tavern featured excellent burgers and a record console (this was 1963) on which you could play any favorite record you found there or brought.

I thought the classes interesting and challenging. And suited to my thinking: much careful framing of the question and logical thought to answer it. I loved the idea that the conclusions were most often based on previous cases rather than a definitive law somewhere.

Room and board, terrific friends, interesting classes, and a great nearby bar, all paid for by my generous father. What could go wrong? Yet I drank myself out of it all. I told people afterwards I could either say I was dumb or drunk. You can be sure I said I was too drunk. Some smart guy pointed out that I could have been *both* dumb and drunk. I think he was right.

But it took a year, in which I had a stimulating time, and the partying on weekends was excellent. Unfortunately, the hangovers were lasting through and beyond Sunday. I try to capture some of that feeling in the following:

Late Brunch

I knew exactly the time I was
going to fail out of law school:

ten o'clock, one satiated and sick Sunday morning
when taking the plump nurse out to her favorite breakfast diner,
knowing I should be studying then
or a little last week,
or some other time that semester.

Guilt breaking through that high LSAT score
and past that nasty little gin love affair,
seducing me now with some sober sanity.
(Had I hit that nurse last night?
Was I Sorry?)
She loved me and I couldn't wait to get her home.
None of this was new:
my parents loved me
and I'd failed plenty for them
even beyond those bad grades,
disciplinary problems, those wrecked cars.

Acid coffee burning my stomach,
shaking cigarette, all ticked a late hour.

The nurse loved those pancakes;
everything made me sick.
The waitresses looked at my untouched hash
and chided,
"What's the matter, hon?"

And I was having a lot of trouble during the week. I stayed at the Pitt Tavern so late so often that the bartender gave me a card to an after-hours club. That didn't help my studying. I was having trouble sleeping, so I also discovered (more honestly, stole from my parents' medicine cabinet) sleeping pills. They only made matters worse. A lawyer friend recently pointed out that the first year of law school is very hard, *overwhelming*, she said. All through Lafayette I had skated near poor grades, but could always pull through. Law school was just too much.

But I had made some good friends. Jay Ruffner taught me about some great popular novels I had missed, such as *Gone with the Wind* and *To Kill a Mockingbird*. He also taught me about Tony Bennett, not to mention some truly sane conservative politics. Pete Veeder was a fine conversationalist and supportive friend, especially when I found myself flunked out. I kept these friends, knowledge, and memories, especially of dinners the three of us would have. I remember Peter asking me to the Fox Chapel Club for dinner early on in that first year. I was too shy and nervous to accept. So I called Peter's mother to hem and haw around about how I couldn't make it, and she replied bluntly with the best suggestion I ever got about invitations. *My general rule is*, she said, *when invited, accept and go!* I still live by her wisdom.

As I flunked out of law school, two myths were crashing: 1. sporadic hard work didn't save me from drinking too much and 2. bad things *could* happen to me.

 One warm day that June I was walking around Shadyside scared and sad as hell, trying to figure out what I was going to do with my life. I ran into a second-year student, who was a schoolmate from Shady Side and a scion of a successful Pittsburgh lawyer family. He was unpacking his car with his beautiful wife. I explained my plight and he sympathized. But life seemed very unfair. Although I knew I was drinking too much, I still didn't accept full responsibility for my situation. My mother continued to be a soothing enabler who often said in my difficult moments, *Have a drink, Jay, and take a nap.*

One of my favorite blues songs from that era contained the following line:

> *Got both hands full of gimme*
> *and a mouth full of much obliged.*

I think I succeeded in being polite, but I sure asked a lot from people, especially my parents. I had decided that I wanted to go to school to study what I really loved, English literature. Part of it was an avoidance of the real world, but part of it was the real desire that I had for a long time and that was fostered by some of the fine teachers I mentioned earlier. My father who was a great believer in education agreed to send me to graduate school.

CHAPTER VI
WEST VIRGINIA: THE MYTH OF SOLITARY LIFE

I had not planned to fail out of law school so I was applying to graduate schools in English after law school grades came out, in the middle of summer. Only two graduate schools I researched that summer were still accepting applications that late, Iowa and West Virginia University. I was accepted at both. Again, I took the closer and easier choice and headed for Morgantown in late August. Housing was a problem at WVU then, and I remember sitting in the housing office trying to connect to an apartment. I finally lucked out with a house being renovated by a local resident, Rick Harkness. It was a real dump at the time. A hole in the roof allowed snow to come right down into my hallway. Wasps had nested in my mailbox, and the radiators were pretty useless. Rick, my landlord, was as accommodating as he could be on limited funds; the huge grass lawn was always cut, even though he didn't own a power mower and had to depend on "Rickey Power." And he was a fun guy. He had gone to prep school with Ted Kennedy and was now a scuba diver often employed by the Morgantown Police. Sometimes he found and pulled dead bodies out of the Monongahela River. Rick had lots of great stories.

So I was able to live alone, both for peaceful studying, when I did study, and not to be bothered when I was drinking. That last reason I have learned is pretty alcoholic. I partly planned and was partly handed a schedule that started on Tuesday morning and ended on Thursday afternoon. That allowed me a four-day weekend to travel back to Pittsburgh and other places, even New York once.

But I did have and enjoy some good courses: Old English and Beowulf taught by a blind professor who decided on where to turn in the English building halls by snapping his fingers and listening for the echo, like a bat. He was an excellent linguist. He was also a big believer in the Viking culture which he said prized democracy and merit, unlike other cultures of the time that depended on lineage. I always remember his saying that if we wanted to understand America today, we should study not the *Bible*, but *Beowulf*.

Another outstanding course was Southern Writers taught by Rule Foster. Students loved to start out their questions or comments with the pun, "As a rule, Dr. Foster, ..." He was an expert on Robert Penn Warren's masterpiece, *All the King's Men* and knew Thomas Wolfe's family. He told us, for example, that Wolfe's mother didn't mind her son's tough criticism of her in his novels "as long as Tom could make a good living off those books." Through those courses I began to really understand what a rich literary heritage I was heir to.

My advisor was a thoughtful man who was also the head of the English Department. He was grandfatherly old, but taught a good Chaucer class. I became concerned about my grades and he advised me and became protective of me. Later, during my oral exams for my Masters, he started off the questions with what he thought was an easy question from a course he had just taught me: *Mr. Carson, aside from the bawdy elements in Chaucer, why do we read the Canterbury Tales?* I froze and could not think of one reason we read the *Canterbury Tales*. He answered for me suggesting among other things, the rich characterization, the humor, the beautiful language. His relaxed thoughtful answer (for me) allowed me to settle my nerves, and I was able to go on and do a pretty reputable job. Later he wrote me recommendation to Carnegie-Mellon's English Department. I remember him saying somewhat wistfully, *I hope you find what you want.*

I was lucky again to meet some interesting people. My best West Virginia friend and later my boss at Robert Morris was Tom Marshall. Tom was a good student, fine guitar player, and excellent drinking companion. He helped and companioned me in all those areas. A native West Virginian, Tom knew much about the state. A collateral descendent of Chief Justice John Marshall, Tom taught me a good deal about early American history. I remember an afternoon driving around West Virginia as he pointed out virgin forest and secondary cuts. I also remember an epic night of drinking when Tom and I finished a night of visiting coal town bars. Our last stop was 7:00 AM at a place that opened early. We looked such a wreck after our debauch, the bartender seemed terrified, saying, *Whatever you want, boys, just take it and take it easy*

But Tom and I also had some surprisingly serious experiences. One tired evening, I was so wiped out from translating Old English, (probably *Beowulf*), I could only watch the wasps die outside my window on my deserted sun porch. My phone rang with an enticing offer, "How would you like to watch a Walt Disney movie?" I was charmed until I figured out this was a come-on for the Church of Latter-Day Saints, the Mormons. I was still a stone-cold atheist, but saw a great prank possibility. I told the caller that I would be delighted to see a Walt Disney movie – and then gave them Tom's address and a good time to come over. I was just going to let it go and listen to Tom complain later, but about an hour before the appointed time, I cracked and called him. Tom said "You better get over here with a bunch of beer right now."

Three sheets to the wind, we watched the two Mormon boys (black pants, white shirts and tie) show us a movie about Mormonism, mostly emphasizing that Mormons were not strange or fearful. The boys then talked about all the cool people who were Mormons, I remember them referencing the great Pittsburgh Pirate pitcher, Vernon Law, who was often referred to in the sports pages as "the Deacon." They followed that with a talk about how family and community orientated their religion was.

Then Tom interrupted, now on his fourth or fifth beer, essentially arguing that our education made us too smart for this kind of simple religion. "Our keenly-honed intellects simply cannot accept this easy explanation of metaphysical matters." I loved "keenly-honed intellects" and never let Tom forget it as I kidded him over our long and close friendship.

But then to my surprise, both boys dropped to their knees on Tom's living room floor and swore they believed what they were telling us and in all the precepts and tenets and miracles of the Mormon religion. I wasn't about to join, but I clearly remember thinking that I wanted to believe in something the way they believed in Mormonism.

I met other interesting people, mostly West Virginians whose authenticity and personality I loved. Some appear in the following story which is based on a real legal case as well as my life:

THE MAGDA JEAN FEVERAUX SONGBOOK

God, it was hot and jungle green late on that August day in 1967 when Ray and I took those trips toward our Morgantown meeting. We were coming from opposite directions, Ray from southern West Virginia, Tera Alta, Taylor County, to be exact, me from a little west of Morgantown, Star City.

Nor were either of us driving. I was chauffeured by my sexy girlfriend at the time, Crystal Truax, and he by his later famous wife, Magda Jean Feveraux. I was headed into Morgantown about a week before classes started to hunt for an apartment for the second year of my Master's Degree in Rhetoric. Two months before, I found out later, Ray had finished his last stint working underground at the Munseem Mining operation. Since then, he had been at home in bed with a recurring stomach problem. Magda Jean, a stay-at-home wife who nursed him during this illness, was later quoted in the *Morgantown Star*, saying that he was getting "way more better care at home than he would in any pop bottle hospital," West Virginia University's Hospital, which although well respected, had picked up its tacky nickname because it was funded by a tax on soda, still referred to in West Virginia as *pop*.

Crystal and I were really appreciating the lush green trees and vegetation around Morgantown. Unfortunately, we were appreciating them so much that the optimistically named Crystal t-boned the Feveraux Chevy. Thank God none of us turned out to be hurt – although Ray was in enough pain from his stomach that it was hard to tell if he didn't have a cracked rib or something. Anyway, that's how we all met.

I jumped out of the car to try and do a little good for the Feverauxs and maybe for me too. Some audience analysis was in order (although I sure didn't know any Aristotelian rhetorical category for angry West Virginia car crash victims.) Also in order was maybe spending a little money - to avoid any insurance troubles, of which I had a few at the time. I could see that Ray Feveraux was laying in the back seat, where I assumed he had been for some time, the crash being way too mild to have displaced him. Even in that pose and sort of doubled up, he was one hell of a big man, and with a set of those coal fire eyes that seemed to burn right out of his head and into whatever he was looking at, which at the time, happened to be me. I thought I ought to be really nice.

"I am so sorry. We just didn't see you," which is what Crystal had told me right after the crash.

"I should sure as hell hope not," the long reddish-brown hair in the front seat said as those tresses swished and swayed and then turned around to become a pretty if mature face.

"Otherwise, we'd think you were trying to kill us. Right, Ray?" His powerful grunt of assent turned what I thought was the woman's rural humor into an ominous warning, even considering Ray's weakened condition.

The Feveraux's green Chevy, maybe '58 or 59, was crumpled in at the side passenger door indicating that the driver, Ms. Feveraux, was not really hurt. And Ray in the back seat seemed to be away from the damage. I was already doing a financial inventory and considering the best approach and amount to mitigate the situation. I barely noticed a small khaki-colored envelope dropping out of that driver side of the car when the brown-haired woman got out and introduced herself,

"I'm Magda Jean Feveraux and unless you got real good *in*surance you are Mr. Mudd." She said that as calmly and purposefully as ordering the turkey and stuffing special at the *Have-a-Lunch Diner*. A bad sign, I thought.

"I just wanted to make sure that everybody was ok." And, as a nice touch, I handed her the khaki envelope which I had picked up as she was checking Ray in the back seat. "I think this dropped out of the car." There was some of what I thought was white gravel dust on the outside of the envelope.

"I'm sure..." she started with that matter-of-fact-shut-up tone until she saw the envelope which she quickly snatched out of my hands. The end sentence came out more sweetly, this time, "I'm sure," she repeated, "glad you found this," as she put it in and snapped her clutch purse shut and snapped her face into a pleasant, grateful look.

While we exchanged insurance information, I offered to make a quick cash settlement (as I said, I was already on thin ice with my insurance company for two previous accidents, one while trying to get inside Crystal's bra when I was driving, maybe a little tipsy.)

"And if you need any medication," I said, "aspirin or something else, my cousin is in the pharmacy program at the University and works in a big drug store in town." I immediately regretted dragging my loud-mouth cousin into this and also mentioning possible extra pain. Ray didn't look so hot, and I thought his could be expensive.

"Let me think about it," she said. "And give me your number."

By the end, it all went smoothly; two days later my fearful obsession had cooled, and I even pretty much stopped yelling at Crystal for her driving.

In the week that followed, I got Crystal's sexy ("You are really going to miss me, you bastard.") butt out of the Hotel Morgan and on a bus back to New York. As well as stood up another pain-in-the–ass date (after she said, "You must understand it's a 4-1 male-to-female ratio here,") and even got to my first class: Old English, not too bad although I sell stocks now.

A week later Magda Jean called and accepted my offer of a cash settlement "as long as it was enough cash." Her figure seemed high to me, but I'd been pretty good about not spending my mother's allowance on anything but winning poker hands (not to say I hadn't had bad years with cards). Mostly, I was relieved not to be losing my license or facing that insurance agent.

She wouldn't take a check, so I suggested a face-to-face at my favorite bar, Sleepy's. She agreed, although it was a bit of a drive in from her motel near the hospital.

The 3.2 beer in WVA worked ok and Magda Jean seemed to be enjoying it by her second, which was fine with me, even though I was buying, since more good will would keep me driving. Turned out, Magda Jean was fun to drink with and not bad to look at.

We talked about life. That was the night Sleepy explained how West Virginians were the most independent people in the country, except for the American Indians. And how both groups paid dearly for that independence. Magda Jean agreed. "People ought to mind their own business, take care of their own problems."

Crazy Bob, the Chicken Killer, so named for his work at one of those factory chicken farms, also showed up that night, but said very little. I could tell he also thought Magda Jean, with her beautiful wavey brown hair and high cheekbones, was a looker.

I talked about what a bitch my long-time girlfriend (before Crystal) was being about Crystal. Feminism hadn't been invented. And frankly, me and West Virginia were slow to get it, even after it was. Even so, I thought it best to change the conversation and so I asked how Ray was. Magda Jean said he was fine and she was going in every day to the hospital to make sure they were taking proper care of him. But that he had had long-time trouble with his stomach and it was slow going. Her voice had a sweet quality even with this bad news.

Just before closing when we were all feeling pretty good, Sleepy said that it was bottle crushing time. He then pulled out a box of mostly beer bottles that was the detritus of the evening, threw a couple of brown bags over them, and started whacking away with a hammer. I guess for economy of garbage space. Sleepy, who was also a little high, asked if I wanted a turn. I got in there behind the bar and let fly for a little. The smashing felt great at that point of the evening. Then, surprisingly, Magda Jean asked if she could try. I swear she went at it with an energy that more than matched mine and Sleepy's.

Crazy Bob piped up. "Wow. We could use her on the chicken farm."

Later, as the conversation was deflating, I tried to wow her with the importance and difficulty of my field of study, but Magda Jean seemed impressed less by my studies than that of my pharmacist cousin. She left with his name and number.

I did arrange to go out and see Ray at the hospital. We left on good terms, if me a little lighter in the wallet.

A few days later, I did go out to see Ray, when I was sure Magda Jean would be there. Ray tried a few pleasantries, but sure didn't look too good and shortly was complaining. The nurses kept asking him about his pain but seemed mystified and unable to help. Magda Jean came in and soothed him and helped feed him his lunch. After Ray fell asleep, we all left. That was the day Magda Jean and I went to Havalunch for their specialty turkey and stuffing. She seemed somewhat upset but ate the good volume that Havalunch served in those days, at very reasonable prices I might add.

I tried to see Magda Jean again to make sure she was happy enough with the cash settlement, not to mention I hadn't had a date in a while. But she seemed busy with Ray. I later found out she had enough free time to see my cousin, who lived near the pharmacy school on the other side of town. But that's all he would tell me, later or ever.

By now, you probably heard about the big Feveraux case yourself. Magda Jean Feveraux was on trial for murdering her husband.

I was still in shock, drinking a beer at Sleepy's one afternoon about a month later.

Crazy Bob came in humming along with the old juke box, I still remember, a Beach Boys song that was pretty popular at the time, "Help Me Rhonda."

"So, Bob, do you think we were safe drinking with her."

"Did you drive her home?" Bob asked.

"No. But I tried. Thought she was cute. She could have put some of that poison right in our drinks. She was bold enough to take it to the hospital and put it in her husband's dinner. Right there with all those nurses around. To say nothing of feeding it to Ray every night for months back in Terra Alta. Arsenic is apparently hard to detect. But she didn't hurt us."

"She musta liked us," Bob chuckled.

"I can't get over it," I said. I probably saw some of that stuff fall out of her car when we had that accident."

"Help me Rhonda," Bob sang and then switched to "Help me, Magda." Pleased with himself, he added "Help me Magda, help me get it out of my soup."

"OK, Bob, cut it out. I'm weirded out." He was way too chatty.

"Maybe not so strange. You should get a woman's perspective." He started softly singing "I Want to Hold Your Hand," which became "I want to fix your dinner…" I didn't want to hear the rest of that and walked down to the other end of the bar.

Sylvia, Sleepy's chubby niece, was on duty that afternoon. I was having trouble getting her attention probably because she thought that rather than ordering, I was just hitting on her.

When she did finally over, I asked her what she thought about the Magda Jean Feveraux case.

"Those men down in Taylor County," she said, "are real tough on their wives, even more than most men. He probably deserved it." Bitches covering for each other, I thought then and told Bob to put that into one of his songs.

These many years later, I'm not so sure. My second wife walked out on me last month.

Although a fictionalized account, the above story reflects the character of Sleepy, a real owner of my local bar in Morgantown. He famously characterized participation in the Vietnam war by saying: *If they want to give me a gun and send them sons o' bitches over here, I'll shoot 'em. But I am God damned if I am going over there.*

But alcohol was catching up. I was drinking too much every night and way too much on weekends. I wonder how I made it back and forth, Morgantown to Pittsburgh. I was driving a new red Mustang when they were so new, boys on the street would yell *MUSTANG* as I drove by. Not incidentally, my father bought me the car as a present for finishing my first year of law school. A college friend later told me that when his father saw his poor first year grades, he slammed him up against a wall and read him the riot act. Maybe that's what should have happened to me. On some of those drunken trips to or from Pittsburgh, I remember just missing a fence post or driving into a driveway at 60 mph breaking in time to just stop before a garage door. Or just getting lost.

Drinking was affecting my daily class life. If I had a presentation to make, I had to drink before, even when it as an early morning class. I would worry about it sometimes, but couldn't imagine any alternative. I just couldn't quit: I didn't know how and was afraid. The only sure-fire way to stop the fear was to drink more. Then, of course, I would forget my worry after a few drinks and think everything and especially me was fine. I remember one night, high, looking from my living room out over the moonlit Monongahela River and thinking *I am a man of destiny*. Alcohol allowed me to lie to myself, to mythologize myself to a ridiculous extent.

Part of my alcoholism manifested itself in my inability to have any relationships with women. When sober, I was too insecure to ask them out on a date. When drunk, I was too obnoxious. This was complicated by the fact that women were becoming much more open emotionally and sexually. That frankly frightened me. I tried to capture some of that in the following poem, which also exposes the cynicism of my outlook at that time, cynicism that I may have glossed over in this narrative.

An Old Confession

Slits, she called all women and herself,
racy even for the English department
at a small West Virginia university in the 70s,
where rutting was more important
than reading and writing.

We dated for a few weeks
at the urging of my roommate
who lusted after her roommate.
Nothing carnal happened between us
although I'd planed something
after we double dated
to see *Who's Afraid of Virginia Wolfe*.

But we all became so depressed
at what Albee thought was
in store for us as teachers
we just quietly got drunk
at the next-door bar
and went home alone.
Our last date.

We drifted even further apart
when she went to Cape Cod that summer.
In August, she phoned, asking me
for the name of an abortion doctor.
She'd had "an ill-advised affair"
and abortion was illegal.

Now I can't remember her name
or why we broke up,
or the doctor, or the arrangements.
I can only remember her nickname
for herself and all women.

And the death of something.

I got through my program just by the skin of my teeth. I didn't finish my last paper for an American Writers course. I didn't have the courage to speak to the professor – Rule Foster, again. I just assumed I would get an incomplete and finish it in June.

My friend, John Flynn was a proctor in a West Virginia undergraduate dorm. He offered a bed in his dorm so I could work at the WVU library. In Morgantown during the weeks, instead of reading and writing, I mostly did what I'd done in Pittsburgh during the weekends: drink. I was so disorganized and out of focus that my course paper was, at one point, entitled "Walt Whitman and You." I finally finished it in late July and put it in Dr. Foster's mailbox, all this time not speaking to him. Three weeks later, I called the registrar's office to see if I graduated. That office told me they had been holding my diploma since June. I guess Dr. Foster had taken pity on me and turned in a "C." I hope my earlier grades at least partially justified my passing grade. But there I was, a Master of English Literature certified by West Virginia University. As Virginia Woolf said about her Masters, it could never be taken away. My grades were not stellar, but I was proud of my accomplishment since I was increasingly aware I was fighting through some serious problems. Like all alcoholics, I thought all my drinking had to be connected to other emotional issues. What I didn't realize was that most of the problems were the result of my drinking, not the cause.

That winter I had started to see a psychiatrist who described me to my father (who wanted to know from the doctor why he was paying those bills – and, oddly, was not talking to me about them) as a "mildly acute alcoholic." After suggesting a number of cut-down methods especially, "count your drinks," he mentioned Alcoholics Anonymous. I was sure that would not work for me. I thought I was more crazy than alcoholic, despite the evidence. Just my drinking and driving and my lack of any meaningful relationships seemed more evidence of alcoholism than weirdness. That I-am-crazy myth would allow me to continue to drink. At first, my psychiatrist seemed to be more interested in deeper psychological issues, like dreams. As our sessions went on, he moved to behavior modification. I think he realized we couldn't get anywhere unless I stopped drinking. Unfortunately, that would take a little while.

CHAPTER VII
THE UNIVERSITY SCHOOL AND MY MYTH OF MARRIAGE

It was now time to get a job. I had stalled enough. But I had trouble interviewing: waking up on time, being alert for the interview, signing paper work with shaking hands. My friend, John Flynn, had begun working at the University School in Pittsburgh, only four blocks from my house. He recommended me to Mr. Lanning, the owner and Head of the school; Somehow, I got it together enough to interview well. Lanning left the room while I shakily did the paper work. Teachers were in high demand at that time, especially at the private schools like University School where the pay was not competitive with the Pittsburgh Public Schools.

The University School was unique in that it was all tutorial. One student and one teacher sat in a cubicle or room for 25 minutes of class. It was pretty intense. Most of the students were bright but had some problems, usually disciplinary. For example, I asked Steve H. why he left his public high school. Steve said he had a disagreement with his history teacher. In reply to my question about the nature of the problem, Steve calmly said he'd broken a chair over that teacher's head. I told Steve if he felt himself getting nervous or upset, just let me know, and we would take a break. He actually became one of my best students, doing all the reading and writing and passing the exams with flying colors.

I had many favorites. In that one-on-one setting, we could focus and communicate. Some students offered to take my car for gas and a wash so they could drive around the East End. One girl was my student for creative writing. I had little idea what to do so I gave her a copy of *The Great Gatsby* and asked her to copy the style. She came back the next week with a story in a style remarkably similar to F. Scott Fitzgerald's. She did the same thing with one of Hemingway's short stories, and then a piece mimicking Thomas Wolfe's *Look Homeward Angel*. She was something of a genius. Unfortunately, she got caught up in the drugs that were more and more apparent on Walnut Street. She would call me late at night and I would try to talk her down from whatever she was taking. I wasn't very good at it since, by that time of night, I was high on scotch myself.

I saw the effects of drugs on much of the school population. Students had started the school year hung over but they were lively and laughing. By Thanksgiving, a pall lay over the school hallways. The students seemed just zonked. But I was no one to talk. Although I always prided myself on not drinking during the school day, I was so hung over that I might as well have been drinking during class time. I once fell asleep on a student, even though it was a one-on-one situation. When I abruptly awoke, I asked *where were we?* My student replied: *You were saying the most important thing in the course is....* He knew and was having some fun with my problem.

I met my first wife, Becky Emerson, at the University School. She was a pretty lovely-skinned and bright-eyed blond with a terrific figure, I remember first seeing shown off in a form-fitting brown corduroy dress. Conveniently, Becky taught in a cubicle just across the hall from mine. Although the relationship didn't end well, we had a hell of a good time in those first years. We had fun preparing together for our courses, grading, comparing notes on students – and drinking. Becky liked to drink as much as I did. We would go to the old Fox Café on Walnut Street after work for beers. I would then go home alone for dinner and several "cocktails" (double Canadian Club) with my parents where I was still living and then meet with her later for more drinks and romance. It sounds like I was abandoning her for another cocktail hour - and that was the truth. Becky was bright and one of the best readers I knew; she just seemed to have a deep feel for literature. As much as I could love, I loved her.

We married at the end of that school year. As a wedding gift, my parents gave us the money for a honeymoon. I contacted Carlos, my Colombian friend from Lafayette, and he arranged an apartment in Cartagena. It was a mixed trip: exciting and different, but I was so hung over from the wedding, alcohol poisoned really, I thought I might have to be hospitalized in Colombia. But after a few days of resting and drinking somewhat moderately, I recovered. I loved the apartment Carlos got for us. It was a modern flat on the Boca Grande with a pool. We had some stores, a supermarket, and restaurants nearby. The views of the Caribbean from our windows were spectacular, especially at sunset. We were both very happy with our access to fine and reasonably priced international restaurants; one French bistro became a favorite. And the local beach had the best body surfing I ever experienced. You could ride a wave seemingly for miles.

Cartagena is a lovely walled city with much to see. I was very taken by walking the fortress parapets and the old churches, especially St. Peter Klaver's that supposedly had the greatest collection of relics in Christendom, including a splinter from Christ's cross. (I have since learned that that honor of collected relics belongs to St Anthony's Chapel right here in Pittsburgh's North Side.) Cartagena was both modern and old fashioned. Our apartment building was just across the street from a supermarket. One day in the liquor aisle while looking over the scotch selections, I heard a loud ongoing swish sound behind me. I turned to see a man hauling a steer carcass, rope around the horns, down the aisle toward the meat section. You don't see that in the Giant Eagle or even Whole Foods. We had everything we needed or wanted, except that occasional power shortages were a problem. A man from the apartment management would come to our door and gesture in mime (I don't speak Spanish) that the power was out. I did however understand his major vocal explanation: *Communistas.*

We stayed in Cartagena for a month and then traveled inland to Carlos's family's home in Medellin. That was an amazing look at the upper-class lives of Colombians. The Londonos had a beautiful and imposing house. Carlos told me an American businessman offered them many thousands just for the doors. But they needed that big house. Carlos had a mother, father, wife, baby, and four sisters. Lucky for us, Carlos had just bought a smaller house for his wife and child that included a guest room. Both houses and most others that I saw were built around an inner courtyard which provided great privacy. I noticed the surrounding walls had broken glass imbedded at the top for security.

One of the Colombian myths Carlos and I talked about was the lack of racism in Colombia. He did admit that throughout Colombia, the lighter the skin, the better the job. Certainly, income equality was a problem. One weekend we went to Carlos's family farm where we rode horses and swam. We also target practiced with a pistol. Becky nearly shot me and Carlos because of the gun's hair trigger. Luckily, nobody was hurt. Over drinks at the pool at the end of the day, Carlos commented on the poor workers employed on the farm. He told me one of the reasons he had gone to New York Military Academy for prep school was to learn enough strategy and tactics to organize a protective force against possible communist rebels attacking the farm. His force was these farm employees. Carlos never told me whether he had had to use those tactics or employees against an attack. He then said, *they are so poor they don't even eat well, sugar bread is a staple. Why they don't just rise up and take over the farm, I don't know.* In keeping with Scott Fitzgerald's definition of intelligence, Carlos could keep two opposing ideas in his head at the same time and still function

We were in time for a great annual costume party at the Londonos' Medellin club. I have never seen such attention paid to costumes. Carlos decided that we would all go as a stained-glass window. For days, he had the maids at his father's house sewing together different colored cloth, the stained glass, separated by black cloth (the lead in the windows). Despite all that effort, we only won second prize, losing out to a group dressed as pregnancy prevention pills, new at the time. Timeliness counts. At that and other parties Carlos took us to, I got pretty drunk, prompting him to warn me about the dangers of too much alcohol. He had always had an older brother protective side toward me, but had never talked to me about my drinking. I paid only scant attention to his warning. It was who I was; I drank.

We returned to Pittsburgh with no real home: we had signed a lease on an apartment but were three weeks early. An aunt and uncle of my wife offered us their mountain cottage for one of the bridge weeks. My wife's mother and my mother and father gave us two other weeks in their homes. One of the myths I've needed to dispel is that my problems were everybody else's fault. In fact, throughout my life, most people have tried to help me. I deal with this myth more fully later.

Our apartment was in lower Point Breeze, only a block away from Homewood, an African-American section in the East End. When we moved to our street, McPherson Blvd was about 80% white and 20%

Black. I was and am a liberal and believe in integration, so I was fine with it. Also, the rent was very reasonable. When we signed the lease, I was asked for a security deposit, which I didn't have, little money being left over after our Colombian honeymoon. At this awkward moment in the Kramer Real Estate office, I spotted my old Shady Side school mate, John Kramer, sitting in the back of the office and asked to speak to him. Although we had never as much as said "hello" before, John recognized me and okayed my signing the lease and move-in without a security deposit. One American myth is that prep schools are supposed to be places where you make connections that benefit you financially in the future. Perhaps more true for others; that's the only time it happened for me. But I was grateful for it.

I taught one more year at the University School, or U School at the students were increasingly openly calling it. I continued to love my students and their light-hearted pranks. My cubicle was very close to those of four women teachers. One afternoon, all four had female students in class. The eight female voices got higher and higher until our section sounded like an aviary on fire. I could barely talk to my student, a weekend singer in a blues band. As a mild protest, he began to sing *Ole Man River* at the top of his big bass voice. The women never heard us.

I was casting about for some way to find a place in work and life as many of my friends had, despite my drinking problem. Too often I ended up with a smaller and smaller group of friends who were too much like me, like the characters in this story:

NIGHTCAP

"You should not have run over his rims," I said.

"He should not have taken my parking place," my cousin Bill answered.

"Not equivalent," I answered. A parking place for nice expensive wheel rims destroyed."

Like most bar tables of drinkers, Hughie, my cousin Bill, and I usually thought we looked, talked, and were thinking great again, there at Artie's on Baum Boulevard. Hurting little of the world with our only slightly damaging, but always to us funny, pranks. Hysterically laughing, and drinking that summer of '74 away.

I had a general sense of the nonsense of our self-appraised OKness, but the repetition of those nights was giving me an almost out-of-body insight that we were just a bunch of burgeoning bums. I was set off by Bill's pulling off (God he was a moose) and driving over a new set of Cadillac-specific wheel rims. And by my loss of a job in a call center selling theater subscriptions and the breakup with Susan, my first real girlfriend.

Sharing my insight was harder than becoming enlightened.

"You know, you guys got to get a grip. We all need to wake up."

"I'm feeling pretty sprightly," said Hughie, the smartest and least accomplished of all his successful brothers. And potentially the most dangerous, alleged to have blown up an oil well field in Texas during his short stay at Texas Christian University. One of the few things he wouldn't talk about.

"We are all doing fine," chimed in my hefty cousin, Bill, still working on the latest 12- ounce addition to his big beer belly.

"We don't have real jobs like all our friends. We live at home. It's already 2:00 AM and we have no reason to go home. Nobody at this table is getting up before noon tomorrow."

"A car like that guy had, he'll have no trouble replacing his rims," Hughie jumped in to my cousin's rescue.

"Hughie's right. Calm down. We just are having some fun now. We all have plans."

"Real plans that contain a future? Grown up jobs?" I asked.

"Maybe you are just feeling emasculated because the city is repaving your street and you can't get your car out. I hate it when I can't drive."

"You guys need to get out of here," the bartender interrupted. "It's already past legal closing. Want me to call the cops?"

"Shut up," my cousin let fly loud with his usual 5-drink charm. "Like your bar? Want us to call the State Liquor Control Board and have this rat trap closed for good or me to come over there and 'splain it to you?" Bill was big enough and scary enough to keep pretty much all of his fights verbal. I never saw him lose a fight or throw a punch, good pretend life, I thought.

I looked around Artie's Bar and supposed Grill although I never saw anything in the food line more than the pickled eggs on the bar that looked like a cholera hot bed and some sausage strips that were at least wrapped. Dirty floor, dirty tables, one ancient pinball I never saw played, and an old toothless swamper, waiting shakily for us to leave so he could mop the floor to earn his last drink of the night. Artie's was stripped down for booze. It wasn't the first night we had closed the place. I was 25. A college graduate. Many of my friends were married, were lawyers, accountants, businessmen and one a doctor. What the hell was I doing there?

"Let's go," I said. "Let's go home."

"I still have my Artists and Models club card," Hughie said. Let's get us a nightcap."

"Or we could go up to the Hill and find that whorehouse again," my cousin offered. "Wasn't that Marie something?"

"We have to stop this," I said.

"Are you ok, Ray? We know you were really bummed by that firing on top of losing Susan," Hughie said.

"Yeah, it's their loss, Susan's and that dramatic theater subscriptions job." Bill laughed at his "dramatic" joke.

"Stick with us and we'll cheer you up," Hughie added.

"I've had it. Take me home," I said.

All the way home we reiterated the same arguments, getting nowhere, but they were annoyingly kind.

"A loss of a girlfriend and a job all in one week is tough." Hughie said.

"I'll buy you a girl on the Hill," Bill offered.

"I'm talking about doing something serious in life. More than telephone sales and worrying about girlfriends and whores."

"You'll feel better tomorrow. You have a chance to feel better tonight if you would come with us. The Photographers and Models Club has a lot of nice-looking legitimate babes."

"Home," I said for the last time and they did, letting me off as close as they could, considering my street was torn up a block either way for repaving.

"Don't try to take your car out. That drop from the driveway will tear up your undercarriage," my cousin said.

"You should ask those workers to build you a little down ramp." Bill added.

More fantasy, I thought.

"Yeah, or call one of us," Hughie said.

I had trouble sleeping even at 3:00 in the morning; I started thinking about some kind of real job I could do. What did people in business do?

Just as I was finally falling off to sleep, I heard the big machine starting.

"Oh, no," I said into the pillow as the earth mover revved louder and louder. I tried putting the pillow over my head, but the noise was relentless.

I knew who was starting an earth mover at 3:00 AM. I don't know whether I worried so much about keeping them out of jail as keeping my neighbors and parents from knowing. Dad was getting sick of me, and I had no other place to go. I ran downstairs and through the front door to the porch.

There on top of a giant humming earth mover, stolen city worker cap atop his head, was Hughie. It looked like only minimal earth had been moved, but Hughie was clearly on the case in the cab, moving levers, getting the scoop up and down, all, I was sure, to build me a ramp out of my driveway.

Down the street now was a City Police car birthing two cops.

Hughie saw them, finally gave up, jumped to a big tread and proudly took off and waved the cap toward me, looking like he just hit the winning run in the World Series.

I knew a couple things at that moment: least important, that Hughie would run, like the track athlete he could have been, through my back yard into the alley and beyond where Bill would have the car running and they would somehow get away as usual. I also knew that to have any kind of adult life, I had to stay away, far away, from these guys. And I knew I would always have a slight ache to be on that big earth mover with Hughie, jumping down to the get-away car.

THE END

My drinking was now pretty much out of control. I drank between a pint and a fifth every night. Our marriage was in trouble, and we went to counseling. Our therapist consoled my wife, explaining "Of course this is difficult," she said. "You are married to an alcoholic." I told them both breezily that I was not an alcoholic and could and would quit. And I did for about six weeks, but then a gift fifth from my brother, who knew nothing of my abstinence, got me started again. I was on and off liquor, mostly on, all that year.

But I did manage to stay off the booze for several weeks during which I had a successful job interview. My old West Virginia University friend, Tom Marshall, had become the head of the English Department at Robert Morris (then) College. He knew and liked me: we had taken classes together and were drinking buddies. Despite my unspectacular grades, he hired me.

Even having been sober for several weeks, I was nervous going into my first class, a survey literature course held at night. There was no lectern or teacher's desk in the room. I thought this must be what it's like for entertainers, such as those on the Borscht Circuit, nothing between you and the audience. I started off haltingly but got into the material quickly which I had prepared carefully. And then, as the students responded well, I felt a sort of electricity around us. It hit me as I think it hits all teachers: *I can do this; I love this.*

I thought back to a book recommendation, Dr. Rule Foster had made and talked about at WVU, *The Thread That Runs True* by Jesse Stuart. The controlling metaphor in that title refers to an old Appalachian children's' game where the students form an arch for other students to walk through, all singing "the needle's eye that doth supply the thread that runs so true." Stuart likens a teacher to that needle's eye that provides *the thread that runs so true*, that is, intellectually prepared students. I was proud of my choice of a profession. Now I had to meet the responsibilities.

It was a busy year. I taught four composition courses and one literature course, a fifteen-hour load. Too many class hours, sometimes with as many as 130 students. But the intense work was keeping me from the scotch until later in the evening. Another myth was gaining credence with me: Hard work could save me from alcoholism.

I liked the students, who were far different than the privileged ones I had gone to school with. These young people were generally first-generation college students, working to pay for school. This was before loans became a big business and easy to get. I was struck again and again how lucky I had been to get an education paid for by my parents – and how less than lucky many of these students were, lots as smart as me and some smarter.

What I loved most was their sense of humor and fresh look at what we were studying, like the student who suggested about Nick's position in *The Great Gatsby*: "Nick is trying to jam with the big boys." Or, my favorite evaluation by a student who said of me: "He reminds me of Colombo; he looks dumb but he ain't."

I worked hard grading eight papers per student, plus rewrites, in four classes, around a thousand per semester. They ranged from so so, to pretty good, to excellent. Often it was drudgery – nights and every Sunday afternoon were devoted to it. But many of these papers provided a glimpse into intelligent, surprising, and sometimes beautiful hearts and minds. I still remember, forty plus years later, a woman student who wrote powerfully about a gang fight, and a night student who wrote about how he hated growing up in a small town because of all the adults who presumed authority over him or at least would call his parents - and why that was just the reason - now that he had children – that he was moving back to a small town.

Although paid poorly, I had an intellectually ideal job situation, one that continued presenting interesting problems. Could I make my students better writers? I sure as hell was going to try. And my wife, Becky, became pregnant. I was very nervous but excited about it. As my friend, Jim said, *Isn't it great that this sex stuff actually works!*

It was great, and my son, John, was born on July 27, 1970. He suffered from hyaline membrane disease and was in the hospital on a breathing machine for the first six weeks of his life. When he came home and I would do the 2:00 AM feeding, I would look and him and think that if he had fought so long and hard to live, I had to do everything possible to help him grow.

But that commitment and the one to my students were in jeopardy. I was now keeping up to nearly a fifth of scotch a day. And weekends were worse. I spent one at a house party in the Laurel Mountains with some of my old Shady Side buddies. Friday, we drank into the wee hours of the morning and got up on Saturday to raft down the Youghiogheny River. I was so hung over I could barely think, but we all had wine skins. So, I squeezed out enough cheap red to pull myself together and start off on the raft. By chance, my wife - who had also been up the night before - and I ended up in the two most important positions in the raft, back and front. It got pretty crazy: two people fell out in the rapids. But they got back in without any damage, and we all finished safely. It was something of a miracle. People die doing those rapids.

I came home Sunday to host a party for some of the same people. I finished the wine and started on scotch. That night, I started throwing up blood. The next morning my brother took me into the hospital. With a tube down my throat, one intern asked the doctor "Is this guy an alcoholic?" Even in that beaten state, I tried to rasp out a defensive *No*. Because I knew that would probably mean I would have to quit. And I couldn't do that. Bad as my life was becoming, I was sure it would be impossible without the aid of alcohol. I spent four days in the hospital on a careful diet until I stabilized.

Afterward, having been abstinent for a few weeks, I asked the doctor if I could have a few "cocktails" during the upcoming Christmas holidays. He replied *Oh, you'll never drink again*. I thought ironically, *I'll just bet, Doc. I'll just bet I don't drink again.*, knowing that it was just impossible for me to stop drinking. I did not say it out loud, of course. I didn't have that kind of courage. What I did have was an incredible amount of fear which I could only take care of one way.

But I tried to quit again and had some success. After three months or so, I was feeling pretty good. My stomach stopped hurting and my wife and son, John, were comfortable, even happy around me. Then unaccountably, I started drinking again. So, it wasn't just fear or outside circumstances. I just wanted to drink. Maybe it was metabolic, maybe it was what I learned at home. Whatever it was, I just drank.

My wife drank with me. While we did still have some fun, too often we argued. One of our topics was who was the worst. The following poem touches on how mutually destructive we were.

Luminary

Just in case you think
I got screwed up only recently,
let me tell you about the fire:

My wife in those days was a candle maker
as well as a crazy maker, like many artists,
just good enough to be impossible.

We were having a big drinks party
to celebrate Christ's birth
although he wouldn't be coming or mentioned.

But the wine much advertised
in his bio would be plentiful.
And candles.

Lots of candles to celebrate
my wife's talent and for atmosphere.
We lit the hell out of the place. And then ourselves.

Drink up was the last thing I heard.
But I woke up in time
to douse out the growing flames

and, like my wife, to sleep
in throat-coating carbon,

each blaming the negligent one.

Did I tell you we had a four-year old?
A boy so tender he unexpectedly kissed
my hand in the park one day.

My mother had been ill for a number of years starting when I was at Shady Side when she spent my sophomore year in Mercy Hospital. She suffered from a severe bone infection and other internal complications. Although she did recover enough to get around the house and out to dinner with the family, she gradually became more and more incapacitated with increasingly frequent hospitalizations, one near death event mentioned above that brought me home from college.

One of those hospitalizations was further complicated by my father's own hospitalization. He fell down his house stairs and fractured his neck. I was drinking with him that night. It was a crisis situation that neither he nor I in our inebriated state recognized. Finally, his housekeeper got him to go to Shadyside hospital. He was in a serious cast with an electric saw next to him to cut through to chest flesh in case of a heart attack.

I would drive from Robert Morris to visit my mother at Mercy Hospital who would offer me a few drinks from the bottle of Canadian Club she kept her room. Then I would drive to Shadyside hospital to visit my father and have a stiff drink with him. In a what-the-hell mood, I would have few more at home. I was not getting much grading done. Of course, my parents' hospitalizations were an excellent excuse: the phrase I heard later in recovery: *poor me, poor me, pour me a drink.*

My mother died in the Spring of 1972. Again, I took solace in my booze. My father was recovering at home with a series of home nurses. From work, I would hire them in the morning and my irascible father would fire them in the afternoon. It was driving me a little crazy until he found a young blond nurse whom he liked - and she liked him. After a short time, our gratitude for that nurse faded away. It looked to my brother Terry and me and our wives that they liked each other a little too much. That nurse started to limit our contact with Dad. One night, that nurse tried to send Becky and me away from his door. Once inside, Becky took her aside, explained our concern, and pinched her hard. The nurse yelped a little, but we saw Dad. My father soon saw how he was being isolated. He fired her. I was back to more happily finding new replacements.

Despite all this increased chaos, I continued to do okay at work, partly because my WVU classmate and boss, Tom Marshall, was a good friend to me (and often drank with me). Also, when I was sober, I worked like hell. But trouble was closing in. I was missing more and more work days and was more and more worried that I smelled of alcohol. I had taken up the occasional morning drink when stressed. At the end of one semester, a student wrote on an evaluation that I was a good teacher but had to stop drinking, that I was hurting myself. That comment made me ashamed. Once again, I didn't know what to do. Quitting seemed impossible. I was frozen, and my life went on pretty much the same way for some time.

In that time, my father remarried an old friend. He and Mary Sandoz had met on shipboard travelling to Europe in the early 1920s. She was going to finishing school in Switzerland and my father was taking one of his first trips to Europe. It wasn't a much-developed shipboard romance: Mary was 17 and had her mother nearby as a chaperon. But they stayed in touch as friends. Mary married Henri Sandoz, a Swiss businessman. My father and later my mother visited them in Switzerland. Mary's son, Henri Stanton, is named after my father. My mother indicated that my father won over Mary's husband by helping them out financially during the Depression when they lost a good deal of money. My mother was much less happy with the friendship, especially after Mary's husband died and she came back to the United States to be Mistress of French House at Smith College. Once, when Mary called to wish my father a happy birthday, my mother answered and held out the phone so that Mary could easily hear and said loudly to me: *Here's your new mother*! It was biting, but my mother did have a sense of humor.

At the end of that Spring term, relieved to get through, I decided to celebrate. I went to the liquor store and bought a half gallon and a fifth of scotch. One of the things I haven't yet mentioned was how much of the family budget was going to my drinking: a lot.

Those two bottles started a real spiral. The brakes came off, and I was drinking around the clock. Only going out in taxis to buy more booze. I had already lost my license in an epic DUI that I wrote about in an earlier poem. Suffice it to say that twelve tickets: many stop sign violations, several stop lights, and a weak *Too fast for conditions*. Terry came down to the station, talked to a few people in that convincing way he had, and got me home.

More painfully, I remember my son who was then three, asking my wife, *Why does Daddy always sleep on the floor?* I knew I was in trouble, but every time I woke up, I would think "I'll have a few drinks and figure this out" – and then I was off again. I remember sleeping under the dining room table so no one would step on me. And seeing my wife's and my son's feet go by as they went to job and school. I felt I was dying.

CHAPTER VIII
RECOVERY AND MYTHS OF ALCOHOLISM AND ME

I finally got it together enough to call my brother and asked if there was a hospital or someplace I could go. He checked around and told me to be ready for his pickup the next day at noon. Terry said we could have lunch on our way. I just laughed; I hadn't eaten for days and couldn't.

I drank my way through our lunch, and Terry drove me to St. John's hospital which had a well-known detox floor. They gave me some medication and I collapsed into bed for nearly 12 hours.

I awoke in the middle of the night totally disoriented wondering where I was. In my drunken deranged state, I imagined my friends had hired a motel and some people in white coats to look like hospital personnel. All to fool me. So I walked out of my room and started down the hospital corridor saying as loud as I could. *You can all come out now. I know. Come on out, I figured it out.* Somebody came out of his room and asked me what was my problem. I told him my theory. He explained I really was in a hospital. I asked why, thinking maybe I had been in an accident. He said rather kindly: *Maybe you drink too much.* One sad thing about my theory was that I had few friends outside of work at that point and none who would go to all that trouble about me.

I learned a lot in detox and actually enjoyed some of it. I hung out with a guy who looked like Slip Mahoney from the Dead-End Kids. He was very funny in his imitations of his famous look-alike. I also met Frank, an interesting and a tragically hopeless alcoholic. He was a war hero, flying jets and fighting North Korean MIGs in that war.

Back home, he began a successful career as an advertising executive. His drinking caught up with him quickly, and he became one of the best-known drunks on the Pittsburgh's North Side, finally living on the street. He was so often hospitalized that he had been barred from most of the city's detox units. St. John's would still take him in because of his personal relationship with Dr. Gabos, the Director of the well-known and respected alcoholic unit.

The humor I initially experienced evaporated one night when I sat with Frank as he went into alcoholic hallucinations that I heard other old timers in the ward refer to as "the rams." I watched and listened as Frank "re-experienced" a sortie over North Korea, complete with fears of being shot down and calling for help, out loud in the hospital night, from other pilots.

The next day in the hospital, Frank was joking again. When the nurse asked if he could at least eat some soup when he was on a bender, he said he didn't want soup. *I want pork chops,* Frank said, which everybody including Frank laughed at, given he hadn't been able to put any food on his alcoholic stomach in weeks. Doc Gabos, reminded him of his recent pain and hallucinating, saying: *Frank, you think you will just be able to keep drinking and then one day peacefully fall asleep and die. But it's not going to be that easy. Your stomach and liver and brain are going fast, and you are in for a lot of agony like last night if you don't quit.*

That little conversation didn't help Frank. I learned he died of alcoholism about six months later. But Doctor Gabos's talk got my attention. When my brother suggested I meet with someone from recovery once I got out of St. John's Hospital, I agreed.

After eight days, I did get out. And I talked to one of the recovery community's most influential members in Pittsburgh, Bill D. He took me to some meetings and talked a little about his own experience. He'd done a surprising amount of drinking for a very successful lawyer. In the meetings he took me to and those I continued attending on my own, I enjoyed the stories of members in their talks, referred to as "leads." (The idea being the talks would lead into discussion that would help those listening.) But I was unwilling to brand myself as an alcoholic even though the evidence was overwhelming. And I certainly was not going to turn my "will and life over to the care of" a God I didn't believe in.

Still clinging to the myth that I was not an alcoholic, I went to the psychiatrist I had been seeing off and on since my West Virginia days. I told him I didn't think I was alcoholic, hoping against hope he would agree. He said, "Then what do you think you are?" That momentarily stumped me. "A heavy drinker," I answered. What's the difference?" he said. I could dimly see that for me there was no difference. I then told him I needed to treat the alcohol problem outside of meetings because "Those are not my people." He also destroyed that proposition quickly: "Who are your people?" I had no answer. I had almost no people, very few real friends anymore.

People in meetings were very kind, letting me find my way. I was impressed with the varied background of the members. And with their patience: I was the one who was often picking arguments. I found someone smarter than me, not that it was that hard. Ed M. regularly answered every one of my verbal barbs with sometimes stinging humor: When I argued that recovery was just some bourgeois idea for the middle classes, he suggested I hang around a while and maybe I'd make it into the middle class. (He was right; by this point, my drinking expenses had driven me and my family nearly into the poor house.) As much as I found Ed to be annoying, I realized his attention was helping me. I asked him to be my sponsor. We were together for more than 40 years, until he passed away from cancer nearly ten years ago. During that time, he helped me work my way through the steps and through a lot in my life. I still think about and quote him to my sponsees.

But at the beginning of my experience, I was struggling, emotionally and spiritually. I was having an identity crisis of the toughest kind. My self-serving rationalizing myths were falling away. I was not the creative genius about to write the great American novel; I was not the world's best teacher. I wasn't even a decent father or husband. And I hated that I was being encouraged to get honest with myself about all these things. But I knew I was down to my last chance. So I went to meetings like a job. At that point, I didn't like my job, but I showed up. So I followed Ed's advice and made six meetings a week (*You drank every day; you can go to a meeting every day.*) I even made some friends. I was particularly fond of a meeting at Sacred Heart church that sometimes had discussion shares so dramatic (one Sunday night a woman, a little high, said she had to continue to drink to continue to have sex) that the gathering was referred to as *The Secret Storm*.

Still, I had trouble identifying as an alcoholic and was tired of what I saw as the *aren't-we-special-and-don't-we-have-it-all-figured-out* nature of recovery. In one meeting, I said loudly that I was sick hearing over and over that people had such a hard time before they came into the Program but now everything was hunky dory. The chair of that beginners meeting simply said that he had felt the same way until his sponsor suggested that he "should either take the first step and admit he had a problem, or go out and try drinking again." A cold chill ran up my spine at the thought of going out and drinking. Given my stomach trouble and my marital and job situations, I didn't think that if I drank again, I could last much longer. I really meant couldn't live much longer.

It was suggested to me (it's all suggestions; nobody makes anybody do anything) that I spend one full year on the first step. That time helped me let my major misconceptions, myths really, drift away. By the end of that year, I had accepted I was a serious alcoholic. Part of that realization came from my wife who reminded me of all that I had done to make our marriage worse. She was not totally innocent herself, but my sponsor and others constantly reminded me that my job was to keep my side of the street clean and not worry about others' shortcomings. I was also told that alcoholics make the people around them sicker than they are. An alcoholic knows what, when, and why they are doing things – usually to get more access to booze, but often just to carry out a drunken idea: such as the time I dressed in full academic regalia, cap and gown for gravitas, and walked next door to ask the neighbors to quiet an outdoor party. The neighbors knew and told me I was drunk and to go home. My wife was horrified. Spouses have to guess at the madness.

The issue of accepting God was helped both by the recommendation that we simply find a "higher power." That higher power for many members does turn into a more traditional belief in God. And like a lot of the program, patience is key. As one thoughtful and humorous member said: *We don't ask that you believe. We don't even ask that you pretend to believe. We just ask that you act as though you would like to pretend to believe.*

The following suggests some of the difficulties I was having,

Quitting

my sloppy kitchen clean-up,
I watch the ants walk out on the slotted spoon
towards the honey-dipped plank end
over my soap and vinegar sink water
and wonder about
focus, attraction, suicide,

their honey over astringent water,
my drink of choice.

Along with the other choices:
to have both hands full of gimme
and a mouth full of much obliged;
to fondle without holding on;
to promise without keeping;
to back down, to lie.

To justify, how others did it too:
John O'Hara having to lock himself in a hotel room
away from the booze to write, Hemingway too.
Fitzgerald giving up, drinking all working day,
all of them various levels of selfish bastard.

The curtain at Friday's abstinence meeting
only half covers the wood cross, still
unexpectedly huge even in a church basement,
affirming my own small size, half commitment.

Inside me, the speaker says,
*lives a creative, charming, witty,
almost irresistibly relentless romantic
waiting to kill me dead.*

In my own ordinary hours,
I walk carefully between the actions
of balance above the extinction below,
and finding enough sweetness to live.

After about a year of my being sober, my wife began to appreciate what the program was doing for me. Our relationship gradually improved even though, or maybe partly because, I spent many evenings at meetings. My relationship with my son also greatly improved. He no longer saw me sleeping on the floor and doing and saying lord knows what. I had spent his 4th birthday in St. John's Hospital's alcoholic ward. A year later, I remember taking him swimming and his asking me what it was like to be an adult. I said it was alright, and then asked him what it was like being a kid, fearing what he might say would reflect anger at my drinking. He said it was pretty great being a kid. I teared up knowing I had made progress.

I had also started to pay more attention to my work. Most of my idealism about teaching had withered in my alcoholism. It was hard getting it back. At first, I just seemed to read my lectures out of the text for the course. I slowly realized that not only was this immoral, but I was making myself and the students miserable. So I started to get more involved with the students, especially in individual conferences. I also tried to be more creative in assignments.

Complicating my emotional adjustment was the getting over the loss of my mother. She passed away under some difficult circumstances. The attending doctor, her physician, put down on the death certificate as the cause of death, *Alcoholism.* Although I knew it was true, I was furious that he would not leave her more dignity in death. In truth, I needed to hear that reason for her death and recognize I was still laboring under the middle-class myth of a person and family looking ok, when it was suffering from a serious disease. My mother's death and my full realization why made me more serious about my own sobriety. I remember her fondly as someone with a great wit who loved me dearly as best she could and often tried to show it by giving me alcohol as a balm. As I mentioned, she often said to me when I was having a difficult time, *Have a drink and a nap, Jay.*

The following poem to reflect some of our closeness and love just before she died.

Last Visit to my Mother

I look down at my dying mother,
the anthropology of my Celtic history, and see
my own skull staring back at me,
beautiful hair gone knotted to a question mark.

Is that papier mâché mask telling
me some secret, in the mysterious unbroken
word stream that could be a keening for lost sisters,
a story from before I understood words?

A hundred runic prayers
run together for their eternity in the airy alleys
of her heaven, with its one incomprehensible God.
I add one more plea: please, get me out of here.

I can offer nothing now, and really
never could, except a hand to a stronger one
helping me perhaps across the street
or squeezing goodbye on the train to camp.

I sneak my fingers away and watch
her hand rise, like a crippled duck,
now swimming somehow
smoothly into a glorious swan,
her wake finally empty of cygnets.

CHAPTER IX
MY PROFESSIONAL LIFE AS MYTH

As my emotions cleared from the loss of my mother, I found myself more and more involved with work and our new union. There had been talk of a union for some time, but many faculty objected on the grounds we were professionals. Like many of my colleagues I came to see this as a myth used to exploit the faculty by telling them they had a sort of class privilege that somehow substituted for decent pay and working conditions. I liked my work at Robert Morris but we were badly paid and overworked: 12-hour schedules (they had finally been reduced from 15 hours a few years before) with no release time for research. Many people think that "only 12 hours of contact with students" is easy. What they don't take into consideration is how much time is needed to prepare meaningful classes, how exhausting teaching can be even in an invigorating class. On top of that, English classes require careful diagnostic and evaluative grading that takes an extraordinary amount of time. Things came to a head when after another profitable year, Robert Morris top administration again offered faculty only a miniscule raise. Only months before, we had voted in the American Federation of Teachers (AFT) to represent us.

There is a great story from the early days of AFT negotiations in New York about its president and co-founder, Al Shanker. A fascinating man in his own right, he both defied and lived up to the myth of tough labor leader. He had graduated with honors from the University of Illinois and was ABD (all but dissertation) in philosophy from Columbia University when finances forced him a take what he referred to as a "lousy job" substitute teaching in East Harlem. He soon became involved with the union movement. In an early contract negotiation, the AFT and the City of New York were down to their last million. The City negotiators said there just was not any more money. Al finally believed them and agreed, signing the contract. Shortly thereafter, the headline in the *New York Daily News* read that New York City spent four million dollars to clean up a record snow fall. An angry Al supposedly walked into the mayor's office holding the newspaper saying "I thought the city was out of money." The Mayor said "Al, this was a disaster," Shanker answered, "From now on, I'm the disaster." In fact, he was generally known as a level-headed, honest, and fair leader but very effective negotiator, who did much to raise the level, not only of teacher pay but also their responsibilities and professionalism.

Maybe we weren't that tough, but we did strike, which was a shock to the Robert Morris administration and, I think, even to us. As a "teaching professional," I walked a picket line, sometimes watching my lawyer friends pass by on their way to their offices. My consolation was knowing that I was right in standing up for myself, for ourselves. I was surprised at our support. One mailman suggested he would not deliver the RMU mail. But fair minded as we were, we insisted and he did.

Other support was more complicated. Once, I tried to stop a truck of fresh vegetables, telling the driver that we needed his union support. He drove right past into the Robert Morris campus to deliver. I asked our AFT union representative what about union solidarity. He revealed the magic words to me. "Just ask him what's his name and local (union)." I did ask the next food driver (hauling a semi of fresh meat), those important questions. He swore, but stopped and turned around and drove away. A picket line fellow and friend from the history department expressed our ambivalence, saying "That's the trouble with this country, Jay: a couple of guys like us can ruin a truck full of fresh meat." My friend saw the conservative position, but stayed on the picket line, once again proving Scott Fitzgerald's dictum: the sign of true intelligence is to be able to hold two opposing ideas in your mind and still operate.

We won with the Robert Morris administration acceding to our negotiation demands, including better salaries and working conditions. I so believed in the union I became Grievance Chairman (AFT Local 3412). It's a title I am still proud of: I helped work out a number of problems between the administration and union members, sometimes siding with reasonable administration positions. I thought but didn't say to one chronic faculty complainer: *You're lucky you're not getting fired.* At one point, a member of the upper administration at RMU confided to me that the union made their life easier: solving one problem for one union member set a precedent that could eventually solve many. Over time, our local and the Robert Morris Administration came to appreciate each other.

If anything, the respect of better salaries and working conditions made us more professional. Personally, sobriety made me a more responsible and civic-minded citizen.

NEH

One day, out of nowhere, a colleague suggested I look into National Endowment for the Humanities Summer Seminars offered by the US Department of Education. These are government sponsored seminars run for college teachers in various disciplines looking to work with experts in their field to learn more about it and improve their teaching. I was concerned that I would not be able to attend because of expense and time away from my family. But the program provided stipends, and it turned out that two of the rhetoric and composition programs were right in Pittsburgh, one at the University of Pittsburgh and the other at Carnegie Mellon University.

I knew the professor running the program at Pitt, Bill Coles. He kindly told me that friends were off limits for applications to his program, but since he knew and liked the writing I showed him, he would recommend me to Richard Young who was running the program at CMU. The first step was writing a proposal explaining what my project was going to be. This requirement started me on the first serious research I had done in a long time, maybe since my paper on Walt Whitman for Rule Foster at WVU. I worked hard to understand what was going on in my field, particularly in rhetorical invention, Richard Young's specialty.

MY PROFESSIONAL COMPETENCE AS MYTH UNTIL...

Richard Young's summer seminar in rhetorical invention was both rigorous and eye-opening. I found Young himself to be amazing. I had seen him speak at a professional conference where he was attacked for creating a PhD program in rhetoric in an English department with no literature at all. His answer was that the United States was in a literacy crisis which was causing failures in job and military training and where people were even poisoning themselves because they could not read the warnings on food labels. I clearly remember him saying that we were not going to solve such a crisis "by doing a little bit of this and a little bit of that."

Young's scholarship is very impressive. He had written for journal submission a long game-changing article, "Invention, A Topographical Survey" that pretty much defined rhetoric scholarship in invention, the most important of the five arts of rhetoric (invention, arrangement, style, memory, and delivery) from ancient to modern times. All Young's subsequent publications had been at the request of various journals.

I discovered that summer that I had been teaching something - English composition, rhetoric really - about which I knew very little.

This was true of the profession as a whole which was undergoing a radical revision by modern composition scholars. I (and the majority of my colleagues in the field) had been teaching versions of arrangements and style, mostly organization and grammar, much of which I had learned back in my Shady Side days. Like other composition teachers, I would encourage students to imitate essays that were too sophisticated for them to master. This emphasis on imitation, organization, and grammar was referred to by Young and other modern composition scholars as the current-traditional method. Interestingly, one of the chief proponents of that method was my old Lafayette College teacher, William Waite Watt (W3). As I mentioned above, Watt thoroughly developed his version of the current-traditional method of teaching composition in his text referred to by his students and many others as *the Little Green Bible*. The chief problem with that approach is that it leaves great gaps in students' writing skill set, especially how to start their writing - the rhetorical field of invention.

Young told us that at a professional conference he had confronted the author of the best-selling composition text at the time and accused him of writing an immoral text. That author in a 280+ page book devoted only 8 pages to invention. That left students with very little instruction on how to start their papers. Yet, as every English composition teacher knows, the question most students want answered when asked to write is "What should I write about? How should I start?"

Young's work in his articles and especially his book, *Rhetoric: Discovery and Change* were ground breaking. After reading the book, one PhD quit her job, packed her bag and dog, and drove from the west coast to the University of Michigan and then to Pittsburgh to work with Young. Richard's book was almost all about invention, methods for finding the writer's subject and relevant arguments.

We focused on the crucial role of invention, chief of the five arts of rhetoric, but we did not ignore the other arts: arrangement (organization), style (a field going much beyond grammar to encompass among others, word choice, sentence structure and variation), memory (not really paid attention to since the invention of writing) and delivery (paid too little attention to outside of speech courses and some traditions, such as the Black church experience). I discovered that summer that I/we are heir to a rich thinking, rhetoric, and teaching tradition that I knew little about. Yet what little teaching instruction I had been given told me I was almost fully informed on the subject: another significant myth. Some of what I discovered that summer was truly astounding to me.

For example, I was floored by the rhetorician, Gorgias (from whom we get the name for beautiful) who said about the nonmaterial world in a famous fragment: *Nothing exists; if it did, we could not know it; if we knew it, we could not express it.* This concept sees the world's ideas as primarily rhetorical constructs where the most effective speaker (most beautiful speaker in Gorgias's case), or, for example, the most seemingly charismatic speaker in John Kennedy's case (to some and Donald Trump to others) creates truth. This drove Plato to write the dialogue entitled *Gorgias* in which he points out the dangers of using such a provisional approach to truth, especially in ignoring values. The knowledge that my profession was so deeply involved with ideas, values, and philosophic aesthetic presentation was a revelation.

Much of the seminar was devoted to how that rich classical tradition had become gradually weaker, so that in American colleges, universities, and high schools, what remained was a composition course that was only the hollowed out current-traditional method, mostly grammar and some arrangement/organization.

Young's answer for the modern rhetorician, which we all were hoping to become, was his neo-classical approach: problem-solving rhetoric. The approach built upon our rhetoric heritage with its emphasis on solid heuristics (such as Aristotle's topoi), based on good theory and systems. Crucial to the method was finding and effectively stating important problems, then methodologically researching and solving them. Whenever one of us questioned Richard about an approach to a writing task, he would always say, *What's the problem?* I finally learned that a well stated problem often goes a long way to solving it. A classic example was the Viet Nam War. American politicians kept asking how can we win the war? The real questions, finally agreed to among those politicians turned out to be: What does winning the war mean? Why are we fighting it? How can we leave with some honor? The solution to the situation was embedded in those questions.

In teaching, I had been having trouble getting students started on their papers, so I was very happy that I was in Young's seminar with its systematic approach: sufficient background, problem statement, question that focuses the problem, and preview of how the writing will approach a solution. It didn't work for all students always, but it worked for most and was far superior to the more haphazard approach I had been using before.

My friend Bill Coles' summer NEH seminar was being taught less than a mile away in Oakland. Bill joked that he had become annoyed that Richard was referring to him in scholarly articles as a neo-Romantic. But I came to believe that the title was apt. Bill spent much time encouraging students to write authentically. And this often had to do with getting to the student's emotions and feelings. One of the ways Bill did that was confrontationally, challenging students to question their own approaches; and staying away from what he referred to as Engfish: a sort of pretend writing: I remember Bill saying about some student writing that it looked like writing; it smelled like writing; but it wasn't really writing. That is, it wasn't an authentic revelation of the writer as a person trying to reach a goal. I remember an outstanding example of the beginning of a successful authentic paper starting out with the old song lyric: *I want to be Bobby's girl,* followed by the student's sentence, *Oh God, did I want to be Bobby's girl.* Again, I felt very fortunate to have access to two of the leading rhetorical scholars and teachers of the time, each mining one of the two great strains of thought in Western intellectual history, classism and romanticism. Less crucial but still interesting was my being taught in my Lafayette days, by William Watt, one of the major proponents of the now discredited current traditional teaching approach.

It turned out that Young and Coles knew each other from their Master's Degree days and reignited their friendship when they both ended up in Pittsburgh. They each taught one of the other's classes that summer, broadening students' understanding of modern rhetoric possibilities and scholarship. Because they were both heads of departments and were hiring excellent rhetoric teachers, such as Rich Enos, the great rhetoric historian and Linda Flower, the equally fine socially conscious problem-solving rhetorician, both at CMU - and David Bartholomae, the respected composition scholar at Pitt, I was in Rhetoric City. The whole seminar felt we were privileged to be part of some ground breaking work. At the end of the summer, we got Richard a t-shirt that said, *Caution: Emerging Paradigm*

Aside from Young's excellent teaching, I benefitted from my terrifically bright and motivated NEH Fellows, many of whom went on to important careers: Chuck Bazerman is probably the most well-known. But equally sharp and influential were, among others, Jerry Mulderig, Dick Easton, and Leslie Olson. We did lots of scholarly and some non-scholarly things that summer and became good friends. One of my favorite memories was attending church at the Pittsburgh Oratory Parish along with my six-year-old son who was just losing his baby teeth, one of which came out during a Sunday mass. John deposited this treasure into the hands of Leslie Olson. After the service, she showed me my son's gifts, and I could only say it was a sign of trust.

I did have some second thoughts about whether I had been earning my paycheck before I knew what I was learning that summer. But, even prior to my CMU experience, I had worked hard at teaching what was the lingua franca of composition instruction at that time: mostly organization and grammar, William Watt's current traditional approach (at that time, adhering to the broadly accepted composition myth that it was the only way to teach). With what I had, I also helped improve students' ideas and ways to begin and develop papers. I have had over the years, many thanks from students indicating they got something from my courses.

CHAPTER X
GRADUATE SCHOOL AT CMU:
THE TRUE MYTH OF GOOD EDUCATION

The NEH summer seminar experience encouraged me to apply to Carnegie-Mellon's English PhD program in rhetoric. I had made that decision early in the summer and worked hard to impress Richard enough to get accepted. It turned out that the PhD program was only accepting full-time students. I couldn't afford to give up my Robert Morris job to go to CMU full time. Luckily, a happy alternative existed. Some years before, CMU had started a Doctor of Arts (DA) program with concentrations available in rhetoric, literature, and creative writing. I was accepted into that DA program which allowed me to take virtually the same program as PhD students did. I was also able to go part time while keeping my Robert Morris job. I took pretty much the same classes with a bonus: a literature and a creative writing class could also earn credits toward the degree. I enrolled in a terrific Thomas Hardy seminar taught by my then advisor who was a Hardy expert. And my creative writing class was taught by Hillary Masters, son of America's great poet, Edgar Lee Masters, most noted for writing *Spoon River Anthology*, (at one time generally considered as great as Whitman's *Leaves of Grass*). Hillary, a talented writer in his own right (author of the excellent, very readable, and award-winning memoir, *Last Stands*) made a deep impression on me and encouraged me in writing poems and short stories. But busy as I was, after our class was over, I had to put such creative writing on hold.

It was a challenging and exhilarating time. Carnegie Mellon really worked me. I was learning so much and was eager to pass on what I could to my RMC students. (We would not become a university for another decade) I was happy to see another academic myth fall. Far from being the stereotypical inaccessible researchers, the CMU English Department faculty were available and worked closely with students in research, teaching, and encouraging. I admired and tried to imitate their attitude. They worked us hard, but they were not slave drivers. I remember Rich Enos, still one of America's foremost rhetoric historians saying, "Nobody here will ask you to do more than you can." But they sure made us do as much as we could. He also taught me that education is like a bank. *When you are reading, you are depositing in the bank. When you are writing and presenting, you are withdrawing. The most important thing to remember,* he joked, *is that on Saturday, the bank is closed.* I worked every Sunday but tried to keep Saturdays for my family.

Because my WVU Masters was in literature and my concentration at CMU was rhetoric, most of my previous credits didn't transfer: I had to take 90 more, allowing me to take pretty much all the rhetoric courses offered. Each was demanding and my Robert Morris teaching course load was now four courses, 12 hours a week. The only way I got through taking, giving, and grading finals was a quirk in both school schedules that allowed me to finish my finals at CMU before having to give and grade them at RMU. It was a very difficult time.

I remember going over to CMU to sign up for the Thomas Hardy literature seminar. I sat outside the registrar's building for an hour just not having the energy and umph to go inside and sign up for a summer course, my one literature course, which should have been a nice break. I was just worn out. I walked away and went home, hoping my motivation and energy would return. It didn't come back until registration closed. At a CMU English department party a few days later, I explained my plight to the teacher of that course; he said it wasn't too late to show up in class and he would fix a sign-up for that Thomas Hardy course. He was so inviting, I did. Great seminar. I still remember being so moved and saddened by *Jude the Obscure*.

The rhetoric courses continued to be a revelation. I saw what my discipline could return to being and how far it had to go to get there. For nearly a century, rhetoric as invented by the Greek masters such as Isocrates, and Aristotle and passed on to the Romans, including especially Cicero, had been the center of education in the West. It was the basis of what we now call the liberal arts education. Now, it often become no more than freshman writing courses with weak foundations: Comp I and Comp II.

But more interest meant more work. I often had contradictory feelings: lucky to be in such terrific ground breaking program (CMU's graduate rhetoric program was singled out that year by the leading academic journal in my field as the best rhetoric program in the US), and nearly exhausted by the work.

CHAPTER XI:
THE MYTH OF FOREVER LOVE

Life was busy, but, in most areas, going fine: Unlike my undergraduate and Master's Degree experiences, I was doing well in my classes; amazing what sobriety does for the mind. I was present in school, in my homework, in the classes I was teaching and the papers I was grading. All of that was because I was present and progressing in my program. With the help of my sponsor, I was doing the work of the steps and even began to support some sponsees of my own.

By this time, I had also bought a house in Highland Park – on Hampton Street, the other end of which ran past my great grandmother's farm, now Heaths Run park and St Raphael's Church and Parish House. Our new home was a big old rambling thing close to Cousin Chick's childhood house. I was able to move into the third floor my considerable and growing library. Across the street at Fulton School, (where his grandfather and cousin Chick had gone) son John had easy access to school and many friends.

Highland Park was a varied neighborhood, home to many families of different social and economic backgrounds. Two blocks either way from us were the mansions of Negley and Highland Avenues. Many spacious and smaller family homes were in between. It was a wonderful place to walk. Busy as I was, I often took an hour with my son. Once when taking a break from studying an obscure rhetorician, Abraham Fraunce, to walk with John, we came across some tough looking teenagers down the pavement. John suggested we cross the street. I was a little hurt and said: "What's the matter, John, don't you think I can handle myself and take care of you?"

John said: "What will you say? 'I don't suppose, my good man, you know who Abraham Fraunce is.'" I treasure that comment for its humor, honesty, and sense of what we could say to each other, how close we had become. When people ask whether we crossed the street away from those tough guys, I say to them what I say to you now. What do you think?

But within our home things were not going so great. At first, my wife was very taken with the academic experience I was having and the people I was having it with. During the NEH summer seminar, she hosted a beautiful dinner for all the participants. But after my third year or so, Becky became disenchanted. "You are always in that little room of yours, working," she sometimes said. Also, she had never stopped drinking; I often remember, while I was reading or writing a paper, hearing the snap and small woosh of a beer can opening. Each of those sounds made my heart sink a little.

I had been cautioned by my mentors not to talk about her drinking, but it was depressing having my wife check out to television with a six pack after 8:00 PM every night. I do know she had her complaints about my spending too much time on work and school. The work in our CMU program was so demanding that many of my fellow student relationships did not survive.

But Becky continued to believe that I needed to do more with the family. It came to a head when she demanded that I coach my son's soccer team. I didn't even play much soccer, nor was I an expert on the rules; and frankly I was not interested. We went to a counselor twice, and Becky quit going. She then suggested we keep our marriage going as a business relationship. I answered honestly that if I wanted to start a business, she would be the last person I would call to be a partner. She then said that the romance was over and a business relationship the only way she would stay in the marriage. It was mid-June. I moved to the third floor and told Becky she had until August 1 to change her mind and agree to work on our marriage. After that, I was leaving. I wanted to leave then, but my sponsor suggested that I do everything I could to keep the marriage together so that if and when I did leave, I would not look back with regret. That proved to be true.

After Becky's refusal to compromise or return to couple counseling, in August, I moved into a nice one bedroom in the Arlington apartments in Shadyside. It was close to both the Shadyside business district and Bloomfield. Although it jumps ahead in my narrative to my son becoming a musician and to my writing poetry, the following poem reflects my surprise at how much I preferred Bloomfield.

Bloomfield, Pittsburgh

Not much is really blooming
except on the one flower bed
under the signature sign
just over the bridge. And the fields
are mostly on the TV screens
neck-stretching above bars where sports
hypnotize their Pittsburgh lovers.

Everybody who moves to preppy Shadyside
eventually ends up happier in bluer collar Bloomfield.
Always a fan, my final conversion came through
my son and his rock band, The Little Wretches,
who asked me to open with my poetry
for their Bloomfield Bridge Tavern gig.

What a place! Tiny and smoky in those days
as if to say this is a corner off the mill floor
where the iron-bending world-builders

can rest with their own.
The food: big, bold commas of Kielbasa
and a standing bet-you-can't-finish this pierogi and haluski
serving.
How delicious, opening for my son's rock band.

They were all so cool in their unbelievable twenties
and I wasn't—but I invited all my friends,
not sure I'd have another chance,
hopefully remembering that Elvis
used to open for the Louvin Brothers
and Bloomfield is all about trying.

I did OK; my son's band brought down the house:
And we both bridged to our friends. But my memory
was stolen by a childhood woman friend with MS
who made me understand Bloomfield, even Pittsburgh,
as on that miserably cold night
she negotiated her motorized wheelchair through
a slog of snow and ice—I nearly hit her when parking.

She was dead a year later,
but not to her friends, not to me.

I had many friends from the program and was busy taking CMU and teaching RMU courses. I had never really lived alone, moving directly from my parents' house to my marriage home. But I was somewhat prepared by my childhood of benign neglect. I found I liked living alone with much more time to work, and more control over what little free time I had. Although I lacked domestic skills, notably laundry and cooking, I did ok. My father's housekeeper was kind enough for a few dollars to do my laundry. Frozen food and cheap local restaurants got me through. I was sometimes sad and missed family life, especially my son. He would come over once a week and we would get some fast food and talk and watch television. I stopped inviting women to join us since they were sometimes horrified that one of our favorite programs was "The Women of Cell Block H," a serious and good dramatic TV show about incarcerated women. Maybe I did have some residual anger in choosing it. John and I also spent Saturdays together, going to the museum, zoo, or a movie.

Becky and I did some separation counseling with a therapist we had seen before. Becky said she had changed her mind and wanted to put the marriage back together. I didn't. I had had enough. She was continuing to drink too much and I found out she had been seeing someone while we were married and still living together.

Now about six years sober, I was asked to give my lead at the Deep Creek Conference. Participants were mostly people about my age or younger, some of whom I knew. One woman in attendance caught my eye, Tina. She was petite with lovely dark hair, a great figure, and a sparkle in her eye. Another attraction was she was very active at the conference and in recovery generally. I still remember seeing her in/as the center of a group of lovely young women, several of whom she sponsored. We started dating. We were pretty compatible at the time largely because of our commitment to sobriety.

One night, while Tina was at my apartment, I got a call from my son who said his mother was acting "strangely" and angrily toward him. I told him to hang in there and I would pick him up tomorrow. Tina had some psychological background and was smart. As soon as I told her the details of what was happening to John, she said "Your wife is having a breakdown. You have to get him out of there. Tonight." And I did. I told him to pack a few things and I drove over and picked him up. Becky indeed was having a breakdown. Getting

John over to my care was the wise and safe thing to do. I will always be grateful to Tina for that insight and encouragement to get John.

I took a leave of absence from my doctoral program and moved John into my apartment. He slept on my fold-out sofa bed. The arrangement was crowded and difficult for him to get to school. The situation also presented difficulties for me to get my teaching preparation and grading done, but John and I both enjoyed it. John is fine company and we had great talks, some about his mother's difficulties that I think were helpful to both of us.

Tina had lost her mother when she was 13 and related well and sympathetically with 12-year-old John's difficulties. She was a real help to John and to me. I had many reservations about getting involved in a long-term relationship with any woman. And frankly, I was still growing and finding myself in sobriety. My history with women had not been very mature. I came to realize I had married Becky as a drinking buddy. This poem, although not totally autobiographical, starts with my early high school myths and touches some of my difficulties with women, especially issues of my maturity.

Lenore

I stenciled my girlfriend's name
on the side of my 10th grade English book,
only Linda wasn't her name. Her name was Lenore,
only I was afraid of misspelling it,
or getting it right and her seeing it.
Because she wasn't my girlfriend either.

I was just alone and waiting, for a long time.
Terrible, but it was my only strategy.
I counted on girls being more assertive,

knowing what they wanted.
Surely, one of them, maybe Lenore, would want me.
It was a sad, boring time, and so I drank,
beer mostly, then cheap Pennsylvania rye.
Suddenly, some of them did want me.

I got Betsy, who I thought had all the American virtues,
but who had only impatience and aggression.
Then I kept getting myself picked—

Some of my women were sexy, others dull;
some beautiful, others transactionally kind,
angry when I didn't reciprocate.

I've been married to three of these witches,
not at all sweet and demure like Lenore,
whom I once saw on her knees at her father's house,
cleaning a rug with a toothbrush,
just a little at a time,
and whom I still wait for.

During the following summer, Becky and I agreed that I should move back into the Hampton Street house with John and she should move into my apartment. Luckily, I had a number of good friends, one with a truck, who accomplished this difficult double move, still somewhat mythologized among my friends as nearly impossible: a few of them said they were my friend, but it was their last move with me. Not only logistical, it was a difficult psychological exercise since Becky insisted on being there. Everything went smoothly until I introduced Becky to one late-comer helper as my *first* wife. My ever-vigilant sponsor, Ed, made me apologize to her. He was, of course, right.

I spent much of that year alone, with occasional dates. John came over on weekends when we would go to the museum or library or other activity and then have dinner. Then, we would watch tv. As mentioned above, I had to curtail dates to these evenings when they became appalled at one of our favorite shows: "The Woman of Cell Block 9." John and I loved it.

Tina and I started dating exclusively, and I was very happy. We both were very busy professionally and had the program as a help and centerpiece to our lives. And, of course, we had John which I was delighted about. Always he has been a fine companion.

CHAPTER XII
MARRIAGE AND MYTH 2 OF THE HAPPY HOME

Tina worked hard at creating a home for John and me while still maintaining her demanding job as marketing Director at Gateway Rehabilitation Center. In many ways, she succeeded. Once, she soothed John when rain and wind wrecked the newspapers for his route. Tina calmed him down, helped him put his papers back together, and helped him deliver them. That memory still touches me. As does the time I came home to Tina dirty and greasy on her hands and knees while cleaning our ancient stove. And she was not even living in that house then. This is a woman, I thought, who is willing to work in a relationship.

Despite her terrific step-parenting, I was still hesitant about a long-term commitment. I even broke up with her a few times. But Tina was so sure that marriage was the right thing for us. Finally, at her continued urging, I agreed, and we married at her parents' church and home in Bloomfield Hills, Michigan.

Tina's parents put on a terrific celebration for us. They had a beautiful old farmhouse in which they staged a dinner and fireworks. We were married the next day at Christ Church, Cranbrook. The elaborate reception was at the local country club. We could not have asked for a more beautiful wedding.

The day before our wedding, we finally saw a minister for "instruction." In the extensive profile test of values and concerns he gave us, we seemed not to agree on anything. Although I can't remember the individual test questions, it seemed our shared commitment to recovery had covered over some very basic differences. I thought about surreptitiously leaving that night, but then thought of all that Tina had done for me and John. I stayed. Tina was very upset about the compatibility questionnaire. I remember I was worried and Tina was in tears To console and distract her and myself, I told her jokingly not to worry: that as a professor who has had much examination experience, *I should be making up that test, rather than worrying about its results.* How foolish and arrogant that was, and I only half believed it as I said it. But I was still suffering from the myth of the happy warm home and white picket fence.

For support, my best friend Jim, my brother Terry, and my old friend Dick Webster, all with their wives, came to the wedding. My son John, now 15, stood as my best man. Terry and Tina's brothers Larry and John were other ushers. I was grateful to my friends, new family, and son, all of whom were very supportive. Among the many memorable dinner toasts, my son commented on how many Johns were in the family, me, him, Tina's father, and Tina's brother. He swore he would name any male issue of his, Sam. Spoiler alert: he and his wife, Emily named their first born, John. At least they call him Jack. They named their second, Evan, Welsh for John.

Although he didn't come to the wedding, my father was delighted. He found Tina, as did most people, charming and beautiful. I remember once having a serious disagreement with her, going over to my father's house, explaining my complaint, and expecting a little fatherly sympathy. He turned to me from his corner in the massive couch and said simply and authoritatively: *Jay, Tina has class*. The implication being I was lucky to find such a woman, should be grateful, and be careful not to lose what I probably could not find again. As always, my father made a good point. Tina and I made up and had a successful marriage for some time.

Having Tina's helping to anchor our home life made my academic challenge of taking and teaching classes easier. She took care of many meals and helped out with John. I now enjoyed being on both sides of the teacher's desk. I was learning much that was helpful to my students, especially about invention, helping start and follow through their writing. I and many of my students became true believers in a problem-solving approach to their composition. *What's the problem*, became my mantra to my students, encouraging them to deal with real problems in their lives rather than hearing them fall back on old formulas such as comparison and contrast. (I finally stopped getting fake papers such as living in the country versus living in the city. Papers, as Bill Coles would say, that looked like writing, even felt a little like writing, but were not really writing.) Several of my students said that improving their ability to search for and state important problems was helping them in other classes as well. I remember coming into a night class complaining about how my purchase of some airline tickets to Portland Oregon ended up being to Portland Maine. Several of the students piped up, "You have a serious problem, Mr. Carson."

Like my colleagues in the NEH seminar, my classmates at CMU were interesting and often fun. As we prepared our dissertations, we formed small groups that were supportive and challenging so that our misconceptions and writing weaknesses might be caught early by fellow classmates, rather than by our professors later during orals or a dissertation defense. My group consisted of Rachel Spilka and Elizabeth Curtin. In my case, my major weakness and Elizabeth confessed in hers, we try to get too much information in one sentence. They were enormously helpful and great company in the process, which consisted of reading and commenting on each other's work and supportive dinners at inexpensive restaurants.

CHAPTER XIII
WRITING ACROSS THE CURRICULUM AND THE MYTH OF IMPROVED TEACHING

At Robert Morris, my Vice-President and Dean, Jo-Ann and Bill Sipple, were a powerhouse couple who did much to improve the institution and raise its profile nationally. At one point, they got us mentioned in *Newsweek's* Best Colleges issue. They were also generous and fun to work with. Both had fine senses of humor. Once commentating on a colleague who changed his sex from man to woman, my VP JoAnn said, "Well, of course, after puberty, childbirth and child raising, and menopause, who wouldn't want to be a woman." One of their most important projects was the Writing Across the Business Disciplines (WABD) program, funded by a big grant from the Buhl foundation. The main idea behind WABD was to use the latest theory and practice of writing across the curriculum to improve student learning at our then business focused college.

In the 1970s, many in the nation as a whole became concerned with the crises in literacy among high school and even college students. This worry crystalized in the *Newsweek* article entitled "Why Johnny Can't Write." Clearly, Johnny hasn't been taught to write. Much government and philanthropic funding such as the Buhl Foundation grant became available for programs to improve literacy. Although some focused on grammar and other surface features, the most successful of these programs used writing as a tool for learning. As the scholar, Janet Emig, famously wrote, writing involves the simultaneous use of the hand, eye, and brain, ideal coordination for learning. (For a summary and further discussion of the problem and solutions, including an extensive bibliography, see my dissertation, "Writing Across the Business Disciplines at Robert Morris College: A Case Study.")

Although they had written and won the initial grant from the Buhl foundation that began WABD, Bill and Jo-Ann turned over the program to me as director. I led seminars for some of the faculty in using writing primarily as a tool for learning, rather than as a finished product exercise. We would then use the each-one-teach-one approach where a new candidate for the program would pair up with one of the previously instructed and qualified faculty. I would act as coach and final examiner of the improved syllabus. I helped develop about two thirds of the Robert Morris faculty in those writing-to-learn principles, ensuring they were anchored in faculty syllabi. A CMU faculty member once asked a Buhl Foundation representative why they gave money to Robert Morris rather than to a larger research university such as Carnegie Mellon. The Buhl representative answered that *a grant to a "star" at a large research university would allow a few scholars to make bigger names for themselves. A well-placed grant to a smaller school such as Robert Morris could cause a revolution.* In our case it did.

Richard Young had already committed to helping Robert Morris as an advisor to the program. He also taught a seminar at RMU on the subject. It seemed a natural to choose that program as my dissertation topic. Again, I felt lucky to be studying a really interesting and useful rhetorical area with one of the leaders in the field. Richard became my dissertation advisor, and Jo-Ann Sipple became a second reader. At Richard's suggestion, for a third reader,

I asked Dan Resnick, a crack CMU historian with expertise in the history of education. I will always be grateful to Dan for his early patient page-by-page assignments and careful readings for helpful feedback.

My final pick was Pete Jones, a terrific Southern (Texas) gentleman, who was great at smoothing away some bureaucratic and personnel problems. One CMU faculty member, also a Southerner, objected that my research was not theoretical enough. I remember Pete and I going into a meeting with her. Pete started by saying that "We two Southerners aren't going to scare this Yankee today, are we?" She loved the comment, and Pete kept the charm up. Turned out my research method was just fine.

So, I finished my dissertation, "Writing across the Business Disciplines at Robert Morris College: A Case Study" and defended it in the Spring of 1991. Richard said in person and in writing that my oral defense was one of the best he had seen and that the dissertation would be helpful to other programs. My old Shady Side classmate and best friend Jim was back in Pittsburgh designing and building CMU's excellent Andrew email and communications service. He kindly came over from his busy schedule and listened to my defense. Jim also complimented me, saying he was surprised I was that good. (His best memories of me were our high school drinking days.) Those were very nice compliments from two of the most intelligent and effective people I've known.

I became Dr. Jay Carson. (I love that the basketball great, Julius Erving, and I are both Dr. J.) I had come a long way from failing out of Pitt Law and just getting by at West Virginia. In the process, I had learned lots of important and useful things, which helped me further develop the thinking skills of many students at RMU by improving their faculty's knowledge of writing-thinking connections. I also learned how fortunate I was to have those second chances. That made me more sympathetic with (but not easy on) my own students. Scott Fitzgerald's supposed myth that there are no second acts/chances in American life proved not to be what he really meant and totally false in my life.

Key to a lot of this academic success was my active participation in recovery and the help I received from my therapist, Mary Jo. Both were teaching me what I could do and how I could do it. For example, I spent a fair amount of time making sure I understood assignments and other CMU work including my dissertation work. I was no longer slipping late papers into faculty mailboxes as I had done with Dr. Rule Foster at West Virginia University. Mostly what I was learning was who I was, what talents, abilities, and drive I had. And how to be responsible with them. I was gaining a sense of purpose.

CHAPTER XIV
LIFE AFTER CMU AND THE MYTH OF NEEDING TO BE LIKED

One Saturday years before, I got a call asking if I would like to do a voice over for an education video shooting at Robert Morris. I was charmed by the director telling me I would sort of be the voice of God. How do you turn that down?

This was my first video experience. It went well. I even took our then-ten year-old son John to one of the shoots and he had great fun. The AV staff used the video for some kind of faculty training. Although I don't remember what it was about, I really saw some of the power of video learning. I also enjoyed working with that group and looked forward to maybe doing it again.

The television/video studio at Robert Morris, although state of the art, had not been used near its full potential. That changed when Bill Sipple as Dean of the Communications and Information Systems Departments assumed control. He began doing video conferencing, especially in the area of writing across the curriculum where Robert Morris had some expertise because of the WABD program. My work in that field both directing the RMC WABD program and my CMU research and dissertation qualified me. Bill asked me to join his production team. We created shows and videos highlighting experts in the field such as Toby Fulfiller and Art Young who had published some ground breaking articles and books on the Eastern Michigan University program. We had other academic stars such as Elaine Maimon as well as Richard Young who also was writing important work on WAC.

My job was to write questions and interview "the talent" on air for the shows which were broadcast at video centers in colleges and universities across the United States. Because these conferences were both instructive and interesting, they became very popular. We estimated, through the number of centers we broadcast to and their attendance data collected from each viewing center, that we were reaching between 8,000 and 12,000 viewers per show. Over four years, we broadcast to a lot of viewers. Impressive, considering the average journal article reaches only 3,000 - 4,000 readers. We also created a number of WAC how-to instructional videos which we marketed to colleges and universities.

Bill, like his wife Jo-Ann, had a very strong work ethic. Sometimes, when outside stars and experts came to our studio, they asked where our full staff was. Outsiders were often very surprised that our little group was it: Bill, Barbara Levine, Associate Producer, Todd Kreps, Director of RMC Television Production and one or two other video people, and me. In short, we worked like hell and put out a series of great products.

There were great perks to this work: I got to meet many of the stars in my field; I got to work with Bill, Barbara, and Todd who were really fun and effective. But creating the scripts, interviewing, and entertaining our guests took much time. I was still carrying a full 12-hour teaching load.

But I managed also to write conference papers and organize panels that showcased our work and examined our place in the ongoing WAC movement. We often turned this work into journal articles. I was honored to be working with other RMU faculty who were part of the WABD program, feeling that I was helpful and learning about other disciplines.

In the mid 1990s, Jo-Ann Sipple suggested I apply for a government grant from the federal government sponsored Fund for the Improvement of Post-Secondary Education (FIPSE). The application was difficult, but clearly Robert Morris qualified under the heading of an effective program able to disseminate our reform to other schools. We partnered with six other colleges and universities: Babson, Bryant (both similarly sized business focused colleges), Mercyhurst, Southeastern, and Golden Gate Universities. Each school had a fledgling Writing Across the Curriculum program that they wanted to further develop. I spent long hours trying to tailor our application to meet the specific requirements of FIPSE. Near the end of the process, my grant officer would send me questions and suggestions to improve the application. I remember saying to him several times that the information he was requesting was in the Appendix. Exasperated, he finally said to me something that stuck with me and I pass on to others in similar long discourse situations: *When are you going to understand: people don't read the Appendix.*

I am proud of capturing that highly competitive grant which went to a little over 3% of the applicants that year including leading reform educators across the country. The award was for nearly a quarter million, which bought me out of teaching, allowing me to focus on the grant work for three years. The money also enabled me to put on seminars for representatives of the six schools, complete with guest experts, and to travel to the schools, also bringing experts in several disciplines. A regular colleague on these trips was Dick Hayes, at CMU a widely respected expert on, among other things, evaluation. He helped the partner schools develop plans to evaluate their individual programs and me to measure the grant program as a whole. He was also a terrific and engaging teacher and an enjoyable travel companion.

It was difficult and uneven work. When the representatives of the partner schools came to Robert Morris, I needed to plan an effective three-day seminar that would convey the essential theory and pedagogy of the program, with interesting presenters who also knew what we were doing. For example, Richard Young and Dick Hayes were great and interesting presenters as were many of my colleagues at Robert Morris. I also had to plan for three days, to feed, house, and entertain about 20 people with RMC campus tours, Pittsburgh tours, and good restaurant meals. I also had some difficult and sometimes unsavory things to deal with. I once had to separate a predatory male from an innocent female from another university.

A burst of such work was exhausting . . . and then it was over. My tendency was to collapse and then slide for a while. Over time, I had to train myself to start to prepare months in advance for seminars at Robert Morris and individual problems that had arisen or might arise on my campus visits to the individual schools. One of the ways I got myself back into a more regular schedule was to regularly go to the office even when not necessary. On the few days there was little work, I began to write poetry. I didn't plan on that; it just happened. Here is an early attempt at the craft. Any serious time commitment to my new craft would have to be put on hold for a less hectic time.

But some good response, including publication in a local journals, to this and other poems gave me confidence for a writing future.

Lyndon Johnson's Hair

November came down to Pittsburgh,
having laid waste the north trees, before
leaving them like mousy thrift shop sweaters,
shrinking on the stick bones
of old tree women. But first,
October came and set the city afire,
as if a maniac god had returned the
steel mills' burn everywhere.

The aging can only envy those
leaves graceful tragedy of turning
without stumble or fearful rant.
How can we learn to be fall?

Must we all become
like Lyndon Johnson's hair,
growing ghost of his late hiding,
immodestly, uncontrollably bleaching
into what he once most feared,
shocking Apache of elder statesman?
A whitening length of rebel, hippie, Ho,
crowning a snowy surrender wave,
to all the glorious red - in yellow, black,
and white - that could yet be.

I became friends with most of the partner school representatives, one of whom was a serious poet. And, as college professors and mostly English teachers, we had many common interests and experiences. The group members worked well together. In written evaluations, supported with data, they reported very effective results using our theory and methods. I sent a similar evidence-based comprehensive report to FIPSE suggesting our work did and would, over the years, improve the learning and thinking skills of more than 20,000 students.

We also did some other consulting at that time. Writing Across the Curriculum was very popular and many colleges and universities were interested in starting or improving their programs. Having expertise through our video work as well as journal articles and conference presentations, as well as our grant demonstrating our expertise, we were often hired. I usually traveled with two or three RMC faculty from other disciplines. One of my favorite fellow consultants was Chris Stenberg, a supersharp accountant, with a great work ethic. He was the only colleague who prepared new material each time we went out and passed it on to me for approval. His work was always excellent.

Most of my consulting was a positive experience for me, and I believe I did some good. I was a little surprised at how many college and university faculty had no goals or obvious means of achieving any objectives in their syllabi. Once established, those goals became my way into connecting writing across the curriculum methods/assignments to disciplinary courses in meaningful ways. Faculty were generally polite but they fell into the categories I had read about in journals: About 1/3 were early adopters, excited to try something new and helpful in their courses. About 1/3 resisted anything new, and often, I found, were afraid of anything that might challenge their teaching. So as academic reformers, we focused on the middle 1/3 who had yet to make up their minds. And might be willing to try new concepts and strategies.

Generally, it went well. Most of the faculty I met were willing to try something that might improve their courses. And many reported positive results. The most recalcitrant faculty member I came across was in an art department in a medium sized university. She kept telling me that she was quite satisfied (and everybody else should be) with her course and was not going to change it. She even sat next to me at lunch to keep repeating the same confidant refusal in a rather annoying way. I usually was very patient on these trips, but by desert of that lunch, I had reached the end of my fuse. I said softly to her, *I don't care what you do; I get paid anyway.* I have been, over time, both proud and ashamed of that comment. I was supposed to be only helpful, but she was such a pain.

One of the benefits of this professional work was travel. I got to see much of the country. Sometimes I could extend a consulting trip into a vacation, and take Tina with me. She joked we should pick out a nice vacation spot and I just had to find a conference or school that needed help and we would have much of it paid for either by Robert Morris or a client college or university. It wasn't quite that easy, but I often did enjoy travel support.

The following story recounts a fictionalized version of a post-conference trip that allowed me to break away from my hectic professional schedule.

KILLER

by

Jay Carson

"So what's the name of my horse?" I asked the young wrangler guide. "I'd like to say it along with my commands."

I was trying to seem more in charge since my wife had told me I looked Quasimodo-crooked on the horse and that I was falling so far back in our line that her horse was trying to bite my horse and then me. So I straightened up and rode up to our guide.

"Killer."

"Why Killer?"

"I'll tell you the reason for the name later."

"Why later?"

"I'll tell you that later too."

I hadn't wanted to go on the ride, but my wife begged me. She had scheduled it three days before, but four other riders had cancelled and Mr. "I'll tell you later" would not go if at least one other person besides my wife didn't ride along (and pay). I hadn't been on a horse since my twenties, when drinking several beers made it a breeze. I had given up riding and beer partly because both caused me terrific heartburn. But trying to be a good husband, I Tums-ed up, ate a very light breakfast, and hoped for the best.

We were at a buffalo ranch in southern Colorado, a dude resort with a small buffalo herd. I was still a little nervous as we rode out past part of that herd when Killer seemed too interested in the buffalo. And then the crooked back comment, which wasn't unusual from my increasingly blunt and cranky wife.

We rode out into the dunes of Colorado, and I thought we could as easily have been in North Africa. The beauty of what seemed endless sand dunes stunned me. Both my wife and our guide stepped it up to a canter and then a run, the guide saying it was the "sweetest part of a horse."

"Come on, sissy, pick it up," my wife yelled back.

I was just trying to stay on. I watched her and thought she was becoming as terrific a rider as she was a bitch. They raced ahead with insolent ease and were talking close together when I finally came up.

The rest of the ride was uneventful, except for the vast sway of astonishing dunes. I was almost sorry when we were coming back to the barn. Clattering over a barn draining ditch, I asked again.

"So, the name, Killer?"

"Some drunk guy was trying to get the horse to rear up, make him feel like John Wayne, kept pulling on the reins until your horse just fell on his back. Killed the guy. His own fault. You can see he's a perfectly nice palomino. I didn't want to make you nervous"

"Thanks for waiting to tell me."

"No problem."

It took me nearly an hour in the hot tub to relax muscles, some I didn't even know I had. As I was soaking, my wife explained how we would go down to Santa Fe and what we would do there. And how I should avoid overeating red meat and not sit out in the patio tonight to watch the stars and should spend the time with her. How it would be more "romantic."

I was starting to wish that she had been the drunk on Killer. And wondered at any possibilities. She had stopped haranguing me about riding tomorrow since others had signed up, and thus she "wouldn't be slowed down" by my "timid riding." She finished by saying with a cheeky laugh, "I'll ride Killer."

Having given up on romance again that night, I was gazing at that beautiful, unpolluted Colorado heaven—like my own planetarium, restful, meditative. About ten o'clock, after my wife came back from who knows where and announced she was going to sleep, I was told I should be extra quiet when I came to bed. I decided to walk down to the barn and say hello to good old Killer. I'd seen a lot of cowboy movies growing up; some included inciting a horse to rear and buck.

Wouldn't that be a surprise for my wife? So on the way down, I picked up some rough vegetation that could pass for a burr, something to put under a saddle to irritate a horse into doing who knows what.

For a city guy like me, barns are primitive in daytime. At night they are prehistoric. And the smell: Ugh. But there the horses all were, neighing softly to each other. Made me think of my daughter and her girlfriends at a sleepover.

My burr plan was collapsing since it could only be effective when the horses were saddled the next day. I felt foolish coming up with such a stupid plan anyway and remember actually hitting my head against a splintering post. I was still angry at my wife. Had she winked at the guide? But my rotten mood dissipated the longer I stayed in the barn. The animals seemed to be emanating a more pleasant, peaceful scent, horse and leather overtaking the manure. I didn't see Killer, but was close to a big roan mare, and wished I had a carrot or something to give her. Wondering if I could pull it off without getting bitten.

I'm not crazy enough to think the horses were talking to me, but the peace of the scene was having an effect. I started to quiet my fantasy that my wife was doing something fast, other than riding, with a good-looking young wrangler. And maybe I should be connecting to other women. We really had married as sex and drinking partners. Both of those favorites had run their course.

"Looking for Killer?" Our young horse guide nearly made me jump.

"Yeah, and maybe a carrot to give him." I tried to sound like this would be a normal thing for me to do.

"It's a little late for rustling up food for the animals, but I'm glad you are feeling more comfortable with them."

"I guess I was a little tight today. Wasn't comfortable making him run."

"You didn't have to make him. He would have loved to just be let go." He smiled. "It's really good advice for much of our lives," he added.

"Aren't you the philosopher," I said, more as an accusation.

"Psychology. Going back next week for the last trimester of my master's degree."

"You think I try to rein in my wife too much."

"More like reining in yourself." The wrangler then, almost

rudely, turned and walked away.

* * *

The next year, after our divorce, I was telling the story of Killer to a seasoned rider, emphasizing how he finished off that drunk guy. My friend said it never happened.

"Horses just don't do those things, especially dude ranch horses. Nobody got killed," he reiterated.

"Something did," I said.

THE END

One conference allowed me to visit with my two lawyer friends in Phoenix: one was Gil a childhood friend whom I wrote about earlier. He was deeply involved with the ecology of
Arizona. We spent a few days walking the nature surrounding Phoenix. Gilbert pointed out how the big land owners, especially ranchers, were damaging the river areas. A day later I visited my old Shady Side Academy friend Jay Ruffner who was a high rise lawyer for some of these same cattle/land owners. And he was the lawyer for the Phoenix Suns basketball team. I asked Jay about all this over grazing of the riparian areas. He said as many in his profession would and as kindly as he could: "It's a real problem. Want to see a Suns' game?" And I answered the way many Americans would: "Sure." It was a great game from some excellent seats.

It was a fine trip where I got to travel around Colorado and New Mexico (first time I ever saw the stars so bright.) But seeing my two friends doing what they do so well was the highlight. This is an important memory for me since both are now gone, as many of my friends are. At least one of this larger group is rumored to have taken his own life. I touch on that and its frightening attraction in the following

Balance

Joe and I were teasing about suicide the other day,
whether either of us would do it,
how awful for the children and spouse,
how to do it neatly. How to use pills, not be
too scared of heights to make a botch of it.

I recalled a friend I met on a long trip;
Sue told me she was a widow
because her husband killed himself,
on the second attempt.
The first time, he missed something vital
and was miraculously saved, but
wheelchair bound.

She told her children
that she was not going to refit their house
with ramps, hand bars, and other equipment
because, Sue said, he would just
do it again when he could.
And he did.

But I have another story:
of a friend who shot himself
over a kitchen drain board
to minimize the mess.
His whole family still does a special
service with his favorite berry pie on his birthday.

I'm told we don't dread heights
because we fear we'll fall;

we're deathly afraid
we'll jump.

After the grant ended, I was excited to get back to the classroom again, but Robert Morris had some other ideas. Our President at the time, Ed Nicholson, had been challenged by a number of Pittsburgh business people who hired our graduates to improve their writing skills. Our Writing Across the Business Disciplines program was designed to improve student *learning* through writing. I had good evidence from syllabi and WABD faculty class evaluations that we had done just that. Now, we were being asked to improve the *writing* of our students as well. Nicholson turned the problem over to my Dean and Academic Vice-President, Jo-Ann and Bill Sipple.

Working with the Communications/English Department, the Sipples came up with an astonishing plan: A nine-course Communications Skills Program. Five of the courses were to be taught in the Communications/English Department. The remaining four were to be the responsibility of the various subject area departments. While I participated in creating two of the courses in the Communications department, I was also asked to train faculty in seminars to create syllabi across the curriculum that embedded communications skills into those subject area courses. It was quite a job, being responsible for communications skills in so many upper division courses. I soon found out that preparing such a seminar was hard enough, but not nearly as hard as dealing with an unhappy faculty. Although they were being paid a stipend to participate, many of the participants felt bullied by the Communications Department especially my bosses, Jo-Ann Sipple and Bill Sipple, both former Communications/English Department chairs. Who were we, subject area faculty thought, to tell them how to teach their courses? I found out later that many of those faculty had been "volunteered" not by their own will but by their department chairs.

The faculty seminars were Friday afternoons, and I woke up many Friday mornings with a stomach ache like I hadn't had since Sacred Heart Grade School. The beginnings of the seminars were especially contentious: complaints about being there, work load and my leadership. I tried to get as much participation as possible and pressed on.

But one Friday, I confronted a near revolt. Why did they have to create syllabi that I would approve? Why did they have to add these specific skills to their syllabi in a specific way? Of course, just like an undergraduate class, most complaints came from the same recalcitrant small group. I just lost patience and told the group that anyone who didn't want to participate should turn back their stipends and leave. A near riot broke out, but I stuck to my guns.

I later reported it all to Bill Sipple. He asked for a list of names of troublemakers that maybe should be fired. Nothing came of that, but I did feel he had my back. In coming weeks, the seminar participants didn't seem to like me any better, but the seminar did right itself and got to work. Many participants began proudly showing their work in presentations.

I went over every syllabus to make sure it had the requisite communications skills goals and that they were tied to the activities and assignments of the course in an obvious way. These syllabi were to be used not only by these faculty but serve as models for other faculty in that department. Sometimes I found myself a little lost in a discipline's specialized language and methods, mathematics or statistics, for example. While reading the first few completed syllabi, I remembered to myself as I pondered over some part of it, *I'm not exactly sure what I'm doing, but I know that goal (or that assignment) won't help.* We worked together until by the end of the seminar we had collectively developed an amazing set of communication skills intensive courses across the curriculum. My greatest regret at Robert Morris is that I didn't collect those syllabi into a book as the examples of what can be done to enrich syllabi in all disciplines with meaningful communications goals, class activities, and assignments to achieve those goals. I was proud of the work of the seminar participants and proud of my work leading the group.

Another of my myths was falling: I had always believed that I could only teach, lead, work with people if they liked me. Many in that seminar and the previous Writing Across the Business Disciplines program did not like me at all, but we got excellent work done. (My therapist, Mary Jo, had to patiently explain to me that not everybody was going to like me.) Later, I ran two more similar but smaller seminars. I am proud to say that counting all those and the WABD seminars, I was responsible for teaching more than 100 Robert Morris faculty plus 50 at partner FIPSE grant schools how to improve student writing and learning.

Because of these language across the curriculum programs accomplishments, Robert Morris won honorable mention as a national Hesburgh Award recipient given annually to universities that have exceptional faculty development programs.

By this time, my Dean Bill and Vice-President Jo-Ann Sipple were moving on to other jobs in New England closer to Jo-Ann's roots. There was credible gossip that they had become too powerful which threatened the RMU President. But they also displayed an admirable morality and never talked about that possibility for their leaving Robert Morris. Bill became the Provost at Bay Path College and Jo-Ann served as interim president at a New England college and later consulted at various colleges and universities on communications issues. Bill offered to take me with him. Continuing to work with him was very tempting. But I had strong roots in Pittsburgh, including family I knew would not want to leave. So I stayed at Robert Morris which had become a university by this time.

I missed Bill and Jo-Ann even more when I had some meetings with my news boss. He was a Vice-President for Enrollment before replacing Bill as Academic VP. He was one of those guys who was compelled to prove he was the hardest worker in the world, sending out email at midnight, staying late and arriving God knew when. These are admirable qualities but were not matched by impressive output. Bill and Jo-Ann had required my attendance at academic administrators' meetings, only on a need-to-know basis. My work was so specialized I rarely went. That changed, and I was now required to sit through long boring meetings where it seemed many people just made up work for each other. I did come to admire some administrators who seemed to be helping students learning. Some of them impressively shouldered the responsibility of what new programs and activities could help students. Those same few worked to help keep the financial bottom line of the university viable; something as a faculty member and grant recipient, I had been shielded from.

Yet another myth was falling: that all administrators in charge knew what they were doing and were working efficiently to help students learn. I am basically a teacher and saw too much administrative bloat in my time. (Serious academic university research was showing the same thing.) Academic administrators like the Sipple's who remembered their roots in the faculty and the purpose of the university, that is, students, had tried to shield faculty from needless bureaucratic work. As Bill said: *I hated administrators so much I became one.*

My new boss set up regular meetings with him to discuss my language across the curriculum programs (Writing Across the Business Disciplines and Communications Skills Across the Disciplines.) Most of our time was spent with my explaining to him what we had decided at the last meeting. He wasn't stupid; but as an Enrollment professional he just didn't have the academic hooks to easily grasp academic issues, especially my program. For example, he never really seemed to grasp what writing as a tool for learning was all about. He seemed to like me well enough, but I no longer needed to be liked

One of my original requirements for taking an administrative job was that I have the right to return to the faculty when I wanted. I surely wanted to then. Within the semester, that was at the top of the agenda I handed my boss at our final meeting.

During this time my father passed away. As I have mentioned, he and I had our rocky times, but he was usually generous and kind to me. We had as good a relationship as possible given our mutual addiction. I have mentioned his losses, mother at 10 and father at 17. In the following I try to capture a little of the sense of generational sadness and loss:

Second Hand Systole

There's a three o'clock in the afternoon
in this saddest ventricle of the day,

an empty chamber two hours wide
that opened congenitally

as my father cut out his valentine
wife as poorly as my father's father and his

choice – roughly outlining men like my son
leaving uneven faces

missing not woman-smelling salt and lavender
or the crusty tease of baked yeasty loaves

but the lost soft touch of tongue and ear:
mama hearing the unspeakable

soothing, until it became a soul's chant
breathe less than the dog-panting chest.

Knife through these generations
cardiac board to nursery

to a home painted once on a heart wall
perfectly all in red.

My father's passing had a powerful effect which I exorcised by writing poems, many of which appear earlier in this memoir.

My return to the faculty had some rocky moments. My secretary, who my now former boss had kindly left in place until the end of the semester, had been great at organizing my office and activities. I had to regain my rusty organizational skills again. And I had forgotten how difficult and time-consuming preparing, teaching, and grading were. But I loved the independence and the interaction with the students.

In another innovative program, before he left, Bill Sipple had started a combined communications and information systems doctoral program, which hypothesized that the best prepared professionals now and, in the future, would be those who could define problems in their fields, effectively research those problems, solve them, and usefully explain those solutions to clients or senior executives. I was happy to be invited to teach in the program. The course I was assigned was writing the dissertation. I was frankly honored the program thought I could teach such a course, so I gladly signed on.

Again, I had no experience, but my CMU problem solving background taught me about picking important and interesting problems, focusing, refining, and researching them for a useful conclusion. And, of course, I had written what others told me was a useful dissertation.

Our doctoral students were professionals already employed in their fields. Many came from Washington and worked for the government. Some seemed unusually private about what they did which led some of the faculty to believe that a few of them were in the CIA. One of our faculty members had a son who got a job with the NSA in Washington. When the son came home to Pittsburgh for a visit, his mother, our fellow faculty member, asked him if one of our doctoral students did indeed work for the CIA. I loved his answer to his mother: *I can't tell you.*

I liked working with adult professionals who had a life plan and wanted to work hard to succeed in our program and to achieve their career goals. Many were already accomplished in their fields. I had a U.S. ambassador in one of my classes. I felt I had much to offer them, and the classes were bright and lively. The only drawback to the program were the hours. Because it was a limited on-site experience, we did all of our teaching during one week at the beginning of the semester and on several long weekends. This led to schedules of many hours of teaching back-to-back extended classes. I also worked at a distance on email going over evolving dissertations. In the Spring with graduation looming, reading and editing a full class of nearly completed dissertations became almost overwhelming. Difficult as it was, many of them were quite good and I learned a lot.

During this time, my wife, Tina, nearly died. She suffered an acute reaction to some medication in an inhaler. Feeling that her throat was closing up, she drove toward the Emergency Room of Mercy Hospital where she was sure she would be safe. Strangely enough, that proved to be another myth. Getting to the hospital ER is not enough. You have to be taken into the examination area. Tina should have called an ambulance. When she got to the Emergency Room, she could not get enough attention to be taken back for examination. Tina believes her time in the ER waiting room was nearly fatal, though the ER doctors did see her in time to get a breathing tube down her throat. While she did not end up having to have a tracheotomy, her time in the hospital was harrowing as she breathed through a tube fitfully all night until her throat opened. Tina then spent several weeks at home recovering. About the same time, we received news that her father to whom she was very close had died. These two events sent Tina into a deep and long depression.

I was a good husband during the first part of this illness. For a decade I supported Tina's needs to see doctors, for bed rest, and for virtually no outside contact. I compensated by staying home and working hard at RMU and increasing my time writing poetry. But, years later, I started going out by myself. We had had a reasonably robust social life that I now participated in alone. I remember several of my friends saying *So Tina's not coming again?*

John stayed in Portland for a while and then went down to Los Angeles. He worked on several movies as a Production Assistant in both places. Unfortunately, he was always competing with other young people, many of whom had better connections. They were often locals who solved the problem of low pay by living with their parents. I sent some support money, but it was not enough. Even then, LA was expensive to live in. I went out to visit him and thought his apartment, like others of young people in the building, looked like a handball court. After two more years of hard scrabbling, John called me and said *If I could last out here six more years, I could get a good Assistant Director job. I can't last six more weeks.*

So John returned to his old room in our house on Kentucky Avenue. I thought it was great having him back. He seemed wounded and needing to stay with us for a while. But Tina objected and wanted him out of the house as soon as possible. It was unclear to me why – it was, after all, a nine-room house with plenty of space. Tina seemed to have an **inexplicable** reversal of feeling for John.

At one point, Tina went to stay with her friend, Susan. A few days later, she called to see if I was going to put John out. The myth of the evil step mother was playing out truly in my mind. I was angry and told her to stay where she was. After a few days' consideration,

I waffled and told John maybe he should think to getting his own place. At that point, John joined a rock band and moved in with one of his fellow members. I still regret that I didn't stand up for him more. That regret makes a small appearance in the following poem, which also reflects my need for further growth.

Jerry, Kobe, and Me

On his friend and protégé's, Kobe Bryant's death,
the great basketball star,
Jerry West, said,
When you come from a place
where there isn't much love
you tend to say "like," not "love," to
people you care about, are close to.

When I come from that place
where there isn't much love
I tend to say nothing,
not get close at all, or care, even
when they walk out the door.

Or I don't nurture a son in need,
maybe when a stepparent brutally staggers over.

I never cry out at night to the moon sickly yellow
or show one damn vein of a blood-filled heart.

When you come from a place
where there isn't much love
you might tend to regularly drop
fans' jaws at your 40-point playoff games,
become the image logo for a sport,

> or strike out, walk away,
> still cool as hell.

Tina didn't get better as I had hoped when John was gone. She never went back to a job, although she had been a successful marketing and communications specialist with some of the biggest non-profits in Pittsburgh. She did less and less around the house and slept more and more, finally, rarely getting out of bed. We had been seeing a couple's counselor since before we were married. Mary Jo suggested everything including a month at an expensive all-inclusive rehab facility in California. Tina wasn't interested. Things came to a head when Tina stood up, waiving her diagnosis of depression from her psychiatrist, and stormed out of the office. I knew right then she was not interested in changing behavior that had become intolerable to me; we may continue to live together, but the marriage was effectively over. I believed that everyone has a life force that makes them want to get well and participate fully in the world. That too was a myth.

About this time, my brother Terry died. Though he had been on an anti-biotic, he had succumbed to pneumonia. Unfortunately, he had built up a resistance to antibiotics because of his prior use of them. I remember him lying unresponsive in the Emergency Room of St. Francis Hospital, where he served on the board and was getting the best care possible. I was relieved that he only had pneumonia. In my ignorance, I thought everybody got pneumonia and everybody got over it. I was even joking around with Terry, hoping he could hear something through his non-responsive haze and perk up. The ER doctor patiently explained to me that he was in a very serious condition: If he could last 27 hours, the doctor said, the more powerful antibiotics they had given him would kick in, and he would make it. Terry lasted only 17 hours, dying at the age of 57. I had believed the myth that modern medicine was magic. What is true was that youthful health is magic.

Terry had been a giant in my life. He could be difficult, but he was always generous to me. They say you never laugh with anyone as fully as you do with a sibling. And I miss that laughter. One issue for us was that he always wanted me close and under his wing, but I wanted to be more independent. Even in his more selfish youth, he was a great reverse model for me. I remember him flaming out with my parents or ignoring them. I watched them get angry, and concluding that whatever Terry just tried is not working. Later in our lives, largely through our experience in recovery, we both became kinder and more patient; as a result we became much closer. As my earlier poem says, he was a tough customer, but an archangel to me. In the following poem I try to capture some of the same care combined with over-protection he always exhibited toward me and my resistance.

CHECK

I stare at the final shreds
of my old checkbook;
little damage can still be done
to the fray of sleek
alligator hide that was
my brother's love,
belt-hard and smooth,
covering my loose expenses.

As a child, he stole
all my dresser change
quickly spending it to nothing.

Later, he learned
to turn a buck
like kicking a bothersome leaf
in the cold wind.

Finding faith then in every
sad thing my father told him,
he tried to invest it back
in me: never to sell capital,
never to buy on margin,
never to co-sign
what you can't pay;
always to talk of money.

He never hit me
after I was twelve,
neither for the way
I mocked him nor how
I stole back
my time from him;
even as his checks
still floated me.

I take out from the billfold
a photograph of my brother, next to me,
formal, dark suits, serious faces,
very much in the bandit tradition.

  Things were getting more difficult for me at home. I was ok with doing things alone and even happy to have time to write poetry, but I was missing a partner in my life. Depression had robbed Tina of much of her life and of mine. I had tried to recommit myself to the relationship and be of help, but after a decade, I was worn out. At one point, Tina told me that I was depressed and ought to take some of the same kinds of anti-depressants that she took. I checked this office.). Mary Jo explained that I was situationally depressed. I figured out that if I changed the situation I would no longer be depressed. In 2004, I took an apartment in the Parklane in Highland

Park. Continuing to support Tina in the Kentucky Avenue house and my new rent were a stretch financially, but I knew I had to do it.

CHAPTER XV
THE MYTH OF SOME PARTNER WAITING FOR ME

The Parklane was no longer the luxury apartment that it once was (when, for example Tina lived there as a single person). But it still had a pool and round-the-clock doormen, one of whom was forming his own musical group, a three-quarters female Hank Williams cover band. I lent him some of my bluegrass CDs after which, Slim Forsythe and I began a long and pleasant friendship.

I managed to keep working hard, and I lived for a short time quietly. But I then decided that at 63, if I wanted to have a full relationship with a woman, I had better start. I had been lucky enough to stay in touch with many friends despite Tina's inability to socialize. I called Patty, the widow of an old high school buddy. We had maintained a friendship over many years, partly because of our mutual interest in writing. We often checked on how each other's efforts were going and had been part of the same writing workshop for a while.

It was an exciting time, and Patty was a terrific person, wise and bright, very pretty with beautiful blond hair. We hit it off and dated for a few years. She was instrumental in helping me get back to somewhat normal. We travelled to parties and danced in Canada, attended a workshop and vacationed in Costa Rica (what amazing birding and zip lining!) and had a wonderful time. One of my great memories is Patty making sure we stopped the car in Ireland to watch one man and his herd dog move more than 50 sheep from one pasture, across a road, to another. A natural miracle with someone I cared about. Even now, I miss Patty's insights and witty personality and regret how the relationship ended. But I still had some issues to work on and out; I may have been too needy at the time, taking offense easily at comments that were mostly meant to be helpful.

AFTER

Oh, her mouth makes a pretty little circle,
I didn't really want to go out with you
again; I mean you could see
we were just rebounds,
but it's all right.

We walk like old friends
in the Renaissance or brothers
in my fraternity ritual,
"two by two, with arms locked firm and tight,"
except that we're old lovers, now finished.

We walk our favorite summer streets,
peering in the big house windows,
now open for fall, frankly snooping,
maybe for a shared old painting, silver,
or secret that holds their circle together.

I dressed in her favorite of my shirts
and took her for her favorite tapas
which I don't like, and
chaste, to her door.

She was as funny as ever
telling of how she won

> a childhood swimming competition
> just trying not to drown.

I then started dating a colleague from the RMU English department, Rosemary. Tall, slim, graceful, with what my friend Tom described as all the right moves. And her hair, I was on a streak of beautiful blonds She was sweet and smart. I particularly remember Rosemary's quiet wit, once telling me about her mother's oncoming dementia. When Rosemary pressed her about what she was doing or eating or watching on tv the night before, her mother simply and repeatedly said, "I don't remember." When Rosemary finally asked if that bothered her, her mother answered, "Not until you bring it up." Rosemary provided much peaceful companionship. But it turned out that too much of our relationship depended on our work experience. And I need more excitement than I thought. I am a little sad about my breakup with Rosemary. I was just too abrupt. Clearly, I had felt trapped in my marriage and was finding it difficult to establish a lasting committed relationship. Rosemary once bought me a beautiful Irish green sweater that I still have trouble wearing, probably out of guilt.

I had other dates and relationships, but nothing came of them. I was discovering how difficult it is to find someone that I really care about and who cares about me.

I then started dating Jolie, another widow of a Shady Side classmate. Jolie is one of the nicest people I have known, often thinking of other's needs before her own. She was always quick to write a note of support or condolence. Jolie was wisely reluctant to become involved, but I forged ahead, probably more quickly than I should (Patty called me a "quick affiliator"). Jolie and I shared common friends and had similar backgrounds, her husband having been one of my best friends. We both liked to attend lots of theater and see the many friends we shared. We also enjoyed all kinds of music. Jolie had been a musician and improved my listening skills, especially to classical music. I took a class to Prague one summer and Jolie accompanied me. It was a fun and meaningful trip. She was a great help in making me and the students feel at home in our apartment. After our return, our friend, Brian, kidded that we did so much, we were exhausting to listen to. In many ways it was an ideal relationship. "On paper" she was everything I (or most men) could want. Once again, I'm not sure what really happened, but I seemed to need or want something else. I was having a hard time feeling meaningfully connected. The following poem, in which the title doubles as the first line, deals with that dilemma.

We're in the Garden of Lost Girlfriends

my ex told me as another old lover
breezed out the gate. She made it sound
not my fault as if they were
just misplaced, like house keys.

We were at a poetry progressive
garden party: poem, appreciate garden,
poem, flowers, you know,
as long as human concentration
or, I feared, nature could hold out.

The evening shade was closing in
when that other old lover stormed through
the gate. I thought I could save her
when the bees came after her;
I offered to change seats with her
and what? Pretend I wasn't afraid?
Take the stings myself?

My commentator, garden-namer
said I should learn from all this.
I acted chastened,
but she was having none of it:
I was like those bees that won't
come back to the hives,
won't appreciate their slot combs
to work and give honey.

They just fly homeless
until they die.

I had been looking for a surrogate family ever since I recognized my failure to thrive in the one I'd been given at birth. My high school friends, including some of my women friends, provided that family. But it too was mythical. My low sense of self-esteem, sense of self, really, was shored up by hanging onto this group and all its members whom I had idealized. As I slowly built a better sense of self through the program and ongoing therapy, I needed that outside buttress less. I take solace in knowing I was genuinely trying to and did form real relationships through these attempts. Many of those friends, including my best friend, Jim, are still important to me. I also realize that I deeply hurt some people in the process. But as I grew in sense of self, realizing I had both good and not-so-good sides, I also realized more of what I really wanted. I try to capture that sense of self-acceptance along with my growing love of poetry and travel in the following.

Hemispheres

It was winter in Argentina,
and everyone in Buenos Aires was coughing.

On La Rocha Street, it was cold,
even when touching
on the whores' couch –
those two with their tattoos:
the charming roses could bloom forever,
one small bud on the shoulder down
and one with a thorn up a thigh.

****

Back in Appalachia's late fall,
my lover takes us to concerts.
At night, her breasts above me,
she explains the music
as she explained the forest's last colors.

When I don't get it,
her face comes close, like my doctor's,
who, when I asked about the origin
of a recurring infection, insisted
It's inside you.

POETRY AND TRAVEL

All through this time I had been getting more interested in poetry. Having started out merely as a diversion from boring meetings, poetry surprised me by becoming an attractive and then a jealous mistress. I have always been interested in beautiful and powerful language from the time as a child when my father read Winston

Churchill's never surrender speech and "The Cremation of Sam McGee," and later when he read Browning's "My Last Duchess." I became increasingly fascinated by the impact poetry could make in such a short space. I started to write poems, first out of boredom at administrators' meetings and then in my office by myself.

One of my indulgences is to take summer workshops, usually abroad. I still vividly remember my first long workshop, two weeks in Spoleto. I was amazed at the beautiful medieval town and the convent where I lived and meetings were conducted. My room was clean and cheap. The convent had been built for hundreds of young women who planned to become Catholic nuns. In the modern world so few women want to study for the novitiate that many of those convents were, at the turn of the 21st century, empty. Lovely grounds and good company rounded out a fine workshop experience. Maybe the most important part for me was understanding that I was writing poetry that others, including the teachers, found worthwhile. The following was written in response to a challenge to write something about food.

BRIDGE CHEESE

My father had his Sunday cheeses,
difficult to pronounce and hard to hear
for a ten-year-old, even one learning
bridge, the Roquefort and Camembert.

The deep steeped tea seemed all grown up,
and the piquant sandwiches squeezed
out silky teasing onion; tangy
potato salad oozed mayonnaise in seas.

But the cheese was the knife
that yerked at my young guts.

They all smelled of rotten crumble,
thoughts of mummies in rut.

Old was just the point
my young hand didn't comprehend,
my father tasting death
to finesse it to the end.

One of the trips allowed me to go to Brazil. In the interest of faculty development, Robert Morris helped finance the travel. The workshop was in Sao Paulo, but I managed to tie in side trips to Rio and Buenos Aires before the workshop. The workshop itself was less concerned with students' poetry than in providing a terrific introduction to modern poetry. Edward Hirsch ran a fine class. I loved our environment and the food was excellent. Sao Paolo was overwhelming, a city built to the sky. I had never seen so many tall buildings, including New York. The big challenge for me was adapting to the workshop/Brazilian schedule. We often had evening poetry readings followed by dinner, meaning we were eating at 10:00, keeping me up and then giving me heartburn when I did turn in. I finally found a nearby restaurant that would accommodate my Yankee dining habits and began eating before the poetry readings and skipping the late dinners.

I was also taken by the culture. Having been raised Eurocentrically by my father and my schools, I knew little about South American art or culture. I had read, however, about the great Brazilian sculptor, Aleijadinho, who worked while suffering from increasing paralysis. I was delighted to find that there was an exhibition of his work in Sao Paulo. In approaching the museum, I saw a long line of what I assumed were fellow admirers of the "little cripple" who was able to flail away, creating masterpieces. In fact, this group was lined up for the Abbey next door. I was told people went in with various pleas, which were written down on little pieces of paper by the Abbey's nuns. The supplicants then prayed and ate the paper. What faith! I had the same sense I remembered in graduate school watching those Mormon boys drop to their knees in profession of their faith. Myth maybe misguided, but a searching in perhaps the best sense of the word. I felt a distant but clear kinship to my commitment to a Higher Power.

Deeply impressed with the sculpture, I found Aleijadinho's successful efforts to be a metaphor for finding faith. I thought of it again along with Cicero's fate when, a few years later, my son was getting married. I had studied Cicero in my graduate rhetoric program and was fascinated by his courage in standing up for a more democratic Rome, even to facing Mark Antony who had his hands and tongue cut off and displayed in the Roman Senate. That courage resonated with my understanding of Aleijadinho's relentlessly searching and finding beauty despite his great physical difficulties.

Communion

At my son's wedding,
from the first pew,
I see how we come forth
for forgiveness and connection,
together and alone.

At first, I would not watch.
As if I stumbled into a confessional
or my parents' lovemaking-
nothing wrong but time and me.
The Gothic church cut stone frees angels and me.

How we come to God:
stone black dressed, jacketed and tied,
frieze of downcast eyes reviewing
cast down days now within reach.

Hands and heads are foremost,
the tools of pleading somehow detached

like Cicero's, hung over the Roman Senate
for pleading his case perhaps too well.

Our open mouths and praying hands
might tell the story of Aleijandinho,
the Brazilian sculptor, the little leprous
cripple, miraculously making masterpieces
with hammer and chisel strapped to his arms.

My brother had a close friend, Harvey Thorpe, who had moved to Brazil. I contacted him, and he invited me to his organic farm in the Matutu Valley, five hours deeper into Brazil than Sao Paulo. Just driving there was a revelation. Such rich vegetation seeming to go on forever. No wonder Brazilians are skeptical at the world's worry they will destroy the rainforest: it seems so vast that it is impossible to destroy.

Harvey, still tall, thin, and athletic enough to climb around the fruit trees on his farm was a great host, showing me over this beautiful valley remembering stories about my brother, and just becoming my friend. I still remember drinking coffee with him at the local collective and looking up at the steep and stunning Tres Marias three-fountain waterfall.

My whole Brazil experience was overwhelmingly wonderful.

I Could Not Understand in Brazil

The Portuguese coming at me –
endless blocks of mysteriously sculpted smoke.

The feijoada stew in Sau Paulo so good

despite the pig's tail and cheeks;
never-ending beef, fish, and vegetables.

And that I ate everything,
with the hungry favela
up the street, so nearby.
The locks and gates
on every house:
Something must have happened
my black, Spanish Harlem friend said.

The fires in the mountain brush:
clearing fires, back fires,
fires for their own sake.

And that story from my friend, Harvey,
about his swimming away from the fishing boat
when it unaccountably went over,
and he the only one with snorkel mask and flippers;
twenty-seven hours of swimming,
exhausted, finally sending back help
for the already dead.

But I see clearly and understand
his tears – and my happiness, alive,
even full, still on top of hell.

I would be remiss if I did not mention Workshops at the Pittsburgh Center for the Arts, especially two that I participated organized and led by Michael Wurster. He ran fine instructive and collaborative workshops that have become an institution in Pittsburgh. I am happy to say he has been supportive of my work. He has paid me the compliment of very much liking the following poem:

Flight

I watch the geese at the park nearby,
soaring in insolent unison to the faintest
heard song of the flock. They follow
wing to wing, mate for life: raise a family.
I watched my movers for evidence of missing silver,
bruised tables, broken family pictures,
stumbling out of joint
on the stairs countless times.

My friends are kind, "supportive," we say today,
but with eyes dreading
endless gloomy pizza evenings,
me sadly trashing an abandoned woman
for being herself.
How do the geese manage
to be always surrounded?
In the steel-encased apartment
I can't call out.

I hear the stories; there must be
thousands of us, but no flock.
I long, perhaps for the children's wilderness camp
where the stubby and tall legs all fit
themselves in canoes, and the children search
the narrow and wide waters, singing
songs they make up of paddle and portage,
brave commitment in high harmony
rising, floating, in the tall Canada pines.

It was at Michael's workshop where I met Joan and Richard. Both are excellent poets, and active in the Pittsburgh poetry scene. Joan curates the Hemingway series, one of the city's oldest and most respected poetry venues. She is also the most dependable source of emails on poetry and other writing news and events. Richard is recognized as one of Pittsburgh's finest poets. They both were kind enough to ask me into a workshop that has greatly improved my writing I hope including what you are seeing now.

My best poetic connection is my close friend, love, and partner, Judy Robinson, poet, editor, painter and beauty. Stunningly beautiful blond hair to match pretty much perfect other features. We met in the poetry community and became close when editing a book of poems by a well loved and respected, now deceased, Pittsburgh poet, Margaret McMenamin. Before she passed away, Margaret asked Judy to edit her last poems. Judy kindly asked me to co-edit one book of Margaret's poems. I remember long summer evenings reading and talking about Margret's wonderful and often romantic poetry. By the end of our project, Judy and I were more than co-editors. She has improved my poetry and my life and remains a light of my life.

FISHING

Do you pace your longing,
time the yearning
so you don't run out of fennel crust
before the salmon, love before desire?

Your love cannot outlast your desire,
especially if you are walking
in a snow-sparkling field
wondering how her hand can be
so warm and small at the same time,
how it fits yours and then wriggles

into your pocket like a hot minnow.

Again your yearning runs away
if she breaks your disciplined line,
with her laugh, almost silent,
but swimming into your heart.

Or if you finally hook her, maybe
with song lines or rock group names:
"Echo & the Bunnymen."
I been thinking about my door bell
Why ain't you ringing it? Why
ain't you ringing it?

Or when you can't wait until summer.

CHAPTER XVI
SON JOHN AND THE TRUE MYTH OF FAMILY

Another best thing in my life at that time was to see my son John meet and settle down with his terrific soon-to-be wife, Emily. They had met while they both were working at a local bank. John said that he needed a ride to one of his band's gigs and Emily was willing to help him out by driving him there. Boy, was he lucky. I didn't quite understand Emily at first because she was so unassuming. She remains in my mind as one of those rare people who are more steak than sizzle. I got an understanding of her quiet wit early on at a birthday dinner at our house for my son. A friend of mine was having difficulty with the death of his father and especially inheritance issues. I got all excited at the birthday dinner table about what John might do if I were to die: who he should call and all his necessary actions around my death. In the midst of my rant, Emily said calmly, "Happy Birthday, John." I saw immediately that she had a sense of humor and proportion that I sometimes lacked.

John had decided to become a teacher. He later confessed to me that one of the reasons he had avoided that choice was my constant repetition that it was a difficult, time consuming, and poorly paid profession. He needed to go back to school to get teaching credentials. I was happy that John thought well enough of our Robert Morris English department to sign up there. I was less pleased to find that the school's complimentary tuition for family members didn't cover him because of his age (well beyond 21). John insisted on funding his own Masters in English Education and finished with flying colors.

Although his personal life was fine, John was having trouble getting a job. The demographics had changed dramatically since I was teaching. The best John could find for a while were temporary teaching assignments. But at each school, the administrators and students liked him. I was beginning to see he was a natural, patient, kind, and wanting to help others.

Luckily, he was working as a full-time temp English teacher when the art teacher retired. The principal asked John if he had any interest in teaching art. *Are you kidding*, John answered, *I was a film and photography major in college.* John ended up with a full-time position teaching his first love, art. He often posts his students' excellent work on Facebook with pride. I am so proud of him.

John and Emily married on Nov 9, 2002 They settled in Pittsburgh's North Hills. Their son, John Stanton Carson IV, Jack - for short - was born three years later on Sept. 22, 2005. I suggested that we had used the John Stanton Carson name too much, but my son wanted to stick with it partly because of its historical connections to Edwin Stanton, Lincoln's Secretary of War, partly for John who is JSC III, and partly for me; hard to argue against all that.

I am delighted that Jack looks a good deal like me when I was younger, but he is clearly his own man. His greatest interest now is a career in the outdoors, environmental science, for example, far different from my own. He has become a bright and fascinating young man (now 17) with a fine outgoing personality. Jack has come down with diabetes and I am so impressed with how he has managed it physically and especially psychologically. He is always open and upbeat about his condition, something young diabetics often have difficulty with,

I was blessed that son John included me in Jack's upbringing. John brought his son over to my apartment once a week: we would often visit the Children's Toy Museum and go out to lunch and then back to my apartment. I was lucky enough by this time to afford a cleaning lady, Lovelyn, who was great at playing with Jack, even putting the top of a clean trash can on her head to play Darth Vader. John and I then had a chance to get caught up on what he and the rest of the family were doing. We all had a great time.

Evan David Carson was born four years later on June 28 2009. John also included me in his growing up by encouraging me to babysit Evan after school until his parents came home and we all shared dinner. One of the great joys of my life has been to see these children develop into such unique selves. Once, Evan asked for help with a first-grade homework assignment that required the student to supply rhyming words. He was doing fine until he reached a picture of a pear which he was to match with a picture of a teddy bear. He got the fruit, "pear" right but was having trouble with what it was to rhyme. I pointed two or three times to the teddy bear asking for the rhyme with "pear." Evan kept saying "teddy." Finally, exasperated, I demanded, *What's teddy's last name?* Evan answered "Roosevelt."

John and Emily have been kind enough to bring me along on some family trips, recently to the Northwest. At the end of the summer, we went to England, Iceland and Paris. Paris was added after I told John and Emily that John's grandfather, my father, saw some of the 1924 Olympics in Paris. A century later we get to see the 2024 Olympics in Paris. Seems like great karma. Four generations and 100 years.

We took the Eurostar from London, saw a woman's rugby match (Great Britain defeated South Africa, 27-19, I think) and were able to get to the Louvre, where John got me a wheel chair to keep up with his family. I was behind about 200 people trying to see the "Mona Lisa." A kind guard came up and asked if I would like to see the painting. I said yes and she rolled me up in front of everyone. I stood up from the wheelchair for John to get a photo. I swear I heard some people gasp. I think they believed the art cured me.

John and Emily continue to keep me connected, including Emily's fine parents, John (another John) and Eileen. They are both warm, gracious and interesting. John Werthman considers himself a true German-American and has encouraged his daughter Emily to become more international by traveling to Germany and hosting a German high school friend in their Pittsburgh home. The young women have become life-long friends. John Werthman in retirement has also become a writer, now working on a mystery, so we have good fun talking about our respective literary efforts.

Another very rich part of my family life is my relationship with my family on my brother's side. My brother Terry paid me the great compliment of naming his first born, Jay Terrence Carson, after himself and me. Because of Terry's estrangement from Jay T's mother and family, I did not see Jay for many years. After Terry was in recovery, he re-established his relationship with Jay T. who, not incidentally, came into sobriety on his own. So I had the double pleasure of re-establishment of my relationship with my nephew as well as my brother. After Terry passed away, I continue to see my brother's great Irish's face with the infectious personality of my nephew, Jay T. Jay was for many years a very successful development professional who, through fate, ended up as Senior Development Vice-President at Robert Morris University. It has been great seeing him in so many parts of my life. And we have had fun in them all. At Robert Morris, for example, Jay was in close contact with the RMU president. Jay's and my email often got mixed up, so I was sometimes privy to upper administration confidential information. At one point, after I was sent, by mistake, some sensitive administrative information, the president said to Jay, "I hope your uncle can keep confidences." Jay said, "Sure, but I tell him everything anyway." Luckily, Jay and the President were on very good terms, and the president appreciated the joke. It might have helped that over his tenure, Jay brought in more than 40 million dollars to the University.

Jay has now retired and become a mystery writer. I have read much of his first book and am very impressed. I think he has a great second career coming up. We have a chance to catch up about this and other things at regular lunches and other activities. With our wives, and son John and Emily, we recently saw the opera, *Il Trovatore*.

I have another nephew, Chris, Jay's younger brother. He is a very nice and bright man whom I have had a chance to meet and be with only on occasions since he has left Pittsburgh. After a very successful career at Bell Labs, Chris has retired and just returned to Pittsburgh from Chicago. So I now get to see him more often. Chris has done some great ancestry work for the Carsons and assures us, among other things, that although we are not related to Rachel

Carson, author of *Silent Spring*, the ground-breaking warning on ecology, we have a very interesting and surprising DNA background which ties in with my theme of myth. More later.

My brother's first wife, Jay's and Chris's mother, I only knew intermittently, more when Terry and Kate lived together and later after Terry reconciled with Kate and their children. She was a beautiful and remarkable woman. A single parent since her late teens, Kate was able to raise and educate (through college) all of her/their children, Jay, Chris and Cathie. Kate later remarried and led an active professional, spiritual, and family life until her much-too-early death at the age of _____ ???? Her daughter Cathie tragically passed away about ten years ago from cancer at the young age of 56. She was beautiful and smart and hard working. She leaves two fine daughters, Katie and, that I get a chance to see at family reunions.

Terry's second wife, Bonnie Lash Carson, moved to Irwin to be closer to her family after Terry died. I did get to know her at family reunions and now miss her great sense of humor, She is not much for driving and is very reluctant to come to Pittsburgh for family reunions, but we do a long telephone conversation at least once a year in which I promise to visit her in Irwin and Bonnie promises me the butler's secretary furniture she inherited from Terry who inherited it from my father.

I am very blessed to have both a great immediate family John, Emily, Jack and Evan and a terrific extended family in which I include my daughter-in-law's parents mentioned earlier, John and Emily Werthman. I see all my family as a gift and am grateful to have them and try to keep connected. The myth of the power of family, going back to ancient times, is true and the most meaningful thing in my life.

I would be remiss if I did not mention the importance of Judy and her family: son Davey, daughter, Heather, and grandson, Grant. They have been welcoming and kind as I have gotten closer to Judy. Davey, Bridget and Heather invite me along with their mother to a week in a South Carolina island beach house. I really enjoy their gracious hospitality and company. I feel like they are also my family.

Similarly, Emily's family, John and Eileen (Bird) Werthman become part of my extended family. Their Christmas and /Easter dinners have become a valuable tradition that I feel lucky to be part of.

MY ONGOING EXPERIENCE IN SOBRIETY

All this time, I have remained an active member of my recovery community, which has continued to give me the spiritual and practical tools that allow me to go on being successful throughout my life. One important aspect of sobriety is the powerful and pleasant effect other sober people have had in my life. They helped keep me sober and greatly enriched my life.

I already mentioned that in my first days in the program my brother hooked me up with Bill D, a successful lawyer who had enormous influence on Pittsburgh East End recovery. And rightly so: he helped begin and ran many meetings, he sponsored or grand-sponsored most of members in the area, and he knew the program cold. Bill was also very generous with his time. Once, years after we met, when someone I sponsored needed a character witness to go with him to a hearing in Harrisburg to get his pharmacist's license back, Bill offered to go with us. He spoke at the hearing, and his argument was so effective, I could understand why he was such a successful lawyer. My sponsee easily got his license back. I am still amazed that Bill was able to sponsor, help, and keep in line so many strong personalities. My brother Terry never seemed to listen to anyone else, but he heard what Bill said and followed his direction. In the process, Terry connected back with his family and became closer to me.

I chose someone else as a sponsor, partly because Bill was so much like my brother, physically (both big heavy mesomorphs) and in personality. Ed M. was smaller, thinner and a very smart mathematics/computer tech guy who used to be in the music business in New York. He had great stories about how this famous singer drank himself into trouble and that one's voice was too icy for good audience connection. Ed came to Pittsburgh while he was drinking. In his words, he was trying to hide out after he misappropriated some money. Terrified that he was moving to a dry town, Ed was relieved to see from his arriving Greyhound bus Pittsburgh's once famous neon Duke beer sign that showed a prince downing a glass of beer. That prince, incidentally, was modeled on the father of my doorman/friend/bluegrass legend, Slim Forsythe. Pittsburgh is a small town.

Ed M. introduced me to the service ways of the program, and its etiquette: come early to meeting, greet people to get to know them and make them and you feel at home, help set up the meeting or tear it down, thank the speaker, be willing to chair and speak at meetings. And be willing to hold office in your home group. It only took me a little while to figure out these are the ways successful people negotiate jobs and other parts of their lives. My alcoholism had isolated me from these common social interactions and responsibilities.

Bill had given me a basic recovery text, written by the founders of the original 12-step program. The story of its founding by a failed Wall Street broker and a failing proctologist along with the stories of many of the first members and others who came after them is fascinating reading. And it is well written: *a masterpiece of the plain style,* Bill C., a writer of some note himself, critiqued. My sponsor Ed guided me through the steps and answered my questions. Many of the questions I had could be answered by his simply saying: *Don't drink and go to meetings.* Other answers were more complicated: "Who belongs on a list of people to whom I should make amends?"

(I loved his comment: *No old girlfriends or bartenders or dope dealers.*)

Most of my amends had to do with my family. I talked myself into believing I was this great fun guy who, if anything, was more sinned against than sinning. While I was working this out, my therapist Mary Jo and I started calling my image of myself at that drinking and just post-drinking time, Saint Jay. A self-myth taken to a delusional level. Through those steps and my therapy, I came to a better understanding of how responsible I was and am for my own actions, my life. I remember hearing a blues song with the lyric, *got both hands full of gimmie and a mouth full of much obliged* which summed me up pretty well. I was very polite but was still manipulative until I could get as much of what I wanted as possible at any cost

Sponsor Ed also worked hard at trying to re-socialize people. Alcoholism is a disease of loneliness, and many of us had been socially isolated for many years; I certainly had been. Ed had parties at his house to re-introduce us to a social life: the first time many of us had been at a party without booze since our middle school years. At one of the gatherings, wickedly funny Lini called such parties "the special Olympics of socializing." Of course, another great benefit was the chance to know better and make friends with the people I saw and often only briefly talked to at meetings.

There was a large group of people about my age or a little younger that I got to know well. I am still good friends with many of them today: Barry Z., Dennis R., Bob Q., Billy P., Thomas S., Pat M. And Johnny M. Newer people have joined our ranks, including Nico M. and Wayne H. And David, and Henry W. and Curran and David. A group of us have dinner before a Tuesday meeting and lunch after one on Saturday morning. More about these guys later.

I have also re-connected with some of my old Shady Side friends who have come into the program. When I first joined, I was the only person not drinking at our reunion weekends. After about six or seven years, there were more people not drinking than were. Several of them had joined the program, including Patty whom I mentioned earlier and Tom T. Brian M. was a long-time member whom I had met in high school. Brian became one of my two closest friends. We had a standing weekly lunch date for 35+ years. He seemed to know everything about economics and technology. More importantly, he had a great heart. Brian passed away earlier this year, and I sorely miss him.

I tried to encourage my other best friend, Jim, to take a look at our recovery community, since he had also quit drinking, but he claimed the logic of his psychiatrist had shown him the error of his drinking. Everybody has to find their own way; I am glad Jim has found his, but I can't help thinking he would have such a great time with all these interesting former alcoholics and junkies, creative and yes, spiritual people I have had the privilege to know: singers, painters, and jokesters. I remember hearing a very unusual tough lead, where the speaker was talking throughout about beating people up. I was sitting next to a friend who said at the end: "Well, let's go thank the speaker, you first."

I have been lucky enough to sponsor some of these people and have felt that I have helped them learn more about sobriety and themselves. But alcoholism is a seductive disease; Jimmy H. and Bill H. for example, were fine men who seemed to be working our program well, at least for a while, but somehow decided to go back out and in one case, drink, and in the other, use narcotics. There really is a mystery as to why some people get recovery and others don't. Years ago, I heard a chilling, only quasi-logical, but effective comment from a long timer: *Many of us have to die so that others can live.*

This program and my friends in it – and as any member will tell you, everybody in the program (maybe with a few exceptions) is a friend – have not only allowed me to develop myself as a sober citizen, but also develop as a contributing member of society. As Ed M. used to say, *There is joy.* Something I once thought had totally gone out of the world.

Today, I am 50 years sober - with a sponsor, Barry Z., whom I also sponsor (this may sound odd, but works out really well.) Ed. M. had been both our sponsors; after he passed away it seemed natural for us to sponsor each other. I also sponsor 8 people directly: Barry, of course, Pat, Rob, Thomas, Billy, Bob, Mason, Brint, and Dennis. I have a number of other friends who I learn from and love to see. As I write this, Henry just texted me he is feeling better and expects to see me at the meeting tomorrow. Another great friend has been Joan, with whom, it turns out, I went to Sacred Heart Grade school. She has a great heart and mind, and has become a fine friend.

CHAPTER XVII
MY CHURCH SEARCH AND MY MOST HELPFUL MYTH: CHRISTIANITY

Participation in my recovery community has allowed me to become active in other areas of my life. I am an Elder in the Presbyterian Church. I can usually get a shocked look from people who remember me a lapsed Catholic who was for many years a pain-in-the-ass atheist insisting you should be an atheist also.

Ed, who was my sponsor at the time, had suggested I might want to look again at the Catholic Church especially since my son was reaching an age when I thought he ought to be getting some religious training. Ed was taking his daughter to the Oratory Parish at the University of Pittsburgh. I joined them, and we all went together. I was very impressed with how much more understanding and open the Catholic Church had become. The preaching, especially from Father Clancy, was excellent. For example, after the Jonestown massacre, I was anxious to hear what he would have to say about the purposes of religion. I was struck with his answer: The difficulties in the world concerning religion are not due, Fr. Clancy said, to a lack of religious interest, but to too much religious fervor. The purposes of the major religions are to civilize the religious instincts in man. I still see that uncivilized instinct around me.

My son found our church experience less rewarding. He did not make many friends among his contemporaries at the Oratory Parish. Whereas the homilies were often impactful, they were also over the head of the children. So getting John to church became a difficult Sunday morning job. It usually started with my reminding him that he had to wear more formal shoes than sneakers. John found this an affront. I still remember him calling out in that pained early teen way: *Do I have to wear hard shoes?* John, now in his 50s, recently confessed that he had, on at least one occasion, set the clocks back so I went back to sleep until it was late enough to have to miss church.

Eventually, my son was confirmed on a rainy day which an Irish professor friend and fellow congregant, called "a Protestant day." Shortly after, Clancy died, and the new man whom I liked personally and who had presided over my return to the sacraments, started to become overbearing in his preaching, especially on abortion. After one particularly intense attack on people who believed in a woman's right to choose, I voted with my feet and left. Ed, my friend and sponsor had already moved to another parish. I was without a church.

After hearing my story, my friend, Fritz, took me to the East Liberty Presbyterian Church (ELPC). What a remarkable building and what remarkable preaching. Pastor Chestnut had taken over a church that was in crises even though in its heyday ELPC had been awash in Mellon family money. Growing up close to it, I had been in awe of the building. The following poem I hope, gives a sense of that, while focusing on my youth in East Liberty. I am grateful to my colleague, Jim, Seguin, who titled and encouraged me to read this poem at his and his son's video show about Penn Avenue also entitled "Collected on Penn."

Collected On Penn

We were a legal 70 only together, but a pure 14 each,
Facing decade by decade, promise before experience,
the way Whitfield lay before Negley, before Aiken,

as we looked up to the top of Penn Avenue,
bright cafés like landing lights; from the days
when the church was called East Liberty Presbyterian
by enough grey-jacketed Protestants,
but dubbed Mellon's Fire Escape by the Catholic
school boys whose fathers had built it.

Eddy had turned his collar up and now
rolled his shoulders to brush and soothe
the back of his neck with it, rebalancing
on the tiny stone edging the church lawn.

We were early for the evening movie
at the Regent, before it was the Kelly Strayhorn,
before East Liberty decayed and was born again.
No one wanted us stone-smelling kids,
the way no one would want East Liberty thirty years later.

Bullnecked, smiling Sal was most open about the wine,
right on the Avenue, pulling it out of his coat
like a sword, choking its neck
put it back; put it back, two new arrivals said.
We weren't ready.

Past Woolworth's, Murphy's, across
to the Cameraphone, down to Bolan's;
and so we walked.
Our after-school job: to make sure
we inherited the street the way it was.

We massed at the cashier's booth
like a good small army

as much for bravado as confusion:
two tactically bought tickets, more chaos
and all five of us were in.

Every weekend, we would sneak in
and be afraid to open the wine,
and open it, and drink, never daring to answer
the question that nosey cashier asks:
Why aren't you at home?
We're ready now. This is our home.

In both my spiritual experiences, my recovery community is where I had to learn to trust a God of my understanding, and in my return to a church, I was coming to terms with the great myth of my own and many others' lives: spiritual faith. I had for a long time thought of myth in a narrow and pejorative sense: as kind of a trick used by any establishment to coerce the masses into a political or cultural belief, sometimes as a commonly held illusion to assuage anxiety. I was now facing a larger understanding of myth as in the definition in The *American Heritage Dictionary*: a recurring defining theme of a people.

After some long talks with my sponsor and others, I came to recognize that Christianity had helped define my background and much of my upbringing. But Christianity also laid some of the building blocks of my cultural view, of how I joined my small part of civilization. When I was about to get married, I told my mother I was not going to be wed in the Catholic Church. Asked why, I simply told her that I quit. Very emphatically and concisely she said, *You can't quit.* At the time I brushed her remark off as a parody of the mafia-like element of the Catholic Church. Now, I believe my mother's remark contained a great truth. I am today a product of the things that have happened to me, including my Christian upbringing. Bill D., who first introduced me to recovery, often began his sentences about something that he believed, *Nobody who was raised as I was can...* So I couldn't and can't quit. I am what my life made me, including my early Catholic spiritual infusion and my later Protestant spiritual teaching.

When I first got sober, I told my psychiatrist that "these were not my people." Turned out that they were exactly my people, partly because I had no other people. Do I know that our particular recovery community has elements of a ritualistic cult? Yes. I pray to God every morning to stay sober and thank Him/Her every night for allowing me to do so. The main point for me is that I do stay sober. I know others who stay sober on their own. But frankly, many don't seem nearly as happy or growth oriented. Every week I see miracles: people coming into the rooms in hopeless conditions. Very often these same people are shortly starting or resuming families, jobs, and responsibilities in society. Most who ask for help, get help and get sober.

This belief often starts, as it did with me, slowly. As I mentioned that my friend, Bill C., used to say: *We don't ask that you believe. We don't even ask that you pretend to believe. We just ask that you act as though you would like to pretend to believe."* So was my returning to a church; as one saying sums up an approach to spiritual and other belief: "Fake it until you make it." It has been a choice that has given me rich rewards.

At this time, East Liberty Presbyterian seemed natural. One of the ways that I was encouraged to join was neighborhood preservation. My friend Tom T. told me that when Pastor Chestnut arrived, ELPC then had 80 members, and was losing 10 a year. "If you and other neighbors don't support it, in ten years ELPC will be a parking lot." While I was there, Pastor Chestnut was revitalizing an aging and shrinking church (although still well endowed with Mellon money, which was meaningless without a congregation). Through great preaching and excellent networking with the local community, Chestnut was growing ELPC into central hub in East Liberty. I still remember one of his homilies in which he revealed that some in his church were accusing him of becoming too Catholic because he has built a labyrinth in the church courtyard. He then asked how many people in church that day were raised Catholic. About half the congregation raised their hands. Chestnut then asked how many still considered themselves to be Catholics. About one third raised their hands. He then condensed an amazing amount of history into a short discussion of the Protestant reformation. This Presbyterian Pastor concluded by raising his hand, in the pulpit: *So I would raise my hand with those who still consider themselves to be Catholic. I am just in the very liberal wing of the Catholic Church.* That sense of identification and community allowed Chestnut to rebuild ELPC and help start the rebuilding of East Liberty.

I was lucky enough to get to know Chestnut in an East Liberty Church men's discussion held at the Pittsburgh Theological Seminary. Over a monthly breakfast, we had some fine discussions of philosophical and practical theological issues. Chestnut left at the end of that year. I cannot remember who replaced him, but I remember that I was not all that impressed. I have come to learn that I am a selfish church goer. Whereas some come to do charity and others to increase fellowship and I support those goals, I come mostly for preaching. I have been lucky in finding some excellent preaching.

I also found that church stimulated my imagination. I even got a poem out of a service where knowing some of the participants reminded me of other experiences in my life.

THE ECHOES OF WIND GAP

It takes two to speak the truth – one to speak and another to hear.

Henry David Thoreau

I listen to the minister in this one-church Pennsylvania town
and wonder if she knows the secret
that her mother wanted me to marry her.

I have become open to arranged marriages
since a Bombay-born woman
told me of the success of such families in her country.

Crazy as my parents were,
they could not have done much worse
at choosing for me than I did—twice, naturally.

We are used to nature here in the Gap, wind
blowing, whistling like hell through the mountains,
over the water, like a ghostly voice.
And don't we pray to hear the words
of the once-dead Nazarene?

Maybe I should write my secret
on my church collection envelope this Sunday,
or on my mirror tonight, next
to my dance club tickets.

About two years later, one of my favorite colleagues at Robert Morris, Ellie Long, also a CMU rhetoric grad, reminded me again that our mutual friend and classmate, Wayne, was celebrating his 20th anniversary as pastor at Community House Church on the Northside. Wayne and I had been good buddies at Carnegie Mellon and had, for example, worked together successfully to get a bad teacher fired. I had ducked his preaching a number of times simply because I was too busy and already was pleased with Dr. Chesnutt at East Liberty Presbyterian, but I thought I should at least go to Wayne's anniversary. I was really impressed. His homily was both thoughtful and thought provoking. I had been working with a man in the program, James, who had a religious background and suggested to him that he might be interested in hearing Wayne too. So he joined me in what became our 25-year spiritual experience at Community House Church.

But Wayne was just part of the Community House experience. The congregation was also impressive. Among its members were Linda Flower, an important rhetoric researcher and writer whose work in problem solving and community rhetoric is nationally known. I was lucky enough to have her as one of my teachers at CMU. She and Wayne and other CMU people had done ground-breaking work in literacy especially for inner city young people. I still remember her brilliant work on teaching young, especially inner city, youth rhetorical alternatives to violence. I often saw them at national conferences. Wayne was sometimes presenting with another of our congregation, a large African American woman known as Queeney. I could go on and on about the congregation, doctors, lawyers, and my vote for Pittsburgh's finest poet and my very good friend, Richard.

Better than their accomplishments were the congregation's warmth in welcoming James, me, and others. Along with that was their generosity in helping us to feel comfortable, interesting coffee hour discussions, and a true sense of community. Rick and I took our turn as responsible for coffee hour, following carefully laid out directions from Linda. When a full meal was being planned, I, who do not cook, would go to Queeney, who was a master in the kitchen, and say *What are we cooking?* She would make something delicious out of what little money I would give her.

It was a terrific time until a few years ago. Wayne quit abruptly. Many of us did not know why, but it emerged that there was some question about how he was handling the finances. The situation was complicated by the fact that there appeared to be two entities for which Wayne had financial responsibly: the church and the literacy center that was the embodiment of Wayne's research and inner city work mentioned earlier. I was on Session (the governing body of the church). The Session and some of the congregation broke into acrimonious sides, those supporting Wayne and those at least questioning his handling of finances, especially since he had retired from the pulpit. I was really torn: I very much liked Wayne and respected his preaching and outreach work. But the documents that were emerging cast some doubt on the exercise of his financial responsibility. I had to let my fiduciary responsibility trump my loyalty to Wayne. It really pains me that I lost some valuable friends in the process, but I learned early in my program a central tenet that has also helped me negotiate in the rest of the world: *principles before personalities*. The Session turned the investigation over to the Pittsburgh Presbytery, who turned it over to the Pittsburgh City Police. Wayne was arrested several months ago and was facing a trial this Spring (2023). His case was later thrown out for lack of evidence. I wish him well, but I feel sure that I did what I was entrusted to do.

All this time I continued to write, read and publish poetry. I have had some success in publishing with more than 120 poems in literary journals, magazines, and collections. I had a great year in 2012 publishing both a chapbook and a longer book of poetry. During that year, Michael Simms asked me to publish a chapbook with Coal Hill Press, a subsidiary of Autumn House Press. That summer Coal Hill released my *Irish Coffee*. Here is the title poem from that book:

Irish Coffee

He sits with me at breakfast
and tells the horrifying story
about his brother's drinking, and stealing,
arrested with his saliva still staining
the rifle barrel. For we are Irish,

dreamy stallions with the bloodlines
that take us back to lost races,
to the knowledge that sooner or later
the world will break our hearts;
for we know the world

of dreams far better than is good.
We know its whiskey surge,
how it gathers to unleash the wizard

of our heart's tongue in a patriot game,
or loss on the water lapping at Innisfree.

I want to be horrified by his brother's excesses,
express sympathetic disgust, but
I am envious of his plans: take, shoot.
After my breakfast I lift coffee for a sip, already
planning for still another before it chills.

Later in 2012 my love and partner Judy Robinson helped arrange the publication of a longer book of my poetry, *The Cinnamon of Desire* with Main Street Rag. My friend, the talented painter, Bob Qualters, was kind enough to let me use one of his excellent paintings as the cover. I am grateful to them, especially Judy who was also an inspiration for many of the poems and for navigating some of the perils of publication. She has also paid me the high compliment of teaching the title (hidden in the last line) poem from that collection. Although included earlier, I happily reprise the poem, so important in my life and in my life as a poet:

Baking the Ginger Boy's Tongue

What do you want?

    The white uniformed voice feeds

my anxious sweet hunger, but iced
with the fear of women's words.

"Them, the ones next to," I said.
Crumb buns? You want crumb buns?
Or the flop overs, which? Her voice, knife sharp
as the red nail of her finger stabbing at the cakes.

Her ruffled pink collar, an old
poisoned plain for her mountain head;
a bumpy nose more sure than Sister Pancratia's
smelling out my neck and side sweat.

But my brother warned me
of the rancid taste in feminine scented,
sweet words. And how to lower
to Bogart's lip and tongue swagger.

I can't give you any until you say.
Her eyes bulge at me,
like muffins rising in the tin.
Finally, timed and done, I rise.

"Crumb buns, crumb buns,"
I cry quickly, through slitted mouth,
cut open for the first of many times,
by the cinnamon of desire.

Shortly thereafter, I convinced my dean to finally approve a budget request to start a literature journal at Robert Morris. I immediately asked my talented colleagues, John Lawson and Heather Pinson to join me as faculty advisors. We easily filled up our editorial board with student volunteers. At our first meeting, I suggested the name *Rune* of the journal. Then rescinded my suggestion, thinking it redundant (there was another Rune journal at the time) and obscure. I am happy to say, I was immediately outvoted and *Rune* still exists and thrives, publishing some of the best poetry, fiction, and drama of the students at Robert Morris along with that of the Pittsburgh poetry community.

Here are some early poems the *Rune* student board thought well enough to publish. I had been wondering about our tech and other material obsession in the face of world-wide hunger. I was also taken at the time with the rhythm and internal rhyme of a phrase I was repeatedly hearing back then that opens the poem.

Man Lives Some by Bread

I know an Internet address
to buy a Spanish ham,
and while I watch starvation
bloat the belly of a rail-thin boy
I wonder how I

eat so much and care so little
for those whose voices
outran their food
in this brutal interface of man's
bloody corrida with man.

Momento Mori

Lost my soul,
lost my locket
with my husband's remains
If found call 412-555-5899.

I wondered at the furnace of love
that can fire a locket of burnt kisses,
sworn commitments, and jealousies,
all shut around a neck.

Heat that can choke out fear
of death: to hold at the throat
the hellish grit,
ashes of love.

I sometimes don't feel close enough
to anyone, my love, to give
even a posy necklace of a devotion
-

I wish, my sweet, that we could
find such love, press it so close
between us, we would fire again,
to more than a dusty frosting
on loyal throats.

Raven

A pitch black arrow thrust
from Akhenaton's bow, a god's
chiseled hieroglyphic from a time
when greatness was shared with beasts;

lightening swift slate spear
shot from dazzling day
through green tree leaves
swooping up dead brown prey.

Still he is Raven
From rat to rook to Ra.

Friends, Mentors, and Mentees

I have been lucky enough to meet a large number of people who have not only helped keep me sober but have enriched my life immeasurably in a number of different ways, some of whom I have mentioned only briefly earlier.

Both Barry Z. and I had over 40 years sober when our sponsor Ed passed away and we decided to sponsor each other. An egalitarian system such as ours would not work out for newcomers who don't know much about the program and are not emotionally prepared to listen to good suggestions from a peer. It has worked out very well for us. Barry is as smart as they come, especially about how alcoholics talk themselves into thinking they deserve what is not good for them. An ex-heroin addict (who departed unscathed and satisfied from a Mexican crack house – to go home with a Mexican addict and eat supper with his family), has probably done more to help people in Pittsburgh recovery through sponsoring, speaking, advising, and simply helping, than anyone else I know. I can always depend upon his wisdom as I did when I was first divorced and I told Barry that I couldn't afford to date. He took one look at my sad countenance and said "You have to; put it on a credit card and be careful." A rebel from his youth, Barry once stole his father's car. His father spotted him in the act and gave chase in another family car, both racing through the streets of Squirrel Hill. Barry ran out of fuel and stopped at a gas station. His father, following, also needed gas. Unwilling to start a family argument that might embarrass them both, his father simply glowered at him over the fuel pumps. After both tanks were filled, they resumed the chase. A year before he got clean and sober, Barry was in the county lockup for another crime. Now he is a retired successful business owner and influential member of his community. I love Barry's line: *As hard as life gets, we have each other.*

Another long-timer whom I met early on, Dennis R., is a remarkable speaker and solid sponsor and helper to many. I love the part of his lead where he explains that all his life, he has noticed there are "some people over here" that have something and "other people over there" that want it. He just wanted to succeed by getting in between them. That "thing" originally was drugs, now it's sobriety. Dennis runs the recovery club on the South Side where anyone can go to a meeting at almost any time of the day or night. To say nothing of getting a great hamburger.

My closest friend in recovery for many years, Brian, passed away early in 2022. Brian and I had been friends since Shady Side Academy. We grew much closer in sobriety. He had had an amazingly interesting life and was and remained perhaps the best conversationalist I knew. Modestly and incisively, he could always explain what was going on with the US economy and how it might affect me. He was Davey Lawrence's assistant at the 1960 Democratic Convention, where he got to meet many of the key players including John Kennedy. ("Nobody could believe how smart he was.") Despite his many connections, he remained an unassuming and helping man. Brian had suffered serious depression and was always willing to talk to people, especially those similarly suffering, about his experience. I know his talks were very useful to many. We had a standing lunch date every Saturday for 38 years. I miss him dearly.

Another long-time program friend has been Bob Q. He has been and, as far as I am concerned, still is, Pittsburgh artist of the year. His paintings show a great understanding of and connection with Pittsburgh and its people - enriched with wonderful wit. (Bob often writes comments, quotes, and poetry on his canvases – I have only half joked that Bob has more literary allusions in his art works than I had in my literature lectures. In several painting Bob extensively quotes William Butler Yeats. I love his quotes from painters, such as the one in my bedroom mentioning Matisse seeing hills and valleys as metaphors for our sexual desires. Pittsburgh is of course great for that idea as is the nude Bob's painting superimposes on our hills. His amazingly rich, vibrant color and his insightful and moving art of the Pittsburgh area just keep getting better. He recently had an exhibition where we were all blown away yet again. Years ago, I thought Bob would enjoy meeting Brian, and I got them together for a regular lunch. That lunch has grown to between 5-8 people every week after the Saturday morning meeting. Once, after Bob came out of the hospital for a minor procedure, we were supposed to meet following a concert on the South Side. I could not find him and went hunting all over several blocks, worried that he had become ill. In fact, Bob had met a few nice - and good-looking ladies with whom he was having coffee while I searched. I finally gave up. Contacting him the next day, I was irate that he had not looked harder for me. As an apology, Bob painted a small paper sheet with the whole story. It was so good an apology and piece of witty art, I framed it and treasure it to this day.

Another of my great friends has been Pat M. Pat has an enthusiastic personality that is a pleasure to be around. It served him well as a music promoter who brought many of the great popular musicians of our time to Pittsburgh. My favorite of his stories concerns the time he brought James Brown in. Pat picked Brown up at the airport in a hired vintage Rolls Royce. The concert was, in Pat's words, "excellent" (Although I did not see that Brown performance, I do remember seeing a film clip of a number of rockers of that era, including Brown and Mick Jagger, where Mick said he was afraid to follow James on stage because of the power of Brown's performance.) Nonetheless, because Brown was not yet so popular in Pittsburgh, the concert lost a lot of money. Pat asked Brown to take a smaller fee, but Brown refused. Pat's reduced circumstances forced him to drive Brown and his wife out to the airport in a several year-old Toyota. Pat's consolation came during the drive: Brown, once a hair stylist, said to his wife, both in the back seat. "That gentleman has beautiful hair."

I have also been lucky enough to know Billy P. one of the great rhythm and blues singers. Billy has gained international recognition underscoring how fine an artist he is. Pittsburgh recently celebrated Billy Price Day, marking his 50th year of creating some of the best rhythm and blues in the country and abroad. We have been able to bond over a number of other interests, including writing, rhetoric, and philosophy. I was also privileged to talk with Billy while he was deciding on a second career. Billy started the conversation by saying that he had to find another career. My response was "Are you crazy? Everybody wants to be you! He said "Think about it: when you are playing, I'm working: New Years Eve, most Saturday nights." Billy did make a good point: I was always impressed with how hard he worked, how professional his shows were. I suggested the Masters in Professional Writing Program at CMU. I knew how good it was from my years at the university and how well those graduates did. Billy completed the program with flying colors and has had a great second profession in various aspects of writing and technology, especially cyber security. More recently Billy has concentrated on his music doing a number of fine CDs and concerts in the US and abroad. I love seeing his energetic and soulful shows. Still maintaining his great sense of humor, Billy says about Pittsburgh's South Hills, *They have a different kind of asshole over there.*

Another great friend has been Johnny M. I first got to meet Johnny at a meeting when I came in late and he was a greeter. At the door, I asked who the speaker was. When Johnny explained who it was. I asked jokingly if the lead was any good. Johnny replied in a straight Damion Runyon manner, *Is the gentleman a particular friend of yours?* I said I barely knew him. Then Johnny then replied, *It sucks*! That was a long time ago, and Johnny says he would not say that today, recognizing that all speakers in recovery have something to teach us.

Another valuable friend has been Joan S. whom I think of as having been "an attorney in Orphan's Court who actually cared about orphans." My father and many lawyers I have known also served in a Court that should have been named (and often is in other states) Court of Wills and Estates. Joan did some of that work but also helped with a number of adoptions for much less than she could have made as a high-rise estate attorney. She has great insight into the program, especially the importance of the deceptively easy admission that we are powerless. Like many people I have heard, she just couldn't understand that meant she couldn't have the first drink. It's hard for all of us to understand that what we think has been our only ally is actually destroying us. Joan is also a great conversationalist and a fine listener. I'll always remember her sympathetic ear when I was so upset about losing my lifelong friend, Gil, whom I've written about earlier,

Thomas S. is another long-timer whom I was lucky enough to meet early on. He has a fascinating software business that is too complicated for me to understand. He was born in Ireland where he occasionally gets back to visit. I love his story about one visit where he confronted the problem of his Irish cousins and friends learning Gaelic. They were especially good at swearing. Thomas begged his mother to teach him some swear words in Gaelic. Finally his mother relented and taught him a phrase, but said it was too awful to translate for him. The next time Thomas was out with his gang, - and they were swearing, he tried out the phrase his mother had instructed. All his friends broke out laughing. Asking what was so funny, they told him he had just asked to be taken to mass. Thomas also generously got my son John a backstage pass to hear U2 from a cousin who is connected to the band. Thomas married a terrific woman in the program and they have adopted a foreign baby who has been a great love child and smart as a whip. I was honored to be a character witness on the adoption application. Their daughter has a successful career now.

One of my sponsees, Brint, has been kind enough to take me to St. Thomas where we celebrated his 35th anniversary. He has done a number of kind things for me including helping me move when I thought the time constraints were impossible. He sent over some of his employees who made it happen. I was best man at Brint's wedding, but unfortunately the marriage didn't work out.

Henry W is another cynic who turned super helpful to new people and took on service positions. He's as likely to hand you an *Oh, Henry* candy bar as to tell you to shape up your program with more serious meetings. I love our conversations. Henry fought a valiant battle with bone cancer and recently passed away. He was a bit of a stickler about meetings, especially about what should be acceptable topics for discussion. But the program needs traditionalists and Henry usually knew what he was talking about.

One of my favorite sponsees is Rob N. Rob attended Carnegie Mellon's Masters in professional writing shortly after Billy did. One of the things I love to mention about Rob is that he achieved a 4.25 QPA on a scale of 4.0. Talk about an overachiever. Rob has been a good friend who runs marathons. He is also a great conversationalist. A kind man, Rob helped me move. We have regular dinners that I think are often more helpful to me than Rob.

Dennis P. is a recent sponsee whom I am always after to meet more often with me, partly to get program work done and partly because he is so interesting. Dennis has been kind enough to give me a tour through his famous church on the Northside, filled with tiffany windows.

Nico has just been added to our group. Much younger, he is sometimes the memory of a group of aging sober guys (not just to help us oldsters remember, but also to pass on some of the wisdom we learned.) Nico did his share of drinking damage and is a studying hard as a nurse in training, but still has finds time to be extremely well read.

Contributions Out Theah

I learned much from one of my favorite quotes in recovery. Nancy B. was a powerful and rich Southern woman. (When asked what she did for a living, she would answer, *I make bishops).* At one meeting we both attended, people began to brag about how good their programs were because of the great number of meetings they were making. Nancy B. responded that we are not supposed to be spending all our time in meetings. In her wonderful Southern drawl she added, *We are in heah so that we can be out theah.* Of course, we must pay attention to our sobriety, but we must grow in other ways and participate in our communities. For me, that has meant a number of things, some of which I have mentioned earlier: I am an elder in the Presbyterian church. (I once said that to a woman who had known me *before*, and I would love to have a picture of the abject shock on her face – you'd have thought I shot someone.) During that period I was on session, we dealt with the very difficult issues of possible financial mishandling by our former and beloved minister. I was also president of my condo board during a very challenging six years of expensive and needed repairs, neglect of which could have been disastrous. During much of my sober life before retirement, I taught just about every course the English Department at Robert Morris offered, helped start a literary journal, and was appreciated enough to be promoted to university professor and given emeritus status after my retirement (where I also taught three alumni literature courses.)

But I think the greatest way I have reached out and grown is through writing poetry and fiction.

CHAPTER XIII
THE MYTH OF POETRY AND SELF EXPRESSION

I don't totally understand why I started writing poetry. Part of my poetic beginning was for relief during boring academic meetings (not all were boring, but as my tenure grew, many of them seemed repetitions.) Another reason, of course: I was an English major who really believed the purpose of literature was to say what was enduring and true. I believed I had discovered some of those enduring truths, at least for me, and wanted to express them in meaningful and memorable ways.

I especially liked poetry's condensation and lyrical appeal. I wanted to learn a little more about writing poetry. So I took the class at Pittsburgh's Center for the Arts taught by Michael Wurster that I mentioned earlier. And where I met Joan Bauer and Richard St. John.

Other fellow workshoppers included the artist, Bob Qualters whom I knew outside the poetry world and whom I consider one of my best friends. Bob's poetic knowledge and insights richly inform his excellent art. He is also a fun companion at a poetry workshop and anywhere else.

We had another artist in that class, Pat Barefoot. Pat taught art at the Center for the Arts. She encouraged me to take an art class, which I did; the results, written several years later, are as follows:

PROPORTION

You must *get a sense of proportion,*
my father said when, at 12, I wanted
to have two members of the Howe Street gang
arrested for punching me.

Later, I tried to convince anyone who would listen
that Lyndon Johnson should be impeached.

A sense of proportion.
To be able to see more and better,
I took a "Drawing the Figure" course
from a lovely artist who,
when I complained no talent,
said she had special methods.

On a bleak Saturday
I wandered into a paint-spattered studio
where all looked giveaway shabby, except
the seven women at easels,
their laser eyes directing mine
to a platform on which a robed woman
was standing, removing her belt
until all those lovely nook and nestle places
fell out, and she was just there.

I hopelessly drew lines
that somehow squiggled this woman,
then pleaded with my teacher
for some of her special methods.

Look! she said.
And it began:
how to do comes from to see,
only partly through the eye,
to see and feel how it all fits together
in its spaces, to own for even a moment
the smallest part of God's iris.

With the day nearly closed,
my teacher came around to look:
:

*If you would only worry less about nipple
placement and more about the line ...*

CHAPTER XIX
POETRY AND THE MYTH OF TRAVEL

All through this time I had been getting more interested in poetry. Having started out merely as a diversion from boring meetings, poetry surprised me by becoming an attractive and then a jealous mistress. One of my indulgences with her was to take summer workshops or classes, usually abroad. I still vividly remember my first long workshop, two weeks in Spoleto. I was amazed at the beautiful medieval town and the convent where I lived and classes were conducted. My room was clean and cheap. The convent had been built for hundreds of young women who planned to become Catholic nuns. In the modern world so few women want to study for the novitiate that many of those convents were, at the turn of the 21st century, empty. Lovely grounds and good company rounded out a valuable workshop experience. Maybe the most important part for me was understanding that I was writing poetry that others, including the teachers, found worthwhile.

I mentioned earlier that I met a great group of young drinkers, one of whom was a red headed wild woman. I was entranced by my new red-headed friend. Little happened romantically although maybe we both wanted it to. But I was still committed to my marriage. I took solace later with some imagination about my "missed chance."

Escape

I have not got away yet
although I began in a trot
last minute, half-hearted for the bus
to the church in Assisi, instead
of the train to the coast she took
with her young friends who could not
stop talking about drinking, hell raising,
the Adriatic beach, and her sacrilegious
outrages throughout that week's workshop.

She would not go with me to the cathedral.
Like all my women
she had trouble entering a church.
God had simply let her down
and neither was making any concessions.
Odd, her red hair made me think
of a martyr, and she certainly burned easily,

Nor were either giving up on me:
over my protestations that she was too young,
she told me that we were just at the beginning,
more true for her than us. I remember
every incidental touch: hand, side, hug, pulse on pulse,
wine lips the night we kissed wobbly on the cobblestones,
after she made us a picnic on the convent table.

But I believe heaven is in art too,
like those shattered, mosaics in Assisi
then reconstructed after the earthquake.
Like me, months after tears, rehab, painstakingly

pieced back together so that the past,
not lost, but a mural for mending:
God's healing magnet of prayer.

She connected at the coast with one young friend,
and wrote about their lovemaking for all to hear.
I said a prayer at Assisi's cathedral
and since have not been able to forget her,
how she lay, hung-over in the convent's shadow,
trembling without a drink for two days
asking me to stay with her.

My trip to Brazil mentioned earlier was the catalyst for the following.

Richard Nixon and Me

There were terrible storms across Brazil
the TV weatherman said, and Richard Nixon's
Press Secretary said that the President's statement
was no longer operative,
and my roommate quoted Dylan:
you don't need to be a weatherman
to know which way the wind blows

I mentioned sluggishly that
we ought to pay the rent,
not move out in the middle
of the night and then agreed
with him: we weren't the real

crooks; we might be drafted.

I am now in Rio
and the warmth is forgiving.
I eat enough for a favela family
of four and throw away
enough for three more.

The real crooks here
we know are the Nazis.

Delirious from my third helping
of meat, I imagine myself
a Warsaw freedom fighter.
Not a Waffen SS colonel in late '45,
checking the plane schedules/from Berlin to here.

I continued to search out and attend poetry workshops that enriched my work and my life. I went to Brazil, Mexico, Greece, back to Italy. Always fascinated by a new country's culture, food, architecture, art. I try to capture some of that in the following.

Assisi Art

I stand in the great room of the restaurant/bar
of the Hotel Giotto and wonder
at the vast plain below Assisi.

My colleagues are right: a chess board strong enough
to build upon, stunning enough to spark
inner fires to want to build for God, the saints,
and their own lives. The fields'
fecundity makes real the full feeding of these people.

Still, how could they build this small colossus of a city,
stone by blister by worn-out back
and then fill it with such awe inducing cathedrals and art?
By holiness, by Christ?

Shocked by Giotto's brilliance, and the stunning architecture,
by my own stupid hands and mélange brain,

I view the valley and town
trough an oversized window
that strangely reminds me of Hitler's study
at his Berghof summer retreat.
Historians say Hitler wanted
to be a painter or an architect,
but was thwarted by mediocrity.

Feeling an edgy itch,
I remember the art critic
who said the first step
in any aesthetic is envy.

My experiences in foreign-based and Pittsburgh workshops encouraged me to continue writing on my own with the terrific help of my own small workshop of Joan and Rick. Our meetings every month or so taught me and continue to teach me a great deal and gave me the confidence one best gets from careful, effective poets who like your work and want to help make it better.

I want to be careful not to attribute or blame all my poetry to or on my friends. Sometimes we left it, as my friend Rick says, "I like this less than . . .."

The following are a few poems that did pretty well in workshop:

The Fault Lines of Cellophane

Paradoxically strong, difficult
until you find the tearing weakness.
My father gave up entirely
even in his 50s,
depending on his wives, one after another,
to crinkle rip the crackers open,
before ordering his dinner
for him, driving him home,
and whatever other slavish thing
they had to do
to tear him from me.

Buzzzzz

I am buzzing now.
I thought at first it was my cell phone;
Then maybe the electric hum
of a nearby appliance.

But now I am resigned

that I am the hum:
my thigh, for example, will vibrate briefly
and then maybe my arm. No predictability:
I hum when they want.

I used to be able to talk to the dead.
Lots of people spend countless dollars
and much difficulty trying to contact the dead.
For a while, I couldn't get them to shut up.

I finally became afraid and just stopped listening
to those beyond, even to Liz, whom I had loved
in that heartbreaking teenage way. And my brother,
who said funny things and woke me up
the night a mutual friend also died
to tell me he was really ok
and they were both laughing now.

I was up on my apartment roof last night
looking at the harvest moon,
as it turned from orange
to a precise punched-out white,
looking almost like an escape hatch
through which, if any signal might pass,
could break through earth, bone, even life,
if only it would touch enough pain in a receiver.

Candomble

followers wear a wonder of whites,
shirts, pants, dresses, and an amazement
on the women's heads, hats like artists'
crushed soufflés of chefs' collapsed chapeaux
or bright meringues of wrapped towels
All dressing them up, strangely, to worship dirt:

the world's prescient environmentalists.

For candomblé is a nature religion
practiced by the descendants of African slaves
first in Brazil and now in every living place
and only lately in the open,
free from insistent Christian shackles.

Tonight I watched Priest Ba Ba Hightower
perform a spiritual earth and water ceremony
in the rites of this earth and flora-loving religion.

I had not heard of candomblé

but I knew a Hightower, descendant of plantation owners,
who suffered Africans a more limited kind of earth worship:
produce cotton and offer self-sacrifice
in any kind of dress some Hightower wanted.

Contemplation

All food is 80% water
a doctor once told me,
When you think about it,
it has to be.

I thought about it:
I didn't think it had to be.
I'm a theological libertarian:
God could do anything She wanted.

All food could be like Jell-O,

which might be a better plan
for no toast stuck in the throat;

If you think about it.

I had a smarty girlfriend
who used the same phrase,
like: *Marriage is the most
logical manner of living for humans,
if you think about it.*

I thought about it.

I live single and alone now.

At the Thanksgiving Party

She wants to tell the story
of waitressing at Cracker Barrel
how she astonished the Polish couple
by singing in their native language the risqué love song,
"When is the Best Time?"

Pausing only for a sip of wine,
She tells how
her cousin became engaged:
A first date, the theater ceiling collapsing,
on her cousin and her cousin's future husband.
She regales us with the follow up:

>   The couple's long and happy marriage.
>
>   But she doesn't want to tell the story
>   of her uncle, and his mob connections
>   and the 35th president who didn't make his 47th birthday,
>   and how Hollywood always gets it wrong.
>
>   What are the stories you tell
>   in place of the one you won't?

The last lines, of course resonate with my own level of willingness to share my personal life experiences in my poetry. Some critics call poets like me *confessional poets*. I prefer the term *personal poets*. I don't feel like I am confessing anything to anyone. I am simply telling/writing what happened to me and the effect it had. I admire and am appreciative of all kinds of poetry. But what strikes me most in poetry is what I think the poet knows best: what happened to the poet and how it mattered.

I gained enough confidence in my kind of poetry to start submitting to journals and had some success. I have now published 120 poems in journals, literary magazines and collections. As I mentioned, in 2012, Michael Simms approached me after a poetry reading and invited me to publish a chapbook with Coal Hill Press, a branch on Autumn House press. The outcome was *Irish Coffee*, a 13 poem chapbook containing some work I am very proud of. With Judy's great help, I published a longer book of poetry. *Cinnamon of Desire*. Excuse my repetition, but I am very happy to say I have complimentary blurbs from Pittsburgh's excellent poets, Judy Robinson and Richard St. John on *Irish Coffee* and from former head of the International Poetry Forum, Sam Hazo and widely respected poet, Jan Beatty on *Cinnamon of Desire*. I am still pleased that Joan Bauer took a moment after I gave a reading at her

Hemingway's series to say, holding up a copy of *Cinnamon of Desire*, "this is a really good book."

I had always written short stories and now felt good enough about my writing to write more and to submit for publication. I have also had some success in publishing them. Some of those appear above. Here's one that that reaches deep into my past with characterizations of some people close to me and myself during an early uneasy time in my life.

THE ZIDDADOOM HIDEOUT

In contrast to the blinding sharp glint of the knife, the rest of the room was filled with a soft autumn light. The afternoon sun came in gently through the quarter moon windows of the old third floor. Although soft, it was a clear light, the dust particles standing out as if the very air was x-rayed. The light shone more weakly through the brown beer bottles scattered on the table spaces around the room. The recent *Time* magazine with the African dictator on the cover, was dated, October, 1964, correcting the September, 1962 Mellon Bank calendar on one wall.

This very place had been the Ziddadoom Hideout. And now - here was Danny McClain out of nowhere after twenty years. Ray Hamilton was his host, if you could call a surprised and somewhat alarmed man trying to get a knife glint out of his eye, a host.

The two young men were about the same age, twentyish, but differently dressed, Ray in a blue button down with khakis, Danny in blue denim pants and black t-shirt announcing "Welcome to the 5th Ave. Bar: DUCK, SUCKER." An ornate red do-rag tied over his hair completed the outfit. But the most outstanding difference between the two was Tommy, while still holding the beer in one hand, in the other was holding a long glinting blade, recently released from its mother of pearl handle with a definite and heavy click. With magical speed thought Ray, now inches from its edge.

"Of course, I can't give it back to you. I'm not God." Ray said as calmly as he could, immediately regretting the reference to the deity.

"You acted like God that day." Danny said as he brought back the blade to point to his own ear, which, although somewhat repaired, was still considerably diminished, the remainder mangled.

"How you like this ear? How'd you like one just like it?" His voice rose as it speeded up.

"No one could have known what was going to happen, Danny."

"I could have. And I go by 'Dan' now."

"Sorry, Dan. We were only trying to get away."

"I should cut you even for that. Always trying to lose me when all I wanted to do was hang around – quiet like. I idolized you guys. You bastards."

"We were kids, Danny. Dan, sorry." Ray hadn't meant to sound patronizing. It was now hard to know what to say or how to say it. Rumors were that Dan McClain, although away in the army for the last three years, had, in his short return, shown himself to be an accomplished, even brutal, bar fighter, and not afraid to use a knife.

"We're not kids now," Dan said. "And there's just us here in the house. I looked on the way up. Still don't lock your doors. You people are in a time warp." It chilled Ray that this little thug had been wandering around his home at will. But his parents probably would not have stopped this old neighbor anyway.

Momentarily feeling protective, Ray was grateful that his parents were at the club.

Both slightly drunk Ray thought and wished that he were more so.

"Why me, Dan?" Ray said. "Why not Will, your brother?"

"Cause it happened here, and I'm pretty sure you thought it up. And now, because maybe I'm just coming out of my time warp."

"We both thought it up so we could leave a littler, boy. Older kids do that. They try to get away from their younger siblings."

"Well nobody's leaving now," Dan said.

Catching the knife glint again in his eye, and afraid of any lull, Ray kept talking.

"We both know the ear's return is impossible? Could I give you something else?"

"What else? Money? – looks like you still got some – or your parents do. You working yet? Speaking of time warps."

"Some more beers? Cards? Arm wrestling? A wrestling match?" Ray laughed, searching for a fuse to disarm this time bomb of a person who'd grown out of a child he knew and even pushed around. And, now, twenty years later, appeared at his third floor door some thirty minutes ago.

"You pussy! I could wipe the floor with you. You were a terrible card player even as a kid, and I hear you're no better now. To say nothing of how weak and scrawny." Dan's voice faded out as he moved the blade closer to Ray's ear.

"The Ziddadoom Hideout was a child's game – with a child's name, Dan. And, like I said, I'm sorry."

"Actually, I don't remember you saying you're sorry. But right now, I want you to think about it. About what happened? Do you ever think about it? Do you?" Dan's voice rose.

Ray had not thought about the Ziddadoom Hideout in many years, maybe he'd worked hard not to think about it ever since the incident. It had all happened here: his own family's third floor with the closet that led to the eaves.

They all had been boys together, Dan, Ray, and Will, Dan's older brother. But Danny had been younger and of little interest to the older boys. Their solution was the Ziddadoom Hideout. Ray remembered the old stripped bathrobes and caps cut out of old stockings he and Will had used for extra-terrestrial uniforms.

"I do think about it a lot, and I'm sorry" Ray only half lied. "But I tried to throw out the sadness and guilt with the space uniforms. I don't even have the communication devises." Ray laughed weakly.

"What were they?"

"Two erector set motors with some tape running in between. I'll tell you more, but would you mind putting that knife away?" Ray really couldn't think of what else he could tell Danny.

"So I fell for that?" Dan's thickening tongue got out.

"You were younger – too young to read, maybe. The knife? Please."

"Only if it's nearby, for later."

Despite all the beer, Dan McClain deftly reversed the knife in his hand so it pointed downward, and with a quick final movement slammed it into the table next to Ray's arm. It thrummed as Dan's hand released it.

"Thanks," Ray said softly. He tried to remember something of the incident that would excuse it to Danny.

"Maybe you won't be saying thanks in an hour." Dan got up and walked unsteadily to the six-pack of Carlings Black Label beers and pulled the last one out of its paper holster.

It had been a summer day, and Will and Ray wanted to be rid of Danny, so they could, what? Play? Play what? One of their endless games of gin or Monopoly that Danny was always interrupting? Ray only remembered the intense desire to get away. Not unlike what he felt right now.

The older boys had hooked up the two motors so the folded up adhesive tape ran between them. They then pretended to read their meaningless pen markings as messages from the Masters of the Ziddadoom Hideout. The messages were always the same: that Danny had to go home and await further orders from the Ziddadoom. To add a little mystery – also to provide some variety and believability for Danny - the latest message the boys had earlier "written" on the white tape and then run between the two erector set motors was different. It had said Danny was to stand in the transporter room, the eaves of Ray's old house accessed by a closed door - now not three feet from where Dan and Ray sat on either side. As always, further, newer Ziddadoom orders might appear. Such further orders never did.

Ray and Will left, with the young boy still in the eaves closet; Danny, standing obediently and quietly among old trunks and support beams was attacked by a family of squirrels, who, unknown to Ray's family, had entered through an unobserved roof hole and established a nest at the other end of the eave's closet. There was no handle on the inside of the door.

Ray never fully knew how vicious the attack had been, nor how awful were the wounds left behind. Ray's mother had heard Danny's screaming and got him out. Seeing how badly he had been bitten, she called the police who had called the ambulance. Ray's only punishment was the usual long talking-to about responsibility to younger and weaker people. Will said he got pretty much the same. Will said Danny had a short hospitalization including the first of a series of painful shots; the hospitalization was followed by continued shots and weekly meetings with psychologists about fear and anxiety. Will said Tommy had many nightmare-filled nights that summer and fall. All three were told how lucky Danny was to live.

The trip into memory, combined with the seven or eight accumulated beers, had oddly also awakened more pleasant childhood moments. For a minute, Ray was back with the warmth of long afternoons of playing capture the flag or soft ball or board games, so much of it fun. Sometimes they were all playing together. Even now, with alcoholic confidence, Ray saw that it should all be all right. He even saw Will coming through the door, as if transported. Ray blinked several times, and saw that, in fact, it was Will. His tall, full frame filled the doorway and loomed over both sitting men. This unexpected sight pulled both of the other men's startled eyes to Will and pulled Ray back to the present.

"Well, a reunion. Nobody told me." Will said.

"Don't worry, brother-fucker, you're next on my list." Dan pulled the knife out of its reluctant scabbard of table top and made a strangely graceful flourish at his brother.

Will must have heard some conversation on the steps up and answered predictably.

"We could not have known about the squirrels, Dan. Nobody knew, and you can't believe we would have left you in an old closet with anything dangerous, let alone some rabid squirrels.

"Why dja have to leave me anywhere?" Dan's voice rose to halfway between outrage and a whine. "And do you know how much rabies shots hurt? A kid of six?"

Jesus, Ray thought, he's like a dog with a bone.

"Well none of that matters now," Will said.

"Yeah, why not?" Dan challenged.

"We're at war. Your unit just called up for you."

"What? What kind of bull shit is this?"

5

"Don't ask me," Will laughed. "I still have a deferment."

"What?" Danny said more weakly. How do I know…?"

"Well, call them and find out," Will's patronizing tone was effective. painful "Where's your phone, bastard," Danny spit at Ray, already waving his knife."

"Let him use the new one," Will said.

As if they had been playing a twenty year-old game, Ray immediately joined in.

"You mean the new safety phone? Sure."

"What….?" Danny sputtered

"We had it put in the closet after you were attacked by the squirrels. So somebody would always have a lifeline out." Ray said.

"You are not getting me back in that closet. How dumb….?"

"All right Smart Ass, I'll call. Ray, give me the key."

"It opens from the outside. Phone inside. Perfectly safe," Ray repeated with only a slight slur.

Will opened the closet and stepped in. Danny's jaw locked as he moved himself and the knife toward Ray; he looked around a little wildly.

Where's your reserve unit?" Ray asked a little loudly.

"If you bastards…."

"Hello, Capt. Dowdy?" Will's voice was clear from the closet.

"This is Will McClain. We talked a little while ago concerning my brother's return to Camp Jackson due to the military emergency. Well, he won't believe the emergency is real."

"Wait, damn it, wait!" Danny jumped up, threw the knife on the table and stepped quickly, if unsurely, to the closet.

Ray heard a quick thump and Will stepped out quickly, slamming the closet door behind him.

"Still no inside handle?" Will asked

"Nope."

Did you knock him out? Ray said looking at Will's unscathed fists.

Will held up an old small, red, erector set motor.

"Found this inside. He's out long enough - until the MPs get here. He's been AWOL for at least two weeks. I called them just before I came over. Mom told me, warned me, that he was over here. That Dumb Ass has been drinking up a storm for a week and cruising this city talking about and settling old scores, no matter with who. I've stayed away from him as much as possible. But then I heard him complaining about the Ziddzdoom Hideout business and thought I should come over. Brother or no, I never did like him much,"

"Is there a war?"

"Always is, somewhere. I hear Vietnam is heating up. But no high alert here."

"Want to play something? While we wait? Gin?"

"The drink or cards?"

"Both!"

I then tried a few nonfiction pieces, especially about people whom I could not seem to capture in either poetry or short fiction. My Aunt Peggy is the best example:

My Aunt the Nun

Of all her sisters, only Peg could talk to my mother when Mother was drinking and angry, which was quite a lot of the time. I saw Sister Alfreda, as the Order of Mercy nuns called her, also perform this magic of tact with her other sisters, either angry, over-determined, high, or all of the above. Aunt Peg quietly listened (a lot) and talked (a little) them out of it. With seven Irish sisters, she had plenty of practice.

My aunt's diplomacy and patience might have served her well in the US Foreign service. To my young eyes, Stalin couldn't be more difficult than my aunts, especially Aunt Ann, on a toot after her husband threatened to leave.

Aunt Peggy was a saint to us cousins, always sweet and supportive of our schooling, even giving us IQ tests that I suspect she doctored in our favor. I was willing to brag my score, but wonder now since she declared my brother a near genius. He was pretty smart but I knew him better than that. She always had amusement park tickets, and, as we grew to a driving and agnostic age, snuck St. Francis medals unobtrusively into our cars, which may have saved some of our lives.

Aunt Peggy was well educated with two graduate degrees and served as Archivist at the local Catholic University.

The emotional and spiritual power that allowed her to listen so well and get us kids to occasionally pray, obscured her slow mental deterioration which went undetected for a long time. I was already in my forties when one of my more observant aunts, a nurse, spotted the encroaching dementia that Peg suffered. It was this sister, Nancy, who stepped in and guided Peg through the medical and Mercy order bureaucracy to a lovely room in Mercy Hospital. My Aunt the Nurse checked in with Sister Peggy after her first night and relayed the following conversation:

"How do you like your room, Peg?" Nancy asked.

"It's fine, except for the talking door." Peg replied

"What?"

"The door over there talks at night."

"Peg, I'm sure that there are just some people behind the door, maybe in the next room, that you are hearing."

"Nancy, I'm 76 years old, hold two Masters Degrees, and have held very responsible jobs my whole life. I know the difference between people's voices in the next room and a talking door."

After hearing that story, I was afraid my own visit a week later would be difficult. But when I arrived, she seemed bright- eyed and lively enough to make me think this would be a real pleasure.

But just before I stepped inside the room, a nurse grabbed my arm and said, "Don't, under any circumstances, give her money. She took a cab out of here yesterday." I disengaged myself and said ok.

"Hi Aunt Peggy, how's it going?"

"It's very nice," she said, frailer now but still with a keen eye which she was keeping on the nurse at the door until we were completely alone.

"Jay, please let me have some money." First thing, not even a hello.

"Well tell me how it's going," I thought might distract her.

"Oh, it's fine, but I need some money."

"Peg, the nurse told me not to give you any money."

"Oh, what does she know?"

"Well, let's just visit a minute. My son, John, is doing fine in middle school, excels in Spanish."

"That's great, Jay, but about the money."

Distractions, small talk, family gossip, none were going to work. I thought about the nurse's desperate grasp of my arm, and her pleading look. But then I thought about my terrific Aunt Peg nurse's and mine. I voted for mine. Besides, she was a saint and saints deserve at least a few dollars. But I thought maybe I could have a win-win for everybody. I'd give Peg some money, but not too much: $15.00. I thought the visit went wonderfully.

After she had passed away (it only took six sad months), the stories of her intelligence, gentleness, and wit abounded throughout the family. But many of them ended with Peg's final remark on my last visit, one that cemented how unequal our loving relationship was as well as establishing me as a minor villain. Aunt Peggy's final comment on my hospital visit - to all her sisters including my mother:

"How far does Jay think a person can get on $15.00?

THE END

So I continue to mine and write about my life, especially my youth because that's where most of the important things that shaped my life happened.

CHAPTER XX
RETIREMENT: THE MYTH OF WORK

One day at work, I was walking past my friend, Lutz Bacher's office. To my great surprise, Lutz *was packing up his books. We had both thought long and hard about selecting our Wheatley Center* offices and I couldn't imagine him moving out of our new building's excellent space. I asked what he was doing and he said he was retiring and that I ought to think seriously about it too. I have great respect for Lutz, impressed by his excellent scholarship in film studies, especially his first-class book on Max Ophuls. I admired his good sense as well. I began to think he might be right about my retirement.

I had talked intermittently about retirement with my therapist, Mary Jo, over the last few years, at least since 2010. Work was becoming less fun. The long on-campus graduate weekends were beginning to wear: I was totally exhausted on Sunday after my share of the three-hour classes and reviewing so many dissertations. Also, increasingly, I was asked to teach on-line classes. I think remote-learning is the wave of the future, but I also believe those classes will be taught by professors far different from me. I got into teaching mostly for the exciting classroom interaction where I was able to see and hear a student feel sympathy for Gatsby (I loved one comment from a student about *The Great Gatsby*'s narrator, Nick: "Nick's trying to jam with the big boys") or admiration for Hamlet ("He's one talented screw up"); or how their personal essay didn't work and how it might be changed to become more convincing and moving. Teaching had changed. And so had I. It was time to get over the myth that my personal presence was so essential and that I had the stamina to teach forever. I did a rough calculation of how many students I had taught over 45 years, and came up with 10,000. That was enough.

Not long after my conversation with Lutz, I was ready. I completed the paper work and retired in June 2013. I was shortly faced with the anxiety most new retirees have: What was I going to do with myself? And like most retirees, it didn't take me long to figure that out. My program and poetry supplied most of the answers. I spent more time at meetings and meeting with my sponsees and friends. I also wrote more and went to more poetry readings. I applied and was accepted into the Pittsburgh Poetry Society, a long-standing poetry group in Pittsburgh with excellent poets who sponsor a monthly poetry contest and meet to hear the poems read aloud and voted on over lunch. Participation has been a good spur to keep me writing, submitting, and coming to terms with how well or poorly I did in the competition; that the important things were participating, learning and appreciating The Society is full of fine people and tough poetry competition. The President, Christine Aikens Wolfe, is a great organizer, terrific supporter and an excellent poet, as well.

I also thought I should spend more time giving back to my various communities. I joined and was elected to the presidency of my condominium board. My choice was not entirely honorable service. Ever since I had moved into my building, I had hated the building's hall wallpaper, a terrible 1950s combination of loud red and orange mismatched colors. I was able to convince the condo board to redecorate. Residents now enjoy a calm attractive grey, blue, walls with very nice complementary carpeting. We also renovated the elevators. I was also president when we discovered that although the building's power generator was fine, the vault surrounding it was collapsing. The meeting and decision making still go on and the resolution seems closer at hand. My tenure on the board is now over, but I feel I did a credible job and have left it in very good hands: my friend, Vince Johnson, served as president for several years and has now turned the gavel over to the capable hands of Elizabeth Russo.

I also was elected to my church Session, the governing body of our Presbyterian church. I mentioned earlier the crisis that faced that board: the discovery that the grants and funds from it as well as the church building ownership may have been mishandled by the previous well-respected and loved minister, Wayne Peck. That issue was resolved when the District Attorney office was ordered by the court to drop charges. Because of the help from the Pittsburgh Presbytery, our Community House Church (CHC) has already received a substantial settlement from the insurance company. But the accusations caused a split in the congregation and the loss of several members. As I also mentioned earlier, Wayne and I have been friends for a long time, and I came to the Community House Church because of him. I wish him well. Although I believe I did the right thing, my service on the CHC was therefore emotionally draining.

And, for a while, I took a service position in my home group. I have always participated in chairing and speaking at meetings. My new position allowed me to meet representatives from other meetings and learn what was happening in recovery on a city-wide and national level, including suggested changes to our basic textbook, to put out a version more in the plain style. Originally thought a revolutionary idea (as I mentioned earlier, it has been considered by some as a masterpiece of the plain style – but in the style of 1930's English prose) the idea of a plainer and more modern styled basic text gained traction during my tenure and that version of it has now been published.

I have also signed up at the Jewish Community Center to work out with a trainer, Molly, twice a week. I ran into my retired physician, Rick Johnson, during my workout routine and told him how I was working out with Molly. He said "I do this on my own." I told him I wouldn't work out on my own. Expecting a guilt-inducing response about how I should be more self-motivated I was surprised when he simply said, "it's a good thing to know yourself that well." I put that comment together with others: from my therapist, Mary Jo, and my friends over the years and my own feelings: yes, I have come to know myself, and am neither enchanted or disgusted. I am pleased at how I have developed from an afraid child of alcoholics, through my own alcoholism, through a difficult recovery to being a helpful and contributing member of my communities (there are several of them: recovery, church, condo owner, friend, and most important, father and grandfather.). Included of course, in all of these struggles, was overcoming or coming to terms with the powerful myths that seemed to direct many of my actions. I really am leading a rich and full life.

More Travel

One of the best ways I have celebrated retiring and life in general is by travel. I had traveled before mostly to poetry workshops or to present papers, often with side trips. Now, I wanted to focus on the trip/vacation itself. In my youth, I used to argue that Americans suffer from the myth of confusing itineracy with sophistication. I was wrong. Travel does broaden and enrich.

Judy and I have taken several trips together. Our favorite destination has been Charleston, South Carolina where, among other things, we have attended the Spoleto Festival. Started in Spoleto, Italy, I saw the very end of that music festival in advance of my first poetry workshop. This 10-day music and drama celebration was imported to the US originally by the opera empresario Carlo Moneta. A few years after, Charleston took over the festival. Judy and I have seen wonderful performances there, the most remarkable by the music virtuoso Rhiannon Giddens, whose appearance was both powerful and wide-ranging. In one performance she demonstrated such excellent ability in a number of music genres: old time, country, bluegrass, jazz, pop, rap. The next year she was asked to write an opera, which she did. I was lucky enough to see *Omar* - one of the most powerful pieces I have ever experienced on stage. Music and sets were brilliant. At dinner afterwards in a wonderful outdoor Charleston restaurant, great tables in a soft Southern evening breeze, over some excellent swordfish, I met someone at an adjoining table who knew Giddens. Along with some others who had seen the show, we reflected on her moving music. This woman spoke of how hard Giddens worked and said that *Omar* was picked up by the San Francisco Opera. It was one of the best entertainment nights of my life.

Judy's daughter Heather and her son David and his family have a house on the Isle of Palms. They have generously invited me to go along with their mother. We have regularly gone there after the Spoleto Festival and spent a very nice relaxing week at the beach.

 Judy and I also took some trips abroad, notably one to England and Ireland. We visited all the great attractions in London. The tower and Big Ben stand out in my memory. We also saw some fine theater. I was struck how small, human-scaled, really, the London theaters were. What amazed me most about London was how cosmopolitan and crowded it was: all sorts of people in all sorts of dress. Just crossing the street was something of an international scrum. A side benefit was the excellent tea served in our Indian-operated hotel. It somehow had more taste than I recalled from tea. It actually caused me to start brewing tea at home for a while.

We then went on to Ireland, where on the first day I left my backpack with all my medications on the bus from the airport. I freaked out. But the hotel manager calmed me down and called the bus company. He then marched me back out to the bus stop to wait for the bus to come around on its second trip. In less than an hour, the bus arrived and the driver stopped and handed me my backpack. What a great and friendly country. Yes, I did tip him.

The most memorable part of that trip was walking around in beautiful Dublin. And seeing a play at the Abbey Theater. We also visited the Dublin Irish Writers Museum for a quick course on how extensive my literary heritage is.

Also significant for me was taking the train up and seeing Belfast for the first time. It has a surprisingly beautiful downtown. We took a black taxi ride to the area of the city now unfortunately famous for "the Troubles," deadly conflicts between Catholics and Protestants. Powerful opposing murals of dead heroes faced each other across domestic back fences. Our taxi cab driver told us things had been quiet for a while, but the area still seemed a tinder box to me.

I was reminded of Bernadett Devlin's challenge to a newscaster: "Just go out in the streets of Belfast and ask some average people, Catholics and Protestants: what's the difference between Catholicism and Protestantism. I'll bet a lot of money they can't tell the difference." I find this to be another generally accepted myth:

some people are taught to think that "only my church can provide the path to God." I know economic and social differences also lie underneath the religious convictions, but the Only-My-Religion one is the fundamental and most dangerous myth.

Judy and I took a taxi out to Stormont, the seat of the Northern Irish government where I was able to see the statue that my father had told me about all my life: Sir Edward Carson shaking his fist at Southern Ireland as if to say we will never become part of Catholic Ireland. This, of course, reminded me of my split heritage, my mother's Catholic background and my father's Protestant one. In many ways I came to think of myself as

Between

Years ago I went out
to Denver to visit two friends,
both lawyers, one who did
environmental law and who showed
me one afternoon on horseback
the desert of neglecting streams and rivers.
My other friend represented many of the neglectors
whose cattle over-grazed and whose manufacturing
over-gulped the water and retched into the air.
The green humble horseback ride with one;
the other's gaseous tank car ride
to his box seat at a Phoenix Suns game.

I have been between most of my life:
my mother's Southern Irish Catholicism
forcing me to Sacred Heart school
that my father's Presbyterianism
made me doubt and dislike.

Between being a smart enough student
to get into a fine college
and irresponsible enough to eak out a gentleman C.

Partying with my very privileged friends
I learned that like Scott Fitzgerald,
in the rich boy's school
I was the poor boy.

Good enough taste to marry
the sparkling witty woman
and bad enough judgment
to end up losing in two divorces.

Between pain for my son's neglect by impaired wives
and my selfish aching that would not to break their hold.

The roughneck Irishman
with my intellectual friends
and the sensitive poet
with my blue collar drinking pals.

But these 60 years have taught me
all are tines on a fork,
now with a stronger handle;
I can now go back to the middle
only this time I get full custody of me

My parents' shared life and my own experience had taught me that the myth that love can conquer all is an overstatement, however, love can conquer much. My parents stayed together and loved each other as much as their disease of alcoholism permitted. The most important thing for me was that I became a stronger self who is in charge of myself.

Whether because of my love of my mother and her family, or my own love of Irish writers, or my liberal leanings, my sympathies were always with the Southern Irish who wanted independence. In Belfast, as if playing out my Carson/Donnelly family dynamic, Judy became involved in a Northern unionist demonstration, literally. Being sympathetic to an elderly woman's plea that she and her fellow demonstrators not lose their right to display their flag in any union of Ireland, Judy ended up getting literally wrapped up in a number of Northern Irish flags to say nothing of the demonstrators and their signs. Neither the local police nor I were very happy with her. I had to unfurl Judy from the demonstration flags and get her back into the taxi. Aside from that small kerfuffle, we had a great time.

Two years later, Judy and I took a river cruise from Paris to Normandy. It was a fine trip, allowing us to stop at various towns along the Seine, including the lovely colorful gardens and home of Monet. The Norman cemetery conducted a small ceremony for our American group which I found very meaningful.

A Simple Norman Thank You

in a French accent
heard in a brief ceremony
on the Omaha Beach
after the quick account
of numbers of young American dead

brought home to me
the Nazi rape of France,
how the Germans weren't leaving
until we kicked them out.
The WWII movies and documentaries I watch
turned now from gauzy celluloid
to rapid fire images burned in my brain.

The Germans invaded quickly,
and stayed slowly, every hour, day,
taking what, beating whom, they wanted.
Monday, Tuesday, all week, all month
all year. Shining brutality
like buttons and boots, they made
the French starve themselves
and pick up after their Aryan trash.

Some of those American saviors had
a shorter walk with their cross than Christ:
a one- or two-minute war; shot in the water
inches from the landing craft or in it.
Some before siring a child, or marrying,
or even tasting a woman's open-lipped kiss.
Some left behind families,
but they all kept coming
doing the right thing.

An old woman opened a window
and held out a little American flag
and waved it to us,
even seventy years later.

Sharing France with my partner was a powerful experience, emotionally and historically, I was deeply affected which I hope the following poem suggests.

City of Light

I did not deserve Paris;
perhaps none of us do,
maybe Napoléon, de Gaulle, Hemingway.

An enticingly dangerous city
that electrified me
into believing I was much better
than I am, as triumphant as its Arc,
grand as any boulevardier
stopping for brioche and cappuccino,
connoisseur enough
to savor Caravaggio
at the Louvre, sense the difference between
Winged Victory and a defeated copy.
All the while, Paris fed me truffles and sole meunière
that I have not the educated palate to understand,
beyond my weak little *so good*.

Once, during the long-ago Algerian war,
beside the Presidential Palace. Suddenly,
I was walking on air
as two French gendarmes lifted me
under each shoulder
and growled *Forbidden*.

This time, I was
walking and pedi-cabing

d'Orsay to Champs-Élysées
dinner on the Seine
with the Eiffel towering behind.

Paris was a prince of Troy,
but only a God could create
a city of such light, love, beauty, art,
gifts which can create a rage

in the deserted heart of terrorists:
in the dead month of November, 2015,
killing 130 innocent people.
They want to destroy
such magnificent presents that mark us
as possible angels
even as we may act devils.

None of us deserve Paris,
but we must live and die to keep it.

Cuba

Judy decided that Charleston and her son's house on the Isle of Palms were enough travel for her. I still had a desire to see some more of the world. About this time, Cuba was opening up. I signed up with a Roads Scholar tour. Oddly enough, about half the tourists on this trip were from Pittsburgh. A restaurateur, her partner and several of her classmates from Alderdice (the excellent Squirrel Hill High School) were the largest Pittsburgh group. The restaurant owner, Pamela, had become well known by serving her famous pancakes to President Obama who then asked her to cook and serve the same breakfast at the White House, which she did with great success. Her classmates were similarly interesting, mostly business women with a practical as well as an aesthetic take on what we saw.

I remember one saying that although one farm we were seeing was beautiful and the organic honey delicious, she did not see how it could be profitable.

Also on the trip was my best friend Jim and his wife Susan. We were early travelers to Cuba and were lucky enough to stay at the storied International Hotel, the bar of which was filled with pictures of Hollywood greats and great mobsters. From my favorite seat at the bar for my afternoon coffee, I seemed often to be staring at a picture of Fred Astaire or Meyer Lansky. While I am taking about that bar, I remember the Russian professor who baited me by saying that Putin had so much more support in Russia than Obama did in the United States. That experience prompted me to write the following:

ONLY CONNECT

> *The representatives at the UN get along fine;*
> *it's the translators who hate each other.*
> *Anonymous*

The Cuban customs agent asked
if I wanted him
not to stamp my passport
so you don't get into trouble
in your home country.

The quick-to-smile people,
a billboard-free city, the Malecon,
the young dancers who seemed to defy
the laws of gravity and physiology,
the aging masters at the Buena Vista Social Club,
the constant refrain of how good the U.S. reconnection would be,

all baked in. I was catching a little communism.

In Havana, one of the best places
to get a fragrant *cortado* coffee
is in the bar at the Hotel National,
where now you find more Russians than Mafia.

The professor's daughter looked like
a cast member out of *Dr. Zhivago,*
hair more at home in a Russian wheatfield
than a famous Cuban bar.

He said he taught history
and started giving me lessons.
Broken English didn't hold him back
from arrogantly asserting that Putin
had seventy percent approval,
and Obama, like the next-to-last little piggy,
had none, - or nearly none.
He laughed at his transliterated joke.
The U.S.A. is fragmented, ungovernable, weak.

All my carefully learned ideas, reading, college lectures:
how Russia has historically occupied the Crimea,
how noble the Soviet experiment was,
my reading of the Motherland's losses at Stalingrad
and throughout the war, to say nothing
of how Russia saved my Cuba,
all of it disappeared like the Russian Third Army
before the German Blitzkrieg; peasants,
reaped like wheat in those western Russian fields -
perhaps this professor's parents and grandparents -
all evaporated from my mind.

All I could remember
was Merle Haggard singing,
When you're running down my country

You're walking on the fighting side of me.

Dark rich coffee dripped down
and off the professor's glasses,
after the waiters separated us,
one more of my country's many famous descriptions
seeped through, but rolled off my back: *Ugly American.*

Aside from the above Ruskie in the bar, I remember our guide and the various guests she brought to speak to us, all painting a grim picture of what American embargo sanctions against Cuba had cost them, especially when the USSR pulled out. That grim picture was nowhere more obvious than in the shabby appearance of so many buildings in Havana. The whole place looked like an old and abandoned Hollywood set. The guide said Cuba could not import paint nor the materials to make it better because of the USA embargo. My friend Jim several times asked these guest speakers, one of whom was in Castro's cabinet, why no one seemed to disagree or have competing ideas. We knew theoretically, but the answer was brought home practically when our restaurateur fellow traveler's partner, who was originally from Peru and spoke fluent Spanish, spoke privately with a dancer from a group we had been watching as a cultural part of our tour. The official spokesperson for the group had been saying how wonderful Cuban life including government help had been to them and by extension to all Cubans. Our Peruvian-born colleague came away from her discussion with the one dancer in the corner saying, "he says don't believe a word they are saying, it's all propaganda that they have been rehearsed to say."

Southeast Asia

My next notable trip was to Southeast Asia: Myanmar, Cambodia, Laos, and Thailand, once again with Roads Scholar. Excellent trip with a knowledgeable and thoughtful guide, along with some great fellow travelers: the sunrise over Ankor Wat and boating down the Mekong River, stopping at local villages and sampling their culture. I still have a picture of me "wrestling" with a huge snake. It was, of course, a tourist trick; the snake was drugged or old or too relaxed to really hurt me. But it makes a great picture. I try to capture some other of my amazement in the following:

Dreams of Myanmar

The children and young girls wear white disks
of cosmetics for innocence and beauty.
I wear a totally white American face to be taken care of.

I saw the sun rising over Ankor Wat
and heard the guides try to explain the unexplainable
with gentle talk and pointing
at the beautiful complexity of chiseled gods,
explanations that stroke at deity.

The rust-robed monks commit
their lives not just to study and service,
but to begging poverty
that itself explains what
the West has lost since St Francis.

That commitment to me now as confusing
as the curly cue written language.

All in a country where
you can see in the fields their inhabitants
work as long as 12 hours a day 7 days a week,
and understand how hard it was for our ancestors
to get us to our comfortable living rooms.
And Buddha looks out from everywhere.

Such a wondrous country;
I am perversely relieved that not all
the food is piquant delicious
nor are the politics serene;
nor all the quiet monks without
traces of intoxicating Beetle juice
in their teeth.

As briefly referred to in the poem above, we did see the later president of Myanmar, Aung San Suu Kyi, make a speech to a medium sized crowd. We were told by our guide of the assassination of her father and the precarious situation she was in. I was sad to see all this play out in the international news later with her imprisonment. Having been there and heard some of the citizens speak favorably of her, I feel a small stake in her situation and that of the country. It is not a myth that that travel really does broaden and connect us. Given the civil strife, such a trip would be impossible today.

Russia

Two years later, I went on another Roads Scholar trip, this one to Russia. My timing was again good since such a trip would also be impossible today. I said earlier that my cultural education was Eurocentric, I should have said Western Eurocentric. Certainly the Russian painters in the museums of Moscow and St. Petersburg were European, but I had heard of almost none of them. And many of their works were rich, vibrant, and evocative. Their painting proved to be a universal art. I also loved the architecture of Moscow, especially the seven sisters, similar imposing Stalinist buildings, one of which was in sight of our hotel. Of course, the prize architecture is the Byzantine Red Square.

Because of the language barrier and the business of the Russian people as well as the isolated nature of tourist groups, we didn't interact much with the comrades. Our tour guide was a lively part-Tarter who also provided guest lecturers, one of whom was so pro-western and reform minded I thought our Russian guide was going to shut her down. But mostly our guide was busy fighting through the Chinese tourists to make sure we got to see the best of the Hermitage Museum. And she did a fine job, angling us good views of the crowded older section and getting us early to an almost empty modern art section of that wonderful museum and, the next day, the Fabergé Museum filled with the delicate, sparkling and complex eggs.

My next-to-favorite experience with our guide occurred after she had spent the day fighting through the Chinese museum tourists and was settling in next to me in the glitzy golden Marinsky Theater. We were all looking around taking in the grandeur when she poked my arm and asked who did I think was in the grand Tsar's box. I said I didn't know. She insisted: *Look*! I turned around to see about six Chinese sitting in that beautiful opera box. Our guide was miffed. I thought we had great seats about ten rows from the stage for Tchaikovsky's *Nutcracker*. Even if not in the Tsar's box, it did feel pretty significant to be watching the same opera that Tsars Alexander and Nicholas saw in the same theater.

But my favorite memory was taking the train from Moscow to St. Petersburg. As usual, I was paired up with a New York attorney who was 82. We were both travelling solo and when necessity demanded two to a room, were booked together. He had a fine sense of humor and I enjoyed his company. He regaled the group with how he made his doctor display his pickleball jersey, after seeing similar jerseys from Bobby Orr and Brad Park in that office. Often when walking over uneven cobblestones, I would warn him, to which he would reply, *Not to worry, I'm a lawyer.* The idea of him suing Putin charmed me. On the Moscow-St. Petersburg train he couldn't sleep, was motion sick, couldn't eat the sparse breakfast they served. He then said woefully, over watered-down coffee in our swaying compartment, *My travel agent told me this was the high point of the trip.*

I loved the tour, the art and architecture, the lectures and the food (lots of good caviar and blintzes). I didn't like the Mercedes taking up all the available parking (even when our vans needed parking), and I didn't like the lack of smiles, or the change in plans arbitrarily given us, for example, cutting out a good part of our Red Square tour.

I tried to remember the trials Russians have been through and was very moved by their celebration of the winning of WWII. But always in the back of my mind was a sense of Russia's history of brutality. I try to capture some of that in the following.

Education of a Prince
Case Study: Yakov

Stalin is not his real name
since his steely father assumed that name…
but you know all that.

What of Yakov?
Who was left motherless

after typhus took her
along with all the love
in his father's heart?

What of Yakov
ordered out of his father's house
to be a man and go fight Germans?

What makes a man throw himself
against an electrified POW fence?
His father's refusal to negotiate
for his freedom?

Or learning from his Polish friends
about Stalin's execution
of Polish officers in Katyn forest?

A prince's education should include
appropriate generalizations from instances--

the even necessary loss of mother's love,
the steel box of a father's heart,
banishment from home to go be a man,
tortured suffering for a father's sins--

What of Yakov?
What of us all?

The Mideast

My latest foreign trip was to the Mideast: Israel, Jorden, and Egypt. Most interesting to me was Israel. It felt remarkable to walk where

Christ walked, especially Christ's pre-crucifixion agony on the Via Dolorosa - although much of it today is in a commercial section of Jerusalem. I was also moved by the Wailing Wall with seemingly hundreds praying. I placed my own message of hope. Many similar images of where Peter and other Biblical personages walked and preached remain in my head.

We stayed in an orthodox hotel, where the elevators stopped at certain floors and not others for religious reasons. A little confusing but sort of charming. We were also able to see a courting ritual of young orthodox Jewish couples since they are permitted to see each other only in public places, hotel lobbies being ideal. Our guide told me that many of the young men would depend on the earning power of their wives since the men would be concentrating all their energies on studying the Torah. I thought that might not be such a bad marriage - for a man. But I was too old and too committed to Christianity to sign up.

In Jordan I bought two gorgeous carved inlaid chairs and had them shipped to my Pittsburgh condo. Our tour guide thought that I needed a rug to go along with the chairs. She gave a hard sell that suggested she had some interest if not commission in the deal, but I also thought she was right. My Pittsburgh friend, Joan, agreed to go with me and the tour guide into Luxor one night to a rug store. The whole evening was beautiful and a little scary. From my seat at the second floor open window of the store, I saw that the city light kept going off, but flood lamps on the ancient ruins were shining bright as was the flashlight of my rug salesman: a stunning ancient city lit by powerful lights and one flashlight.

I settled for one of the smaller rugs that I thought would look good with the ornate chairs and in my living room, and it has. The tour guide assured me, <u>after the sale was final</u>, that the only safe way to get the rug home was to carry it. Thank God for Joan's help. Coming home, we looked a little like refugees getting through airports. The chairs showed up at my condo as promised - six months later.

I also really enjoyed Egypt where I did the customary camel ride. In this case, thank God for the camel herder who was used to hoisting tourists on and off those huge animals. The ancient city of Petra was astonishing, a stone city hidden away in a canyon of rocks and requiring a two mile hike in. I happily took advantage of a handy carriage ride to get out. Although not geographically specific to my Mideast trip, I try to capture some of the wonder I find traveling in the following:

Confessions of a Time Traveler

I'm a fair weather Anglican
who only occasionally thanks God
for the Chilean sea bass or soul-tearing sunset
over Cartegena.

I appreciate every moment
of my first-class upgrade on Cathay Dragon airlines:
Loving God's gifts - isn't that a form of prayer?

But when the stomach goes bilious
or my feet to slush, I fervently ask for help.

I know seriously spiritual people
think this is childish heresy,
but they are good, often getting better;
I'm getting worse, older, and more fearful.

You can laugh at me, but wait till you open
the last quarter of your amputated century
and a flight of 20 stairs becomes a terrible trudge
say to the top of the Gaudi Cathedral. The magnificent
skyline of Barcelona makes it *almost* worthwhile,

until you realize that all the immortal edifices were created
by men like you, not just aging, but dying,
while the sea and distant mountains continue
to look on with indifference.

Covid

My life was just settling back into its pleasant routine when Covid hit. Like everyone who lived alone, I felt really isolated. My companion, Judy, initially isolated herself and we didn't see each other for six weeks. My son and his family similarly isolated. Most of my friends did the same. Meetings were by Zoom only. And, of course, the dreaded illness and its consequences was a dagger over us all. Here is a poem I wrote during those early awful days.

Night in the Time of Plague

My salty sweat stings like an astringent
on finger-picked nail quick.
My mind-hunt for foolish foods
(the sex of the old) sings
like an endless mosquito choir.
Do I have enough meat? Tums?
Apples? Will she love me at arm's length?

Hope: the last glass of honeyed vinegar
I drank before bed, a month ago.

In the weak humidifier light,
I try to meditate,
on what? God's test?
My last inhales?

This breath, excellent breath;
This moment, the guru says,
Excellent moment.

Like everybody else, I was very happy when things returned to some normal: in-person meetings, a chance to again see my family and Judy as well as my other friends. I learned how gregarious a person I am, how much I need others. One myth I came to believe more fully is that we humans are certainly clan animals, maybe herd animals.

CHAPTER XXI
MY FAMILY MYTH

I have had a good time here and elsewhere remembering and retelling my father's family lore about interesting French and German ancestors and even suggesting their national/cultural bloodline influence on me: perhaps French for creativity and good taste and German for discipline and persistence. I simply ignored my ancestor DNA which suggested I was mostly Irish. My nephew, Chris, Jay's younger brother, whom I have been lucky enough to recently reconnect with, has done much family research. Chris argued that a well-researched analysis of my family DNA and other evidence argues that my father was adopted. For example, birth records indicate my grandmother was 53 (my grandfather in his late 60s) when my father was/would have been born to them, an unlikely scenario at that time. Additionally, at that time, Chris found no DNA matches to connect my father to afore mentioned German or French relatives. Nor, for example, had I received at that time any Ancestor.com connections from that side of the family.

I was really stunned by this information. But it made me think and feel some important things. The first is, what did my father know? If true, he must have known or suspected something. Otherwise, his family was remarkable at keeping secrets. As it was, his mother died when he was 10. That would have meant two abandonments. I have suggested to my therapist, Mary Jo, that despite his alcoholism, my father was/is the real hero in our family, holding everything together despite his disease and what I see now as great loneliness.

And who was I? Without my cool linage, just another Irish guy. But as my partner, Judy, said: "You ought to be happy for all the literary heritage the Irish have created." In truth, I have always been very attracted to the Irish, from my mother's family to the friends I have made. And, of course, have been fascinated by the literature. Even the music has had great appeal: In my youth, I was addicted to the Clancy Brothers and Tommy Makem and later to the Pogues and Van Morrison. So I have always been most connected to "my Irish side." Some readers of my work have suggested that there is a certain Irish sensibility to my poems. I certainly don't place my work anywhere the greats such as Joyce and Seamus Heaney but my writing does deal with the complexities and hardship of life. I often think of Senator Danial Patrick Moynihan"s statement after John Kennedy's assassination: "To be Irish is to know that, in the end, the world will break your heart."

But, more importantly, in almost 50 years sober and 30+ in therapy, I have made myself into an interesting person, someone I like to be around, and a lot of others seem to also: I'm lucky enough to have many friends. My departed and very much missed friend, Brian, used to compliment, when I talked of my luck with friendship, *That's because you are a good friend.*

So as long as my family relationships are strong, I don't care about my DNA. My son John thinks it all a myth anyway. Who knows what our ancestors were doing in Ireland and Scotland and, in our case, even France and Germany.

As a **Final Twist**: I am now starting to get ancestor DNA alerts/messages from that German and French side of my father's family that my nephew said we weren't really related to, suggesting my father was not adopted. After all, nothing has changed. I thought nor think anything different about my father. He remains the generous, brilliant and flawed person who appears in my writing above.

 I am who I have made myself. From a frightened child of alcoholics to something of a drunk myself to a free man. Our literature promises that if we work the program, do the steps, and follow direction, we will be rocketed into a fourth dimension of existence. I often feel so at peace with my Higher Power and grateful for all that has been given to me that I feel that promise has been granted.

From being a nearly hopeless alcoholic, virtually unemployable, I have finished a doctoral degree from CMU, considered the number one school in my field at the time. I have had a significant career allowing me to help many other faculty and students do something important, learning to think and write and teach more effectively. In the process I raised the best son anyone could ask for. And I became a poet and writer.

From now on my general rule will be to cherish my family and if I have a great ancestor story, like Sir Edward Carson, claim it.

And What a Fine Family to Cherish

Perhaps my greatest accomplishment should be counted as not mine all: as I just mentioned I have been lucky enough to the raise one of the best sons in the world. John is an art teacher now working in an inner-city school, doing what I think of as, and tell him is, the Lord's work. I have had a chance to watch him teach (I was proud that he took me to Bring Your Parent to School Day– even though the day was designed for the students.) John's knowledge, compassion, and ability to connect with the students deeply impressed me. He and they produce terrific art. John is kind enough to tell me what an important influence I have been on him. I'll take a little credit, but I know he is just a remarkable man. And what a pleasure to be with. Just last week we were laughing about his childhood complaint about wearing "hard shoes" to church and how today tailored (non-sweat) pants which now outsell regular fitted pants, are now referred to as "hard pants." With his son Jack, we saw Willy Watson recently at the Club Café. John has invited me to do a podcast on Bob Dylan with him, and I just might.

Some of his gifts to the world and me were marrying such great wife and producing two fine boys. Emily is smart, witty and committed to her family. She is a successful banker and active in the community. Best of all she is a great companion to John and loving and super competent mother to the boys. I love being with both of them.

Jack is now preparing to go off to college. An excellent student and lover of the outdoors, he will major in forestry. I love how he has grown into such a capable and caring young man: Eagle scout, honor student, musician (bass and sax), hard worker, I will miss him. Jack just went out to Wyoming to check out the University's environmental science department. Jack said a friend told him *there is a beautiful girl behind every tree but there are no trees*. He always makes sure I am safe and steady when we are walking together. Late breaking news, Jack has been accepted to and decided to go to West Virginia. We all went down there last weekend, which happened to be their St. Patrick's Day celebration. All the beautiful girls in green, tank tops certainly didn't give Jack buyer's remorse.

Evan is a runner and a French horn player. Also a scout, he enjoys camping with his brother and father, and incidentally took the author picture for this book. Evan has a fine sense of humor: I recently told him how rising sea levels may, for example mean the end of New Jersey. *Finally*, he energetically replied. He has endeared himself to me with his reference to "Dr. Pap" as when he gives me the passenger seat in a car, "Dr. Pap always gets shotgun."

I have also established a rich and growing relationship with my nephew, Jay. He has become a writer in his retirement and has impressed me with the work he has shown me. Jay is close to publishing his first mystery. We often have lunch and a good time. He just took me to an Eric Clapton concert that really knocked me out. I am planning to take John's family and Jay and his terrific wife, Anita, to *La Traviata* in a few weeks.

Jay's children, Mac, Jake and Ryan are warm, friendly and real gentlemen. Their children, Frankie, Louie (Mac and Kelly, his fine wife), and Charlie (Jake and Erica) are a riot of fun: keeping their parents' handsome gene and generally being good boys. I love a picture I have seen of them crawling all over their grandfather, Jay.

I am so sorry my brother, Terry, the little boys' great grandfather is not here to see them all.

I am just now connecting with my other nephew Chris who has already contributed to my knowledge of my family, which appears above. Chris worked in science and technology and was away from Pittsburgh for many years. He has now returned and I am looking forward to getting to know him and his family better.

Their sister, my niece, was a lovely and bright woman who passed away at the age of 57 from cancer. It was a great loss. Her excellent children, Katie and Emily are thriving, but of course, missing their mother enormously. They have such busy lives I don't get a chance to see them often enough.

The importance of family and friends is a myth in the best sense of the word, allowing us to better understand a central part of our culture.

Final Thoughts on Living with Myths

My early interactions with many of my age and culture's myths were not easy, from the happy home behind the white picket fence (not my experience) to the belief of white and class superiority, that the important people I knew and liked could save me from the rules of life. (In my drinking days, I summarized that myth as *cool connected guys like me don't have problems, at least ones that aren't easy to get out of.*) Other near-deadly myths I have mentioned above include my being helped by alcohol and after that, alcohol at least made life bearable - and I was only hurting myself. In fact, my self-medication made sense for a time but quickly stopped making sense. Another related myth was that I could work myself out of my alcoholism (*stay busy, Jay, until 9:00 PM and then you can drink safely.*) And then, that I was too special for recovery among other recovering people.

The other night I re-watched *Ben Hur*. I was struck by how much early Christianity must have seemed like a dangerous myth, especially to the Romans who had on their side centuries of traditions and history going back to the Greeks. Similarly, Christianity appeared like a dangerous myth/trick to me in my youth when logic was paramount. The problem of evil seemed to lock it up: no all-knowing, all powerful, all loving God could be possible with all the evil that exists in the world.

And then I found the key. It took my almost being dead from the progressive deadly disease of alcoholism. The idea of a higher power and a belief I could live successfully in this world seemed equally outrageous. But sobriety made them both possible. What can easily be seen as a myth in the best sense of the word saved me.

For better or worse, all the myths I have struggled with, overcome, accepted, or come to terms with have made me into who I am. I feel that I have overcome the most damaging myths: those of race and class, that my family's whiteness and mildly distinguished European heritage (as I said early on in this memoir, *Dukes don't emigrate*) placed me above others; that because of my education and friends entitled me to a greater share. *I have also come to realize that some of the most dangerous of those myths benefitted me.* That realization has been so important to me, I will take the liberty of repeating a poem I included earlier.

Lucky You

my Jewish friend replied
to my comment that I
am divorced from most of the antisemitism
she witnesses and fears daily.

For I have been a WASP, raised
in the patriarchy with a faux love
and respect-but true advantage
thrown at me everywhere, benefitting

from cheap black mother-maids
as a child, easier passage to prep
and college schools, and not
much trouble finding work
that certainly wasn't back breaking;
open invitations to all neighborhoods
and some powerful friends,
all brokered by an influential father.

I wasn't the guy who made
all that discrimination.
I was the guy it was made for.

So rather than thinking I have mastered the myths in my life I feel I have come to terms with them. And not too badly. I have stayed the course, lost, then found, and kept the faith, and am finishing the race. I have been active in recovery, speaking at and chairing meetings, holding office in my home groups. Additionally, I have, over time, sponsored more than 20 members in the program. I currently work fairly closely with six.

I have taught about 10,000 students to (I hope and trust) write more effectively, trained some 200 faculty at Robert Morris and more elsewhere to have more solid syllabi that include goals and means to teach their students to write more effectively. The various school reports from the FIPSE grant that I directed estimate our work having had a downstream effect on an additional 20,000 students.

I have also stayed active, holding responsible positions in my church and my condo. I spend just about every Sunday morning in my small Community House Church on the North Side. Pastor Steve Werth and my friends, Sue, Doug and Lynne, Joe, Flo, Peggy and Paul, Bob and Sharon, David and Sarah, to name just a few, do indeed create a community, small but mighty, as Peggy says, which I am happy to be part of.

Equally or more importantly, I have maintained and been a supportive part of a number of friendships in and outside my program, for example, I recently renewed an old friendship with Ken J., a retired lawyer who has taken up DJ-ing at a local university radio station so he could stay current with today's music. He has been kind enough to share recommendations and tickets. A great companion and friend at music or anywhere. I was also able to spend time with Henry, no new-comer, but someone who kept me in touch with younger members (Henry recently passed away from a painful cancer after a long courageous battle): or like Nico, the most active service-oriented young person I know. Or my other friend Maurice who knows more 12-step history than anybody. We learn much from the people we work with in recovery. Johnny M's thoughtful notes and generous help to me and others reminds us all how to pay attention to our fellow human beings.

I have also had to come to terms with another self-serving myth. My parents were not the cause of my drinking or my other problems. My mother and father had their difficulties, many of which became mine. But I was taught long ago that my problems, especially my drinking, were my inappropriate reaction to those difficulties. My poetry has helped me respond to that sometimes tough youth, not always in a kind way. I try to touch on my response more affectionately in the following:

Capsicum,

I
my father used to say
it's what makes ginger ale's pop and taste.
The ginger ale was for me,
his glass was full ale or gin,
then, his memory would explode:

II
first, with the wonders of his youth:
the onion sandwiches seemed plucked whole
fresh from his Grandmother's Heth's Run garden,

and her new made
ice cream, refreshing as her willingness
to sell the farm to Catholics.

Dad looking out the back
of his uncle's new 1909 Packard
for his cousin' Chick's broken arm.
Not just broken, he thought, but broken *off*.

Watching the skin of his Aunt Sadie turning green
because, everyone said, *of eating too many olives.*

II
Then, I could hear about the 1924 Olympics
he saw with law school classmates.
The beautiful mademoiselles he met
and later, the frauleins in Germany.
Until those "bastard Prussian officers,"
similar to those who had pushed his grandmother
off the Berlin sidewalks 40 years before,
bullied him down a flight of Beer Hall stairs.
All the while, Dad yelling *sal bosch (dirty German).*

Oh, he knew and spoke well of many friends
and followed the Pittsburgh Pirates,
was wicked smart in American history,
and cordially exchanged stories with me
during some of our great dinners.

But he was a foreigner to me.
Until my wise Aunt Clara
came to my father's funeral,
encouraging and answering
my bubbling obsession
in my writing about him:
You are writing your father's poetry.

Another of my self-imposed myths is that I could never be a poet. I leave it up to the reader to decide if I succeeded. But perhaps more important is my self-description., self-awareness, definition.

Perhaps it just comes with time as the following poem suggests, starting as it did in my early graduate school days.

Watching the Wasps Die

In the fall from my desk
in my Morgantown apartment
when dying was distant,
what they did on tv
what my grandfather had done.

I enjoyed watching wasps' late Fall
agony. They deserved it.
After all, they'd invaded my sun porch
making it unlivable, almost impossible
to get my mail, frequently attacking me
in my apartment.

I started to write then,
first notes, then jokes,
then poems and stories,
no plan, just winging about
until something hurt. I avoided
that pain at first
and stopped.

But looking out my window,
watching those wasps
curl and hollow in death,

I learned that whether
turning a lancet attack-out
or somehow self-wound in,
the stinging time is a short summer.

I have lived long since then
and regret my pleasure
in those wasps dying.
And learned more to respect other's
and better use my own stylets,
before winter.

Along with other myths, I have come to terms with being a poet. In all my life, I have done much better than survive. I am a lucky man, retired for a decade, with reasonably good health, a beautiful caring partner, and many friends. My retirement savings are supporting me pretty well although I'll never be rich. As my partner, Judy, wisely says *There's no money in poetry, but there's no poetry in money.*

I'm still getting to operas, rock and folk concerts, plays, and some travel. I was delighted to be with my family at 2024 Olympics. The above poem, *Capsicum*, makes a reference to my father's attendance 100 years earlier at the 1924 Olympics. Stanton would be happy and, I think proud.

Judy and I plan on going to the Spoleto festival in Charleston in June to see some pretty great dance, music and theater. Afterwards, we have an invitation to go to her son and daughter's beach house on an island off Charleston. I'm looking forward to another relaxing fun week with Judy's fine and generous family.

My life is good. And the process of writing this memoir has helped me understand how lucky I have been and how good my life is. I have done the work and struggled through and come to terms with my life's controlling myths and have reached a peace.

No good writing is ever finished, only abandoned. Thanks for reading and good luck to you.

Made in the USA
Monee, IL
19 July 2025

30e1f9bc-8b38-4a80-8137-ea4a8a19cbdbR01